"So many of us carry the scars inflicted by a wor
from its addiction to violence. We are injured by t
thy and isolation. We are plagued by the systemic
ism, racism, and classism. We are broken by the c
and war.

So many of us are connected to the institutions that do the scarring –
indentured by our paychecks, our loyalties, our histories, our fears.

In this, we are both perpetrator and victim. And we are not okay. We
need a different kind of journey. I think that for a lot of us, this book can be
the first steps on that odyssey."

Cornelius Minor, *Brooklyn Based Educator, Author*

"This book gives students a voice to show how they belong and connect
with their community members."

Melissa, *Public Montessori Educator*

"Your work is greatly needed, and I admire your passion."

Melinda, *Teacher of Gifted & Talented Students*

"As a peacebuilding professional and now as a grandfather, I've long been
looking for a book that would help teachers and parents introduce our field
to children in their formative years. Here it is."

Charles Hauss, *Senior Fellow for Innovation, Alliance for Peacebuilding*

"Julie Lillie and Carey Seeley Dzierzak have adopted World Citizen Peace's
Five Peace Actions to create a well-researched and deeply grounded
framework for peacelearning. If we want to see peaceful change in our
schools, we must take up the challenge and be the change. **Empowering
Peace and Justice Education** demystifies that challenge, offering teachers
and students a transformational path to becoming peacemakers and world
citizens together. We are proud that World Citizen Peace's Five Peace
Actions have inspired this important work."

Caren Stelson, *Author, Educator and Board Chair of World Citizen Peace*

Empowering Peace and Justice Education

Learn how to thoughtfully embed the tenants of peace education into your own life, classroom, curriculum and school culture with this practical and timely guidebook that features action steps across developmental levels. Rooted in hope, empowerment, culturally relevant pedagogy and trauma informed care, this book provides an overview of peace education and the peace actions; sample lessons and practices; and resources for supporting you in implementing these ideas across content areas, with an emphasis on literacy, language and social emotional learning. The book details how creating a culture of peace is an opportunity for all students and educators to flourish, to create the space to meet students where they are, bringing their assets to the forefront and building culturally affirming systems. Providing kind, practical recommendations in an accessible and eye-opening way, *Empowering Peace and Justice Education* is an essential read for any teacher or school leader who wants to move from vision to action in co-creating brave democratic spaces and realizing a more just and peaceful world.

Julie Lillie, M.S., is a peace-centered educator with over 15 years of experience in diverse PreK-12 settings, including as a teacher, instructional leader, literacy specialist, equity coach and curriculum developer.

Carey Seeley Dzierzak, Ed.D., is a dedicated social-justice-centered educator involved in education for over 25 years working in diverse settings. She has been a 1st-grade and literacy teacher, instructional coach, curriculum director, assistant principal and principal.

Other Eye On Education Books Available from Routledge

(www.routledge.com/eyeoneducation)

The Meditation and Mindfulness Edge: Becoming a Sharper, Healthier, and Happier Teacher
Lisa M. Klein

What Do Great Teachers Say?: Language All Teachers Can Use to Transform Student Behavior, Parent Relationships, and Classroom Culture K-5
Hal Holloman and Peggy H. Yates

Purposeful Educator Connections: Five Principles to Strengthen Relationships with Students
Marcela Andrés

Building Dynamic Teamwork in Schools: 12 Principles of the V Formation to Transform Culture
Brad Johnson and Robert Hinchliffe

Empowering Peace and Justice Education

An Actionable Framework for Elementary Educators and Learners

Julie Lillie and Carey Seeley Dzierzak

Routledge
Taylor & Francis Group

NEW YORK AND LONDON

Designed cover image: Getty Images

First published 2025
by Routledge
605 Third Avenue, New York, NY 10158

and by Routledge
4 Park Square, Milton Park, Abingdon, Oxon, OX14 4RN

Routledge is an imprint of the Taylor & Francis Group, an informa business

© 2025 Julie Lillie and Carey Seeley Dzierzak

ISBN: 978-1-032-58251-1 (hbk)
ISBN: 978-1-032-58079-1 (pbk)
ISBN: 978-1-003-44924-9 (ebk)

DOI: 10.4324/9781003449249

Typeset in Palatino
by KnowledgeWorks Global Ltd.

Contents

Acknowledgments

We are grateful to the people and organizations who supported and inspired us throughout this writing journey! To the board members and staff of World Citizen Peace, we are honored to lift up the Five Peace Actions. Many thanks to the educators who participated in our peacelearning circle series and empower students daily. Elizabeth, Jodie, Kyra, Melinda, Melissa and Robyn, thank you for sharing your perspectives, trying out our lessons with your students and providing us with feedback. Deep thanks to our insightful sensitivity reader, Helen Thomas. Your guidance and comments propelled us and made this book stronger. We extend gratitude to our peer reviewers: Odia, Cathy, Khrisslyn, Mary, Caren, Amanda, Kate and Naomi. Thank you for reviewing our early drafts and providing an array of feedback, all of which created a more compelling and accessible text! We cherish the insights and leadership from our Peacemakers in Practice: Mandar Apte, Moses Abolade, Dr. Naomi Taylor, Helen Thomas, Omar McMillan and Munir Shivij who graciously shared their words and wisdom. Special thanks to the team at Routledge, notably Alexis O'Brien, for bringing this work to a greater audience. We are so thankful for the experiences, (un)learning and support from our colleagues, friends and families!

I (Julie) first wish to thank Carey, who leads from the heart and planted a seed that grew into this book! I extend deep love and gratitude to my partner and best friend, Brady Lillie. Thank you, for sharing your light, listening, inviting me to pause and for being my rock. You created the space for me to put my whole self into co-creating this book and The Peace Pad. Thank you for helping me lean into the process and trust myself. To my Mother, Patty Schulz, I will forever cherish and reciprocate your openness, support, advice, friendship and love. Thanks to my Dad who encouraged me to write and emphasized the importance of humanitarian education. Miigwech to Ida Downwind, your patience, humor, wisdom and guidance were elemental in shaping me into the peace and justice educator I am today. To all who have been a part of my journey, exploration and healing, I hope you can feel my love and appreciation!

I (Carey) would like to thank Julie who is an amazing writer and editor; this book would not be possible without your partnership and hard work! Many thanks to my love – Lou, you are an amazing husband, father and editor! I appreciate all of the ways that you support me and our family, including editing at all hours of the day. Emily, Jack, Taylor and Claire – thank you all for being amazing people and children. Your actions embody the peace education practices in this book – love you to Pluto and beyond! To my brother, Krishna – thank you for being a great brother and inspiration. To my parents, Jane & Bill Seeley, your love, modeling of peaceful practices and dedication to social justice made me the person I am today. I wish you were here to see this book in person, but I know you are both beaming with pride. With peace, love and gratitude, Carey xxoo.

We honor that these words were written while residing on the traditional, ancestral and contemporary land of the Dakota, as well as the Akimel O'Odham, Piipaash and Yavapai peoples. Miigwech and respect to our Indigenous teachers and guides, you have taught us so much about the importance of caring relations with all life.

Foreword

I am delighted and honored to write this foreword for *Empowering Peace and Justice Education: An Actionable Framework for Elementary Educators and Learners*. The book offers a useful framework for those interested in exploring the study of peace and justice as a topic and/or engaging in the teaching and practice of peace and justice efforts within classroom or community settings. Congratulations and thanks are owed to the authors, Lillie and Seeley Dzierzak.

The book is published at a time when the world finds itself at a crossroads. On the one hand, there is a rise in military spending, armed conflicts, and the threat of new wars and nuclear wars, along with escalating climate change, inequalities and polarization, as well as concerning declines in peace and democracy. On the other, there are glimpses of hope all around us, as more and more people mobilize to challenge war, violence and injustice.

As H.G. Wells (1921) suggested, *"Civilization is in a race between education and catastrophe."* From this standpoint, Peace and Justice Education (PJE) has a key role to play in influencing our transition away from current realities towards more preferable alternative futures. PJE is crucial not only for *"Saving succeeding generations from the scourge of war"* (UN Charter, 1945) but also for empowering current and future generations to pursue new versions of peace – within ourselves, with others, across systems and the cosmos.

Throughout my 15-plus years of involvement in studying, teaching and organizing for peace – within prisons, schools, colleges, universities and alongside youth and communities in different parts of the world – I have witnessed significant developments in the field. Multiple efforts by civil society organizations, UN agencies, academia and the private sector have made substantial contributions to policy, practice and research. The United Nations General Assembly's decision to dedicate the International Day of Education in 2024 to the theme *"learning for lasting peace"* represents another step forward in the ongoing global efforts to legitimize, mainstream and institutionalize peace and justice-oriented education.

While much has been written about PJE in schools, university and community contexts, comparatively less attention has been paid to PJE in primary and elementary school settings. The more I interact with individuals and organizations around the world, the more I hear calls to 'put younger generations at the center of peacebuilding efforts,' echoing Gandhi's enduring plea: *"If we are to reach real peace in this world, and if we are to carry on a real war against war, we shall have to begin with the children"* (Bylund, 2011). This book not only joins the conversation about PJE during formative years but also offers ways to envision and participate in Gandhi's vision.

With over four decades of combined experience in the study and practice of elementary education, socio-emotional learning, and peace and justice issues broadly defined, authors Lillie & Seeley Dzierzak are well suited to write such a book. Its chapters highlight the importance of trauma informed and culturally responsive approaches, with hope recurring as a central theme. But the book goes beyond the notion that hope alone suffices. It serves as a valuable resource for those seeking to translate hope and empowerment into 'transformative possibilities' for learning and action. Apart from curating scholarly insights, featuring exemplars 'Peacemaker In Practice' and offering thought-provoking 'Pause & Reflect' exercises, the book also provides conceptual resources, pragmatic tools and lesson plans to 'Put It Into Practice' its principles and concepts.

Whether you are a new or experienced educator, or just someone with an interest in these topics, this accessible book offers a wealth of valuable insights. It lays the groundwork for others to build upon. The onus now rests with you. The hope is that you will not only read and reflect on the materials within the book, but also use and adapt them to your specific context. We look forward to hearing about and learning from your efforts in promoting peace and justice education in the years ahead.

Phill Gittins, PhD
World BEYOND War: Education Director
Rotary Peace Fellow
Rotary-IEP Positive Peace Activator
KAICIID Fellow
Editorial Board: Journal of Peace Education

References

Bylund, L. (2011, December 10). *Gandhi spoke at Montessori London 1931*. Ahimsa Peace Institute Worldwide. https://www.gandhiforchildren.org/gandhi-spoke-montessori-london/

United Nations. (1945, June 26). *Charter of the United Nations*. https://www.un.org/en/about-us/un-charter/full-text

Wells, H. G. (1921). *The outline of history* (Vol. 2, Chapter 41, Section 4). Macmillan Publishers.

Introduction

Peace is not just the absence of conflict; peace is the creation of an environment where all can flourish.
~ Nelson Mandela

This powerful Mandela quote (1994) has been a visible reminder throughout our process of envisioning and writing this book. Our hope is that this framework and practices empower your peace and justice education implementation and truly result in environments where all flourish. As educators and leaders, we recognize that schools and communities are complex spaces. Daily we can experience joy and conflict, love and disconnection, peace and stress. Students also come with a myriad of gifts and challenges. This book highlights our love, passion and commitment to support folks who are seeking justice, peace and want to celebrate joy, even in the midst of conflict and trauma.

Peace is complex and we all have our own experience and journey with what seeking and living in peace looks, sounds and feels like. Our contributions to the multifaceted views of education are guided by a selection of peacemakers who have inspired us and expanded upon from our own lenses, experiences and visions. We feel honored to add to the essential field of peace and justice education and are proponents for its mainstreaming across PreK-12 systems.

We created this book and offer this framework for anyone who is interested in learning about peace education and in implementing its practices with primary and elementary learners (ages and/or developmental levels). And, this text is quite applicable for people at all ages and stages of life. We hope you find the insights and practices valuable personally, as well as professionally.

We invite you to join us in being peaceful allies and co-conspirators and to extend this call to action to others in your community.

We offer research-based grounding and implementation guidance for peacelearning that is rooted in culturally relevant and trauma informed practices. **Peacelearning** (yes, no space there!) is a powerful word that demonstrates the compound and interconnected nature of learning and peace. Pursuits of peace cannot be separated from learning. Our usage of

DOI: 10.4324/9781003449249-1

this word is inspired by a book we read and deeply discussed together before deciding to write this one – *Peace Education* (2013) by Ian M. Harris and Mary Lee Morrison.[1]

We have the utmost respect for peace guides and educators. Therefore, we trust that you will utilize this book and flexible framework, lessons and practices in the way that best aligns for you, learners, the space and context of your implementation. We would be honored to partner with you in this journey, please visit www.thepeacepad.org.

Figure 0.1 The Peace Pad

◎ **Pause & Reflect:** A few notes on text features. Throughout this book, we invite you to **'Pause & Reflect'**. Trace the spiral icon next to this feature to truly pause and breath. Engage in reflection independently and collaboratively. We share over 100 lessons and **'Put It Into Practice'** guidance to illustrate how to take the ideas, research and theory into peace action. The unit of lessons in Chapter 12, as well as many of the practices, indicates three levels: emerging, intermediate and advanced. The level you utilize will depend on the developmental, cognitive, emotional and social needs of learners. You might start at emerging for scaffolding and move into intermediate and advanced later on. If thinking about grade levels, here is the approximate translation:

- ◆ **Emerging:** PreK-2nd grades
- ◆ **Intermediate:** 3–5th grades
- ◆ **Advanced:** 5th grade and beyond; many of these practices extend to adult learners!

We encourage you to add to these ideas, strategies and lessons, melding them into your own style and practices. Think about what your students need and what they are interested in, as well as the context of your site and community. We hope you are inspired by the **Peacemakers in Practice**, leaders in the field who share compelling ways to engage with each peace action in our framework. This book is intentionally organized and sequenced, but you may jump around in your reading and implementation to fit your needs.

We invite you to approach your journey of seeking and guiding others toward justice and peace with the humbleness of a lifelong learner. This process is complex and vital. With humility, we acknowledge the privilege and resources we have in our lives. We encourage you to go far beyond this text as you embark on your peace and justice journey. Feel the gratitude we extend to you and the many amazing peacemakers, peacebuilders and peacelearners in our world. Let us support and empower all people to be, work and live in alignment with the actions and pursuits of peace and justice education.

Note

1. From Peace Education, 3d ed. © 2013 Ian M. Harris and Mary Lee Morrison by permission of McFarland & Company, Inc., Box 611, Jefferson NC 28640. www.mcfarlandbooks.com

Reference

Mandela, N. (1994). Documentary. Mandela Documentary.

1

What Is Peace Education?

Peace education is both a philosophy and a process of learning and being that creates a world in which all people live in harmony with oneself, each other and the environment.
~ Julie Lillie and Dr. Carey Seeley Dzierzak

The creation of cultures of peace is realized through living in accordance with the following Five Peace Actions, which were developed by the non-profit organization, World Citizen Peace (2014).

- *Seek Peace Within Yourself And Others*
- *Respect Diversity*
- *Protect The Environment**
- *Reach Out In Service*
- *Be A Responsible Citizen Of The World*

*In our framework and work, we use Protect <u>Our</u> Environment; see Chapter 6 to learn why.

World Citizen Peace empowers us to create a just and peaceful world. Consider supporting World Citizen Peace by becoming a Peace Ambassador, as an International Peace Site, or committing to living in alignment with these peace actions. We both are Peace Ambassadors with World Citizen Peace and invite you to join us!

Learn more at: https://worldcitizenpeace.org/

DOI: 10.4324/9781003449249-2

We believe that learning, living, being and acting in alignment with these peace actions are the foundational necessity of an education that truly honors the whole child and their place as leaders for the future of humanity. When we create nurturing and child-centered spaces and experiences that cultivate the exploration of gifts, values, beliefs and wonders of the self, each other and the natural world, this is educating for peace. Children are precious treasures who are capable of developing a world in which all humans hold a deeper awareness and love of their true nature and their integral connection to all who inhabit planet Earth.

Peace education is a transformational process that affects ways of being, thinking, relationships, opinions, values, behaviors and ultimately the very systems and structures that make up our society and world. It occurs over time and space.

Peace and justice-centered questions, behaviors, discussions, analysis, pursuits and actions become a natural part of the day-to-day experiences of those engaging in peacelearning. Feminist peace scholar and pioneer Betty Reardon (1988) described the goals at the heart of peacelearning.

> *Peace education, as I understand it, is to promote the development of an authentic planetary consciousness that will enable us to function as global citizens and to transform the present human condition by changing the social structures and the patterns of thought that have created it. This transformational imperative must be at the center of peace education. (p. x)*

As advocates for this deep and transformational process, we understand this is not a small undertaking. A change in the human consciousness and society will need to go beyond this book and its practices. However, this transformation, through the power of nonviolence, is already in motion within the larger space-time continuum. Every individual impacts the collective. We call on educators, leaders, parents, community members and children to be aware of and engage in their evolutionary role of creating a world in which all people, beings and organisms have their basic needs and rights met and are in harmony with all life. We dedicate these ideas, framework, practice and lessons to whom we view as the seeds of peace, our children. We very much believe that children already have all they need, deep inside, to seek peace and grow into peaceful adults. It is our role as educators to provide experiences, opportunities and environments for discovery, stories, action and sharing of their gifts into the world. Let us cherish children as they shine and open into their light!

Peace & Identity: Belief Intersections

Cherishing our children means that we work toward and prioritize peace in our lives and with others. Peace begins within and then can externalize with our families, communities, cities, nations and throughout the world. Knowing that children and their families do not leave their beliefs (part of their identity) at the school doors, we feel it is important to highlight a few of the inspiring views of peace through belief systems, spirituality & religions (see Figure 1.1).

The U.S. Department of Education (2023), provided the following guidance:

> *Public schools may not provide religious instruction, but they may teach about religion and promote religious liberty and respect for the religious views (or lack thereof) of all. For example, philosophical questions concerning religion, the history of religion, comparative religion, religious texts as literature, and the role of religion in the history of the United States and other countries are all permissible public school subjects. Similarly, it is permissible to study religious influences on philosophy, art, music, literature, and social studies.*

Put simply, beliefs may be explored in a non-devotional and inclusive manner in public schools. Visions of peace are a part of human histories and identities around the world and therefore an important resource to be honored and shared within peacelearning.

Concepts of peace have always been embedded as part of the mission of world religions, though as sociologist Elise Boulding (2005) noted, major world religions often follow two ways of approaching peace, called the *"Holy War Doctrine"* and that of the *"Holy Peace."* As humans moved into cities, more stories, fables and religious activities around concepts of conquest and war emerged. Table 1.1 is not meant to serve as an exhaustive overview of the spiritual or religious beliefs of all people. There are many, many more faiths, religions and types of (dis)belief systems! We wish to highlight the connections to peace that exist and the freedom of expression that children have in exploring and expressing their identities and beliefs and learning about others.

◎ **Pause & Reflect:** As you review Table 1.1 consider:

- ◆ What are your personal beliefs?
- ◆ How does this intersect with ideas and goals of peace and justice?

Table 1.1 Visions of Peace Within Religions and Beliefs

Beliefs, Religion & Spirituality	Visions of Peace
Islam	The universal greeting in Islam is *"As-salaam alaikum,"* meaning peace be with you. Prophet Mohammed preached of creating one community under Allah and to help others less fortunate than you.
Judaism	The greeting *"shalom"* means peace and prosperity and conveys ideas of well-being and contentment. The concept *"tikkun olam"* envisions an ideal world and promotes social justice.
Buddhism	The ultimate goal is to attain enlightenment, often through the tranquility of the mind (meditation). Buddha condemned greed, crime and war and spread ideas of compassion for the suffering of all people.
Taoism	Promoting peace from within and a universal connection with others and the natural world. Philosopher Lao Tse wrote of peace in the heart to then create peace in the home, with neighbors, citizens, cities, nations and the world.
Hinduism	Respect all beings. Violence or aggression in this life will lead to being a victim of it in the next reincarnation (karma). Inner peace can be achieved, in part, by ending the forces of egoism, greed, lust, selfishness and anger (the causes of war).
Christianity	Peace of/with God is also the harmony of body, mind and spirit. One of the Ten Commandments prevents the taking of another's life. Prophet Jesus Christ, called the Prince of Peace, practiced nonviolence and preached love for all, even your 'enemies'.

(continued)

Table 1.1 Visions of Peace Within Religions and Beliefs (continued)

Beliefs, Religion & Spirituality	Visions of Peace
Baha'i	Harmony with self, family, community, nation and the world is valued.
	'The Promise of World Peace' invites people to see themselves as members of a universal family.
Indigenous (spirituality views)	Ways of knowing and being that center on the relationship with the creator, land and all who inhabit it. Cosmic visions show the connection between all things.
	Language translations of phrases similar to 'All My Relatives' or 'All Our Relations' embody cultural practices, views and ways of life.
Esotericism and New Age (spirituality movement)	Belief in the coming of international peace and a heightened spiritual consciousness.
	Utilizes ancient and mystical and metaphysical knowledge from the universe to assist in personal transformation.
Agnosticism and Atheism ("No belief" is technically a belief!)	Does not believe in the existence of a spiritual power or god(s) and/or views the ultimate reality (such as God) as unknown and likely unknowable.
	Focuses more on the understanding of directly human concepts and seeking inner peace. Practices non-judgment of others' beliefs.

As we described in the Introduction (p. 2), throughout this book, we share **'Put It Into Practice'** ideas, lessons and strategies to support your peacelearning implementation. The practice level you utilize will depend on the cognitive, emotional and social needs of learners, working within the zone of proximal development and providing necessary scaffolding.

Table 1.2 Belief Intersections

Put It Into Practice: Belief Intersections		
Emerging	Intermediate	Advanced
Honor that all people have different beliefs and that none are better (more right) than another. Invite learners to share something about their beliefs.	Invite learners to journal and then share how their identity and beliefs connect to ideas and goals of peace.	Set up a research opportunity and create a table (like ours above) that explores a variety of beliefs and how visions of peace connect with each.

Peacemakers

Peace education is both a philosophy and a process, focusing on empowering people with critical thinking and problem-solving, skills, knowledge and attitudes. The pursuits and actions of peace education create a sustainable environment, love and compassion for all. Though there are many organizations, resources, books, articles and websites around the world dedicated to peace, the majority are geared toward teenagers and adults, which is why we feel passionately about a need to increase peacelearning at the elementary level. Additionally, peacemaker representation in text and media is limited in comparison to the depictions of violence, conflict and war, which is often done in a glorified manner. To embody nonviolence, children need models, examples and experiences with diverse peacemakers!

Through viewing and hearing transformational people-based stories about the power of peace and peaceful actions, adults and children become inspired and empowered. Peace scholars Harris and Morrison (2013) wrote,

> Peace education can help to get students to see themselves as causal agents capable of contributing to the effort to bring peace to the world. By learning how peacemakers have practiced nonviolence, students' imaginations may be inspired by visions of a peaceful world, where ordinary citizens can realize their dreams. (p. 106)[1]

The Five Peace Actions are designed to create a sense of self-love, connection, belonging and hope that fosters a peaceful global citizen of the world; a peacemaker! When students see themselves as a peacemaker, an agent of change, they are empowered in their role in making world peace a reality.

As peace educators and writers, we appreciate that we are building upon many of the ideas, learnings and actions of other peacemakers. We are grateful for and humbled by all who guide, speak and act toward peace and justice. As such, throughout this book, we honor a few of the many inspiring peacemakers, who also firmly believe(d), as we do, in education as a means to peace. There is a list of more peacemakers who inspire us on our website: www.thepeacepad.org

◎ Pause & Reflect:

- ◆ Who has inspired or empowered you in your journey of seeking peace?
- ◆ Who are peacemakers in your community and how might you connect them with the children you serve?

In addition to the peacemakers we highlight, you might also uplift the work of national and international non-governmental organizations (INGOs) who have helped accelerate peace education efforts. The Union of International Associations (2017), listed 75,000 profiles of INGOs in their Yearbook of International Organizations, many of which have an emphasis on peace studies, civil society, civic dialogue, justice and international relations.

Peacemakers in tribal communities, non-profits, community and grassroots organizations focus more on local humanitarian needs, justice and peace efforts. They can be less bureaucratic to collaborate with and offer networking and educational opportunities, work to address sources of structural violence and provide examples of justice and peace at local, national and international levels. Incorporating learning and exploration of peacemakers and peacemaking organizations in an important aspect of peace education. We encourage you to discover and connect with the people and organizations most aligned to the needs and peace education efforts of your students, school and local communities.

We emphasize the importance of sharing stories of a wide variety of people. The stories shared with children are so influential in how they understand and view the world. Stories that empower and inspire students to see themselves as peacemakers are just as important as stories that challenge stereotypes and the dominant narratives about diverse people of peace. Storytelling is a culturally relevant teaching practice that includes many perspectives, voices, identities, narratives and explores the varying depths of human nature. Peacebuilding is possible through stories and storytelling that provide opportunities to connect and/or learn from the shared experiences of others, which builds empathy and compassion. These bridges, established through storytelling, are also a trauma aware practice that humanizes issues and builds community based on shared humanity. The many benefits of storytelling including healing, connection, critical thinking and inspiration. Hearing stories from diverse people and sharing your own is transformational, which is why it is a key feature of this peacelearning framework!

Table 1.3 Peacemakers

Put It Into Practice: Peacemakers		
Learn about past and current peacemakers. Who are some of the peacemakers that have come up in your learning this year? Make a shared list. Review available mentor texts and media to grow this list! Invite local community leaders, family members and organizations to empower learners with messages of peace and justice.		
Emerging	*Intermediate*	*Advanced*
Create a circle map with the word peacemaker in the center, write down some of the descriptive words generated. How can you be a peacemaker in our classroom, school and the community?	What qualities do these peacemakers demonstrate? Examples: • Care for others & environment • Take action to help • Practice nonviolence How have they helped work toward peace? How does their message support peace in our classroom, school, community?	What inspires you about this peacemaker? What challenges/barriers did they have to overcome? Is there a cause that you wish a leader would emerge to solve? (climate change, conflict, injustice, etc.) If you took on a cause, what would it be and which peacemaker (living or nonliving) would you want to consult with?

Harm, Aggression & Violence

Peace is much more than an absence of violence and war; it is a raised consciousness that begins through the creation of a sense of harmony within. Visionary Dr. Maria Montessori (2007), proclaimed in a 1937 address that *"Peace is a practical principle of human civilization and social organization that is based on the very nature of man"* (p. 29). Despite peace being our nature, many have instead asserted that war and violence is innate to the human experience. We discuss this further in Chapter 10, p. 211, but for now consider…

◎ Pause & Reflect:

- ◆ Is war and violence an effective path for humanity?
- ◆ How much peace is actually happening at any given point in human history compared to war? (hint: peace > war)
- ◆ Why is history often marked by war and not peace?

The World Health Organization's Report on Violence and Health (Krug, et al., 2002) defined violence as:

> *The intentional use of physical force or power, threatened or actual, against oneself, another person, or against a group or community that either results in or has a high likelihood of resulting in injury, death, psychological harm, maldevelopment or deprivation. (p. 5)*

Though one might distinguish bullying on social media, for example, as aggression, it may still equate to violence based on the resulting harm. Models and experiences of aggression and violence are prevalent in all levels of humanity: global, national, cultural, institutional, interpersonal and intrapersonal. There are pursuits and goals of peace for each level of humanity, and all hold concern for the forms of violence that currently exist within it (see Figure 1.1). **Our goal with this book and framework is to support the pursuit of peace within all levels of humanity.**

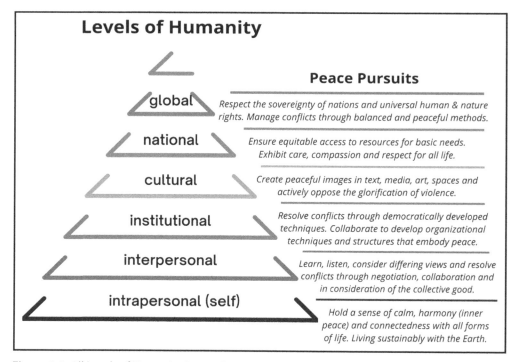

Figure 1.1 All Levels of Humanity Pursue Peace

Adapted from: *Peace Education,* 3d ed. (p. 15) (Harris & Morrison, 2013).

Violence, in its many forms, exists, in a very large part, due to the systems and structures holding it in place; those who wish to keep and gain power over others. Capitalism, colonialism, militarism, the patriarchy and some displays and acts being called 'patriotism,' are upholding and perpetuating these inequities and the continuation of civil violence. When a person's needs are not being met, this leads to types of violence on an individual, community, cultural, institutional, national and global level. Trauma and post-traumatic stress disorder (PTSD) are the results and causes of violence. Violence, in its many forms, is a public health issue and is something peace education can help change.

According to the U.S. Department of Health and Human Services (HHS), the effects of violence include:

◆ Premature death
◆ Physical injury
◆ Pain and suffering
◆ Negative physical health outcomes
◆ Increased mental health needs and disorders
◆ Behavioral health issues
  – Substance use
  – Risky choices and behaviors
◆ Engaging in violence

The Crime and Violence summary also warned *"Children and adolescents exposed to violence are at risk for poor long-term behavioral and mental health outcomes regardless of whether they are victims, direct witnesses, or hear about the crime"* (U.S. Department of Health and Human Services, n.d.).

Aggression and violence take on many forms. Children may be exposed to or experience it within their family, at school and in their community. Virtual violence is also a major concern. Peace educators should consider the presence of all types of violence in their lives, within learning and share research and recommendations with students' families.

Put It Into Practice: Limiting Virtual Violence

The (AAP) American Academy of Pediatrics (2016), *"continues to be concerned about children's exposure to virtual violence and the effect it has on their overall health and well-being."* They offer these summarized recommendations:

➢ Guide content and quantity
➢ Be mindful and co-play and view games, videos, media, etc.
➢ Realize that very young children may not be able to distinguish reality and fantasy
➢ First-person shooter games (killing others is the theme) are not appropriate for any children
➢ Enact legislation that would provide more specific information about media content and laws that help limit access to violent media for children
➢ Advocate for more child-positive media in the entertainment industry
➢ News and information media acknowledgment of the scientific connections and consequences of virtual violence (from peer-reviewed, vetted research)
➢ A federally developed caregiver-centric rating system for the entertainment industry

Set an intention for limiting virtual violence in your home. How will you support families in understanding the importance of limiting virtual violence?

Sadly, there are many instances of bullying, aggression and violence that exist. Consider the possible root causes (see Table 1.4) and its effect personally and on people you know. Notice the presence of varied types and levels of violence in the news, media, books, music, magazines, videos, games, podcasts, television, social media and your daily experiences and interactions.

Table 1.4 Root Cause Theories of Aggression and Violence

Root Cause Theories of Aggression & Violence		
Wants, rights and needs are not being met or addressed (e.g., lack of access to education, healthcare)	Economic inequality and poverty	Repeated frustration, anger and/or fear
Expression of behavior deep in the human psyche (human nature, biological)	Trauma; intergenerational trauma, historical trauma; post-traumatic stress disorder	Observation of behaviors (learned by models, media, culture)
White supremacy (beliefs and ideas that the White race is superior to other racial groups)	Prejudice and hate; biases and microaggressions; stereotypes	Ethnic, religious, racial and cultural misunderstandings and differences
Glamorization of war and violence	Political instability	Competition for resources or power
External influences such as colonialism, proxy wars, foreign interventions, militarization, arms trades		Extremist ideology
Adapted from: *Peace Education*, 3d ed. (p. 136) (Harris & Morrison, 2013).		

◎ **Pause & Reflect:** Before engaging in this, ground yourself.

- Make an accounting, observe and become consciously aware of the many encounters you have that present harm, hurt, conflict, bullying, aggression, violence and war.
- How does violence, in its varied forms, affect you and your community?
- What are the (likely) root causes of this violence?

> We have personally experienced acts of aggression and violence. We know we are very much <u>not alone</u> in this. We have also witnessed violence at many levels. Some of our favorite shows and movies regularly expose us to violence. Glancing through the news headlines reinforces its prevalence. In many ways, we feel desensitized or numbed to some of it – and that's what peace education can help change!

Disagreement and conflict will always be a part of human society; however, violence need not be. Peace education has the capacity to ultimately change, transform and end the many forms of conflict, aggression and violence. Transformation does not seek simply to manage the conflict. Instead, it digs down and asks us to observe, question and explore the core causes of structural violence and inequities. It looks at systems, not just the individual. Ghanaian diplomat Kofi Annan (2011) provided this guidance:

Making peace ultimately requires firm commitment and extraordinary courage, on the part of all sides, to ensure a permanent end to violence.

Indeed, rooting peace within human consciousness takes courage and commitment. When we have transformed our ways of thinking and being, all will celebrate this evolved state. Your courage and commitment are crucial when guiding students in considering root causes of harm, aggression and violence and in seeking peaceful alternatives for handling conflict and repeating violent historical patterns. We suggest that discussion, analysis, critical thinking and problem-solving in regard to harm, aggression and violence be focused on the system (systemic issues), not the person(s).

◎ **Pause & Reflect:**

- What thoughts and feelings are coming up for you in regard to the systematic issues in front of you?
- Have you sought out and listened empathetically to varying perspectives from those most impacted by the root causes of systemic violence?

Educators, families and communities play a crucial role in helping foster a culture of peace that ultimately impacts all levels of humanity (see Figure 1.2) For example, a child who holds a sense of inner peace and self-love will be less likely to self-harm or bully others. Likewise, a child who has strategies and skills for peacemaking and values them, will be less likely to engage in violence in their school and neighborhood when conflict arises and can aid in resolving it. A child who treasures the basic needs and rights of all humans

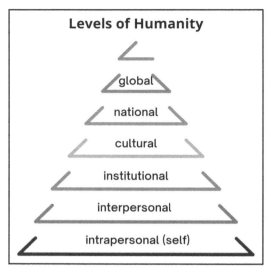

Figure 1.2 Levels of Humanity

and the natural world will grow up to help remove and change practices, systems and structures that exist solely as a means to maintain control and power (i.e., racism, sexism, classism, ableism, ageism, heterosexism, antisemitism).

A child who has experienced aggression, violence and/or trauma can find personal and collective healing through peace actions, pursuits and practices. When we use our ingenuity, action and care for all to fully address the core issues, we continue our transformation into a peaceful world and way of being. Peace education can have the power to help people end cycles of harm, to heal and to create a just and peaceful world.

Creating spaces for children to share their noticings about harm, ask questions and explore peaceful alternatives is the role of a peace educator. When people wonder, hope, care for and act toward peace, they will propose and create solutions, alternatives and changes that reduce and ultimately eliminate violence. If we are to realize this for all beings on Earth, we need peace education to go beyond safe to co-create brave spaces. There are many similarities and differentiations made between the meanings of safe and brave spaces, and language is important. The distinguishing factor we want to bring to your attention is that brave spaces allow learners to engage in critical dialogue, which may not always feel comfortable (safe). Brave spaces are inclusive of all voices.

◎ Pause & Reflect:

- What are your thoughts & feelings about safe and brave spaces?
- Are you engaging in conversations that are safe? Brave? How do you view the similarities and differences of these terms?
- When have the conditions around you created an unsafe space for you? How did this feel and what did you do?

Table 1.5 Exploring Harm, Aggression and Violence

Put It Into Practice: Exploring Harm, Aggression & Violence		
Emerging	*Intermediate*	*Advanced*
Invite learners to share what they think harm means and create a shared understanding. Develop a shared anchor chart that provides guidance and strategies for what learners can do if they feel upset and what to do if they feel harm has occurred to them.	Set up a trauma aware 'brave space' for students to share examples of harm, aggression, or violence that they've seen in various forms of media. Prompt learners to propose peaceful alternatives.	Set up a trauma aware 'brave space' for students to journal about an experience or observation of harm, aggression, or violence. Suggest learners first explore an event that they didn't directly experience (in media, heard about in community) or those that they have healed from. This is meant to bring shared awareness and to provide learners an opportunity to propose peaceful alternatives to what happened. Create a class anchor chart that explores possible root causes of harm, aggression and violence, as well as peaceful alternatives.
Chapter 4, p. 81: Co-creating brave spaces guidance Chapter 9: Trauma informed best practices		

(No) Justice & (No) Peace

Peace and justice walk hand in hand – and in our estimation, they always have and always will. Throughout US history, there have been many civil rights leaders, peacemakers and people who have spoken, written about and engaged in protests that ultimately connect back to the relationship of (and with) justice and peace. Since the mid-1980s, many slogans (e.g., "*no justice, no peace*") with differing word arrangements and nuances in meaning have been declared in response to harm, aggression, violence and police violence primarily against African American people. As with many slogans, it's unclear where it originated, but it is often linked back to a speech that Dr. Martin Luther King, Jr. shared in 1968 outside a California prison where Bill Coffin and other anti-war protestors were arrested and put in jail for resisting the draft and challenging the Vietnam War. In that speech, King said, "*There can be no justice without peace. And there can be no peace without justice*" (Green, 2021, p. 2).

During the civil rights movement, Dr. Martin Luther King, Jr. was not necessarily revered, rather, he was seen as an agitator. Many political leaders asked him and other civil rights leaders to *"wait,"* and be patient. After demonstrating and ending up in a Birmingham jail, Dr. King wrote the now-famous 'Letter from a Birmingham Jail' in April 1963, *"This 'Wait' has almost always meant 'Never'. We must come to see, with one of our distinguished jurists, that "justice too long delayed is justice denied."*

Peace educators take an active role in acting against injustices. An injustice is when there is unfairness or something is not just, such as human and nature rights violations. Peacelearners need spaces for exploring concerns, ideas and solutions, as well as to share their hopes and dreams in creating a world of <u>both</u> justice and peace <u>for all</u>.

◎ Pause & Reflect:

◆ What are examples of injustice that currently exist in your life, community, local environment and region?
◆ What are the possible main causes or reasons for why justice has been delayed and/or denied?

Table 1.6 provides some examples of injustices you might see and explore with children.

Table 1.6 School Injustices by Peace Action

Peace Action	Examples of Injustices
Seek Peace Within Yourself And Others	• Not feeling able to share all of yourself or safely try out different identities • Lack of opportunities for students who have different learning needs (light sensitive, noise sensitive, etc.) • Behaviors (dysregulation) caused by trauma
Respect Diversity	• Not being inclusive of multiple cultures (language, cultural norms, etc.) • Curriculum & materials that are stereotyping: lack of windows, mirrors and sliding glass doors in curriculum/texts • Microaggressions (implicit, explicit bias)
Protect Our Environment	• Water quality issues • Food waste (Federal school lunch rules) and composting • Single-use plastic and recycling • Access to clean and safe natural areas and parks
Reach Out In Service	• Limitations on afterschool and enrichment/club programs for students (fees, lack of free transportation) • Lack of clubs/programs that fit your needs
Be A Responsible Citizen Of The World	• Students' voices are not being taken into consideration when decisions are being made (classroom, administration, school board, community) • Lack of opportunity to voice concerns, don't feel safe or have a brave space in a classroom community

All forms of oppression, marginalization, racism, sexism, classism, ableism, ageism, heterosexism, colonization, anti-Semitism, microaggressions, bias, prejudices, stereotyping and discrimination can and should be explored through developmentally and trauma aware peace education.

There are some people who hold the opinion that children should not have these types of conversations in schools. Our response (discussed further in Chapter 10) is: how can they not be discussing what is happening in and around their lives, which is impacting possibilities for their futures and ultimately impacting and intersecting with all levels of humanity and the environment! Children all around the United States (and the world) are experiencing differing types of harm, aggression and violence. This sentiment has been shared by countless people and their lived experience: **if a child experiences racism, then all children can learn about racism and respecting diversity.**

Author's Perspectives

➢ As a teacher and a school principal, I (Carey) appreciate the need to have conversations with students about the world around them. This includes injustices! Children have an awareness of what is happening in their lives, communities and the natural world. They receive even more input through television, radio and social media – it impacts them, just as it affects us as adults. Children seek spaces to feel connected and valued, to process, ask questions and to have brave and critical conversations about what is happening and how justice and peace might be realized.

➢ When George Floyd was murdered, I (Julie) was coaching and teaching at a school just a few miles away from the site (Cup Foods). We were in distance learning due to the pandemic, and yet my colleagues and I continued to support each other and all ages of children in processing the lived experiences and current events. For example, I facilitated virtual seminar circles with 4th and 5th graders who listened, asked questions, learned and supported each other in deep conversations about what was happening in our neighborhood.

➢ Exploring complex emotions, having the opportunity to share stories and engaging in critical thinking about systematic causes requires brave spaces like those we seek to support peace educators and guides in setting up through this framework. We are mindful to offer developmentally sensitive and proactive approaches (circles, discussion, journaling and reading) to engage in brave conversations of this nature.

We all must take a stand and prioritize co-creating brave spaces that honor all identities and allow for developmentally sensitive conversations about harm, structural violence, systematic oppression and the exploration of peaceful alternatives and solutions. American philosopher and professor Dr. Cornel West (2011), profoundly spoke, "*never forget that justice is what love looks like in public.*" When we align and act from love, we strive to transform injustice at all levels of humanity.

Our students' voices and experiences are integral to this work. How will you raise up the voices of children and provide opportunities for critical feedback? Peacelearners need these brave spaces for exploring ideas and solutions, to give feedback and to share their hopes and dreams in creating a world of both justice and peace for all.

◎ Pause & Reflect:

- ◆ When feelings of vulnerability, unsureness or discomfort arise in courageous or critical conversations, how does this impact you? Others?
- ◆ How might you stay grounded and engaged?

Unfortunately, King's words "*justice too long delayed is justice denied*" (1963) and the ideologies of White supremacy still resonate strongly in the United States (and the world) today. As peace educators and allies in social justice, we hope this book will inspire a spirit of action and urgency around systemic racism and oppression. You are not being called upon to single-handedly address or end all the injustices, harm and violence in this world. That thought, for us, creates feelings of uncertainty, anxiety and despair. However, we join so many voices in calling upon everyone to advocate and actively take steps, every day, that will allow us to collectively realize justice and peace for all. We believe that by living in alignment with the peace actions and in guiding and engaging children in this process, we can ultimately evolve into a culture and society of sustained peace … and justice!

Table 1.7 Exploring Injustices

Put It Into Practice: Exploring Injustices		
Emerging	*Intermediate*	*Advanced*
Introduce vocabulary: injustice and explore common examples.	Define injustice and explore common examples.	Identify injustices in school and/or within the community.

Ask students to think about a topic/cause that they want to change in their school or community. Hold a class discussion about topics that are coming up for them that are identified as injustices. This could be related to inclusive playground equipment, more opportunities for sports, conversations related to race, gender, climate, etc.
 	
A seminar circle is a good discussion format. The lesson plan The Great Peacemakers (p. 255) provides further foundations for conducting seminar circles, but here are the basics:
 	
1. Pre-seminar preparation:
  ○ Review 'text' (evidence)
  ○ What do I think / I know?
  ○ What do I wonder?
2. Gather in a circle: all voices honored, active listening, questions, connection to 'text' evidence, ask follow-up questions, make connections
3. Post-seminar: summary, reflection and goal setting		

Create posters with labels to make their claim and argument	Write a speech, letter or poem and create a poster to make their voices heard	Extend from our intermediate guidance and have students take action with their speech, letter or a poem • How can they advocate for justice and get out into the community?
A mentor text you may want to read together is, *Something Happened in Our Town: A Child's Story of Racial Injustice* by Celano et al. (2018).		

Positive Peace

Practices rooted in justice, care and love, are by their very nature a strategy toward positive peace. As shared by the Institute for Economics and Peace (2018), positive peace is multi-dimensional and focuses on the exploration of attitudes, beliefs, systems and structures in order to create lasting peace at all levels of society. When there is positive peace, the conditions are present for all in society to thrive and flourish. Conversely, negative peace is when there is no violent conflict or war, however, the underlying causes of conflict (inequities, injustice, tensions) haven't yet been addressed or resolved. Negative peace often uses the threat of violence as the means of peace. For example, when a ceasefire is declared, this is an example of negative peace, it stops the violence. Yet, an absence of violence or war does not necessarily mean that there is just, sustainable peace. This is why we need both positive and negative peace, they are complimentary in the peacemaking, peacebuilding and peacekeeping processes.

In our schools, it is unfortunately common for many students to feel unsafe and anxious due to bullying and harassment. Unaddressed or ignored mental health needs can lead to even more conflicts. This bullying and harassment may not be physically violent, but instead can look like tension, exclusion or discrimination (negative peace). Environments anchored in positive peace actively address contributors to negative peace in order to create an inclusive, safe and supportive school culture. The practices, strategies and guidance in this book are designed to promote empathy, foster mutual respect and develop brave inquiry – all crucial for positive peace and the well-being and development of young learners.

The foundations for positive peace begin within ourselves and in our relationship with others and our environment. In order to evolve to living in positive peace globally, our educational systems need to shift the emphasis from only academic content knowledge, competition and personal gains, to education that fosters learning experiences through multiple intelligences, creativity, cooperation and belonging.

◎ Pause & Reflect:

◆ Consider your community and nation. Where there is peace, is it a positive or negative peace?

Empowerment Education

It is necessary for the teacher to guide the child without letting them feel her presence too much, so that she may always be ready to supply the desired help, but may never be the obstacle between the child and their experience.
~ Dr. Maria Montessori

Peace education is deeply rooted in empowerment and creates a sense of hope. Hope for one's future, that others have all the possibilities they will need for a fulfilling life and for the protection and restoration of our planet. Through peace education, we wonder about the current state of life and create a vision of a more just future for all. One flows from caring solely about their own needs and wants (and perhaps that of their close relationships), to a person who values their uniqueness *and* honors their interconnectedness with all. As Dr. Montessori (1914) shared, the teacher's main goal is to be the guide; we should follow the child and allow them to find their own way toward and within learning.

Through peace education and empowerment, children lean into their imagination, wonder and curiosity as they explore the possibilities they can envision for life on this planet. Structural changes take time and having a sense of longing, hope, patience and a futurist outlook is an important quality of peacelearning.

An empowered child has voice, choice and autonomy in their learning and feels valued. They learn to listen to the trickle and stream of their inner compass, exploring the waves of questions and ideas about the self, life's meaning, social constructs and power structures. Full of hope, an empowered child grows into and remembers their power to act in accordance with the love and connection they have for themselves and all that is around them.

◎ Pause & Reflect:

- ◆ When do you feel most empowered?
- ◆ How does this impact your journey in seeking peace?

Empowerment is linked to culturally relevant teaching practices. Being able to listen and be a champion and an ally for students is essential in this process. Culturally relevant teaching asserts that educators form partnerships with students.

This peace education framework and practices are designed to provide space for students to explore their own emotions, grapple with questions and empower them to use their voice and agency. We believe students who interact with peace and justice education lessons will have a thoughtful curiosity for the world, seek out varied perspectives and be empowered to stand up and advocate for what they believe in through nonviolent action. They will be inspired to make a positive impact on the world around them. At its essence, peacelearning is education for hope.

Table 1.8 Art Empowerment

Put It Into Practice: Art Empowerment		
Emerging	*Intermediate*	*Advanced*
Create art that represents something learners are excited and care about!	Art can serve as informative inspiration for the community. Study art that has been used in protest (e.g., civil rights, environmental protection, other human/animal rights issues) and then guide learners to create artistic messages related to an issue they care about.	Going a step further, students can create art as a persuasive campaign. Create a series of art pieces (3–5) that make a case for their topic. What are they interested in standing up for?
Arts can engage and empower learners, while teaching children critical thinking skills, collaboration and creativity (National Endowment for the Arts, 2013).		

Sustainable Peace

A child with self-love and awareness, a connectedness with others and our natural world is one who may embody peace and live in harmony. Children, if provided the opportunities, can be the largest ripple of change toward sustainable peace on Earth. Peacelearning fosters creativity, imagination, connectedness, critical thinking, problem-solving, hope and love. It is also through these characteristics that peace educators neutrally guide children in exploring their thoughts, ideas and hopes for the future and how they might realize them peacefully. Peace education emphasizes there are many paths, visions and possibilities to create a transformed future humanity based on universal human rights and social justice.

Far too many lives are impacted by harm, aggression, violence, fear, anger, injustice and hopelessness. We are mindful that peace education's futuristic views, ideas and aspirations are continually impacted by the realities of current lived experiences of people around the world. Peace is an ongoing journey, with a meandering path that we are on as an individual, collective humanity and interconnected planet. This framework provides foundations for accessible, relevant and developmentally sensitive peacelearning. We believe that in raising up the efforts of peacemakers across time and place; and in the implementation of the peace actions, pursuits, and practices, we can transform and raise our collective consciousness.

We also encourage readers and implementers to go beyond these lessons and practices as you deepen your implementation of peace education. With an open heart and mind, continue your own learning through listening, sharing stories, seeking critical feedback and collaborating with the children and your community. We invite you to actively join us in the effort to live in alignment with the peace actions and pursuits, as well as to be ambassadors for justice and peace for all people, beings and the planet. **We may not see the acorn grow into the mighty oak in this lifetime. Yet, we are planting and caring for the seeds that will become the anchored roots of an evolutionary way of living – in just, positive peace.**

Note

1. From *Peace education*, 3rd ed. © 2013 Ian M. Harris and Mary Lee Morrison by permission of McFarland & Company, Inc., Box 611, Jefferson NC 28640. www.mcfarlandbooks.com

References

American Academy of Pediatrics (2016). *Council on communications and media*. Christakis, D., Hill, D., Ameenuddin, N., Chassiakos, Y. (Linda) R., Corss, C., Fagbuyi, D., Hutchinson, J., Levine, A., McCarthy, C., Mendelson, R., Moreno, M., & Swanson, W. S. Virtual violence. *Pediatrics, 138*(2), e20161298. https://doi.org/10.1542/peds.2016-1298

Annan, K. (2011, October 19). *International conference to promote the resolution of conflict in the Basque country*. Kofi Annan Foundation. https://www.kofiannanfoundation.org/speeches/international-conference-to-promote-the-resolution-of-conflict-in-the-basque-country/

Boulding, E. (2005). Researchgate.net from https://www.researchgate.net/publication/230284090_Two_Cultures_of_Religion_as_Obstacles_to_Peace

Celano, M., Collins, M., & Hazzard, A. (2018). *Something happened in our town: A child's story about racial injustice*. Magination Press (American Psychological Association.

Green, R. (2021). *No justice, no peace: The origin and meaning of a powerful statement of resistance*. A Little Bit Human.

Harris, I. M., & Morrison, M. L. (2013). *Peace education* (3rd ed.). McFarland & Company, Inc. Publishers.

Institute for Economics and Peace. (2018). *What is positive peace?* Positive Peace. https://positivepeace.org/what-is-positive-peace

King, M. L. (1963). *Letter from a Birmingham Jail*, shared with pastors from the Southern Christian Leadership Conference.

Krug, E. G., Dahlberg, L. L., Mercy, J. A., Zwi, A. B., & Lozano, R. (2002). *World report on violence and health*. World Health Organization. https://iris.who.int/handle/10665/42495

Montessori, M. (1914). *Dr. Montessori's own handbook*. Guides.co. Retrieved June 16, 2022, from https://guides.co/g/montessori-handbook/31837

Montessori, M. (2007). *Education and peace* (Vol. 10). Montessori-Pierson Publishing Company

National Endowment for the Arts. (2013). Engaged and empowered. *American Artscape Magazine*. https://www.arts.gov/stories/magazine/2013/1/engaged-and-empowered

Reardon, B. A. (1988). *Comprehensive peace education: Educating for global responsibility*. Teachers College Press.

Union of International Associations (Ed.). (2017). *Yearbook of international organizations: Vol. 1, 1990/91* (27th ed.). De Gruyter Saur. https://uia.org/yearbook

U.S. Department of Education (2023). Guidance on constitutionally protected prayer and religious expression in public elementary and secondary schools. Retrieved December 31, 2023, from https://www2.ed.gov/policy/gen/guid/religionandschools/prayer_guidance.html

U.S. Department of Health and Human Services. (n.d.). *Crime and violence*. Health.gov. Retrieved, December 31, 2023, from https://health.gov/healthypeople/priority-areas/social-determinants-health/literature-summaries/crime-and-violence

West, C. (2011, April 17). *Cornel West: Justice is what love looks like in public*. Howard University. https://www.youtube.com/watch?v=nGqP7S_WO6o&t=21s

World Citizen Peace. (2014). *World Citizen Peace*. https://worldcitizenpeace.org/

2

Peace Actions

A Flexible Framework

If we are to teach real peace in this world, and if we are to carry on a real war against war, we shall have to begin with the children.
~ Mahatma Gandhi

Before we dive into the peace and justice education framework, we want to underscore that our peacelearning centers the view that **children already have everything within to seek peace**. There are some programs, curriculum, professional guidance and methodologies that come from a deficit view, a need to conform or keep to the status quo. **We believe that children have the internal instructions to cultivate peace.** As educators and leaders, we must do our best to protect, create, make and foster supportive and brave spaces for them to access the intuitive genius within. (Note: guidance for co-creating brave spaces is in Chapter 4, p. 81).

Education cannot be separated from identity, personal experiences and actions. As educator and philosopher Nell Noddings (2005) outlined *"Who we are, to whom we are related and how we are situated, all matter in what we learn, what we value and how we approach intellectual and moral life"* (p. xiii). When love, universal human rights, our interconnectedness and well-being are prioritized, then we can realize and sustain just, positive peace. To truly create cultures of peace, as Gandhi said in the opening quote, *"we shall have to begin with the children"* (Bylund, 2011).

Yet, to cultivate peace with children means that we must also focus our ongoing peace education efforts with the adults in our children's lives – you,

DOI: 10.4324/9781003449249-3

our elementary educators, leaders, caregivers and communities. As such, our peacelearning approach connects with multiple lenses of identity; student, educator, leader, school vision and community to create culturally affirming systems.

The Five Peace Actions, created by World Citizen Peace (2014), are the core of our flexible peace and justice education framework. They are:

◆ *Seek Peace Within Yourself And Others*
◆ *Respect Diversity*
◆ *Protect Our Environment*
◆ *Reach Out In Service*
◆ *Be A Responsible Citizen Of The World*

These peace actions provide a powerful framework to support learners, educators, leaders and school communities in deepening personal and collective identities, as well as building cultures of peace.

In This Chapter:

Foundations: An Action-Oriented Framework

At the core of this framework are the Five Peace Actions. As long as implementation is grounded in empowerment, culturally relevant pedagogy and trauma sensitive/informed practices, this framework can be implemented with a great deal of flexibility.

Throughout this book, we explore research, our relationship, understanding and recommended practices that connect with each peace action. There are many ways you, learners, families, schools and communities can implement the peace actions – and in all aspects of life. The universality of the Five Peace Actions provides a shared language to inspire and engage people at all ages and stages of life.

Figure 2.1 Five Peace Actions

This book and flexible, adaptable, action-oriented peacelearning framework provides crucial structure, guidance and language to support the creation of sustainable cultures of peace. We provide:

◆ A systematic, holistic, whole-person and inclusive approach to peace education.
◆ Comprehensive, researched and evidence-based peacelearning.
◆ Clarity and focus on key skills, pursuits, priorities and goals.
◆ Common language and shared practices grounded in culturally relevant pedagogy and trauma informed care.
◆ Practical lessons, ideas and resources for supporting learners in taking peace action.
◆ Best practices for peace guides and educators.
◆ Leadership and implementation guidance.

Consistent implementation of this framework is important because of the long-term impact it will have on individuals, schools, our environments and beyond. When we prioritize taking meaningful, consistent peace actions in our daily lives, we can truly evolve into a more just and peaceful society for all.

◎ **Pause & Reflect:**

- ◆ Which peace action(s) do you feel most strongly connected with personally?
- ◆ How do you already bring this peace action to light with children?

Peace and justice education prioritizes empowerment and enhances resilience, problem-solving, critical thinking, creativity, connection to all life, collaboration and mindful self-awareness. The Five Peace Actions foster meaningful learning and exploration across all intelligences, extending through lifetimes. Before we get into the technical aspects of the framework and implementation, let's consider what it will take to truly transform and evolve education.

The Time Is Now: Transform & Evolve Education!

Our education systems are on the brink of collapse. For years, they have failed to serve the needs of far too many children. The time for real change is upon us, and we believe that mainstreaming peace and justice education will be the catalyst for this transformation. We offer seven areas of focus for the evolution of humanity through our children, educational systems, practices and ways of being. While the supporting statistics are from the United States, these needs exist globally as evidenced by the United Nations Sustainable Development Goals (discussed in Chapter 8, p. 175).

1. **Address structural oppression and systemic racism:** Poverty is a result of structural oppression and racism. As of 2023, 11 million children live in poverty, including 1 in 7 children of the global majority (Children's Defense Fund, 2023). To evolve humanity, we need to evolve the individuals and complex systems that are interconnected to it.
2. **Increase per pupil funding and access to quality education:** In 2023, 12.7% of public funding went toward K-12 public schools education, which again fell short of the international standard of 15%. Additionally, the national gross domestic product grows 13.5% faster than public education budgets (Hanson, 2023).
3. **Value the profession:** Teachers earn 24% less than professionals in other fields with comparable degrees. "*From 1996 to 2021, weekly*

wages for public school teachers, adjusted for inflation, increased by only $29, in comparison to an increase of $445 in professions requiring a college education" (U.S. Department of Education, n.d.). To recruit and retain diverse, high-quality educators require respect and equitable wages.

4. **Reconstruct teacher preparation programs and professional learning:** Regardless of geographic location, training in peace education competencies, technology, culturally relevant pedagogy and trauma informed care will ensure all students have the knowledge, skills and practices to thrive, heal and help evolve our society to cultures of just peace.

5. **Extend educator planning and collaboration time and update curriculum:** To have regularly protected student-free times requires intentional decisions from departments or ministries of education, districts and schools. A ~50-minute daily prep, usually spent responding to needs of that day, weekly team planning and a few days a year of professional development are not sufficient. Educators need space, time and funding for ongoing peer mentoring, coaching, observation, research, planning, reflection and collaboration. Responding to the strengths, needs and growth areas of children takes time and coordination. So does enhancing and re-designing learning and teaching methods to culturally relevant peacelearning.

6. **Honor student voice and development:** Supportive systems include and honor student voices and provide a sense of personal agency and choice. To prepare students to positively contribute to society, an emphasis on practices, skills, strategies and intelligence that can be applied across content areas and one's life ought to be prioritized over isolated content standards and memorization of facts.

7. **Support mental health and social emotional learning needs:** More on this in the following sections of this chapter.

If school, community and government systems and structures continue to operate as they have, how can we expect different results? We do not need to 'rebuild,' we need to transform and ultimately evolve education!

◎ **Pause & Reflect:**

◆ As you review these seven areas of focus, what stands out to you? Why?

Evolution signifies a process of continuous change to a higher state. We echo the wisdom visionary educator, Dr. Maria Montessori spoke in 1949,

> *Humanity cannot be constructed only by one-half of human life. The entire world today is based upon the adult, and we have a world that is terrible, that is hard, and which people say is unchangeable. But I ask you, is anything unchangeable?*
>
> (Montessori, 2019, p. 43)

Nothing is unchangeable. We can evolve our educational systems to be responsive to the actual challenges, needs and gifts of ALL children! This transformation begins with prioritizing mental, social and emotional well-being.

Understanding Mental Health & Trauma

When this peace and justice education framework and practices are fully implemented in schools, it will positively impact the mental health and social emotional needs of learners, educators, leaders, families and our communities. Let's begin by deepening our understanding of why this inner work is so needed.

According to Substance Abuse and Mental Health Services Administration (2023) in the United States (U.S.) in 2020:

◆ One in five adults experienced a mental health condition.
◆ One in six children had a major depressive episode.
◆ Suicide was the second leading cause of death for youth age 10–24.
◆ Signs of mental health disorders appear before age 14 for half of all disorders.

The COVID-19 pandemic compounded the mental health crisis worldwide. Take for example these statistics from the U.S. (National Center for Education Statistics, 2022):

◆ 69% of public schools reported an increase of students seeking out mental health services from school.

- 76% of staff express concerns related to student dysregulation, depression, anxiety and trauma.
- Only 13% of public schools strongly agreed that their school can provide effective mental health services.

The effect and impact of mental health needs ripples through our homes, schools, economically and across all systems (healthcare, judicial, housing, families and community). Educational systems must continue to shift toward a greater emphasis on preventing and intervening early in regard to mental health needs, in part through the inclusion of social emotional learning (SEL) systems and resources that are evidence-based and culturally responsive. Understanding trauma, in its many forms, and impact of trauma on the brain, nervous system, body (physiology), behavior, relationships and learning is crucial. We go deeper into understanding trauma in Chapter 9, but as a foundation Table 2.1 provides key terminologies and understandings that will be important as we explore each peace action (Chapters 3–8).

Note that sometimes this terminology may be explained differently, such as in a therapeutic setting; however our peacelearning approach and guidance align with these meanings and the additional contexts contained in this table (2.1).

Throughout this book we embed trauma awareness (consciousness), guidance and sensitive practices. When we refer to trauma, we mean to be inclusive of the varied types and onsets of trauma included in Table 2.1. In Chapter 9, we expand to related neuroscience and best practices for being trauma sensitive and informed educators and leaders. Comprehensive implementation of these approaches and practices creates caring and supportive environments where all children can thrive.

Table 2.1 Types of Trauma & Peacelearning Connections

Terminology	Meaning	Connections to Peacelearning Framework
Adverse Childhood Experiences (ACE's)	A 1995–1997 study found that adverse childhood experiences and potentially traumatic events correlate with increased risk of substance abuse and negative physical and mental health outcomes later in life. It linked educational, social and economic conditions and consequences, as well as the transmission of intergenerational trauma (Centers for Disease Control and Prevention, 2022).	Transformative trauma informed peace and justice education addresses many ACE's and toxic stress risk factors such as aggression, conflict, violence, social and environmental disorder, disengagement and isolation. Evolving systems at all levels of humanity is a longer-term aim of peace and justice education, ultimately reducing the risk factors and toxic stressors of poverty, abuse, neglect, racism, discrimination, housing and food insecurity (Centers for Disease Control and Prevention, 2023).
Toxic and Chronic Stress	Tolerable stress is normal and can even be positive. But when it is excessive, occurs frequently and/or for a prolonged duration it becomes chronic or toxic. Toxic stress impacts development, relationships, mental, physical and emotional health.	
Trauma	The American Psychological Association (2018b), defined trauma as: *"any disturbing experience that results in significant fear, helplessness, dissociation, confusion, or other disruptive feelings intense enough to have a long-lasting negative effect on a person's attitudes, behavior, and other aspects of functioning."*	Our DNA is 99.6% identical to every human (National Human Genome Research Institute, 2023). Yet our experiences and environment impact our unique, limited knowledge and view of the world. Peace and justice education plays significant short- and long-term roles in addressing the many forms of trauma: • Emphasizes self-care and supportive practices for intrapersonal well-being • Anchors whole child and social emotional learning • Builds and encourages empathy, compassion and understanding for others
Post-Traumatic Stress Disorder (PTSD)	PTSD may develop after traumatic events. The person may be easily triggered, startled, have disturbed sleep, difficulty concentrating or remembering, flashbacks or nightmares and exhibit avoidance behaviors and/or guilt related to the trauma (American Psychological Association, 2023).	

(continued)

Table 2.1 Types of Trauma & Peacelearning Connections (continued)

Terminology	Meaning	Connections to Peacelearning Framework
Secondary Traumatization Secondary Traumatic Stress Compassion Fatigue Vicarious Trauma	A person listening to, witnessing, caring for and supporting those impacted by trauma can be negatively impacted even if they have not directly experienced the event. Burnout (physical, emotional and/or mental exhaustion) from high levels of stress and secondary trauma is common in service-oriented vocations such as educators (American Psychological Association, 2018a).	• Provides meaningful practice and application of peacebuilding techniques such as de-escalation, managing and resolving conflicts, dialogue, collaboration and peacebuilding • Fosters understanding and addresses the root causes of conflict, violence and trauma • Advocates for social justice • Encourages community engagement, collective engagement and solidarity, thereby creating a sense of belonging • Grounds us in culturally relevant pedagogy and trauma informed care • Fosters a socio-cultural evolution to eliminate systems of oppression
Intergenerational Trauma Multigenerational Trauma Transgenerational Trauma	There is more research demonstrating the impact of trauma, oppression and extreme social adversity on future generations. Descendants of a person and/or community who have experienced trauma can have epigenetic changes and responses that negatively impact behavioral, mental, emotional, social and spiritual health (Dubois & Guaspare, 2020).	
Historical Trauma Cultural Trauma Historical Trauma Response	*"Historical trauma is cumulative emotional and psychological wounding over the lifespan and across generations, emanating from massive group trauma experiences"* (Brave Heart et al., 2007, p. 177). Historically traumatic experiences such as internment camps, terror attacks, genocide, slavery and Indian boarding schools impact(ed) future generations. Responses vary and include self-destructive behavior, substance abuse, survivor guilt, mental health disorders and somatic pain.	

(continued)

Table 2.1 Types of Trauma & Peacelearning Connections (continued)

Terminology	Meaning	Connections to Peacelearning Framework
Trauma Aware Trauma Consciousness	Understanding the prevalence of trauma and being empathetically aware of how traumatic experiences (known or unknown) may impact a person's sense of self, behavior and relationships.	• All schools, organizations and communities need these foundations! • Tier 1 of Multi-Tiered System of Supports (MTSS). More about MTSS in Chapter 10, p. 217
Trauma Sensitive Trauma Responsive	Approaches that focus on the specific needs of individual(s) and are responsive, accommodating and provide targeted interventions, services and support.	• Primarily Tiers 2 and 3 of MTSS. • The basic neuroscience behind the approach to regulate, relate and then reason is important here. (Chapter 9, p. 187)
Trauma Informed	Approaches that focus on creating an entire school culture, policies, operations and interactions that promote healing, prevent further traumatization and foster a sense of trust, safety and empowerment. The majority of adults demonstrate trauma awareness and responsiveness. Recognizing biases in yourself, site and community is a crucial aspect.	• Sustaining just cultures of peace at your site may require this approach, which takes time and training. • When in place these understandings, approaches and practices become Tier 1 of MTSS.
Protective Factors Coping Resilience	The possibility of experiencing ACEs is reduced with protective factors. Protective factors can be within the individual and in connection with caregivers, family, relationships and the greater community (Centers for Disease Control and Prevention, 2023). Resiliency is our capacity to cope and adapt from the presence of toxic stress and experiences of trauma.	Examples of protective factors that are tenets of our peace and justice framework and guidance: • Social emotional and mental health supports and awareness • Safe, stable, caring, nurturing and positive environments, role-models and relationships • Focusing on cultural assets and practices help build resilience in students and strengthen self-identity. • Partnerships and connectedness (in service and also with families and communities) • Violence is reduced and not tolerated • Peaceful conflict resolution and problem-solving • Ultimately addresses basic rights and needs of all life

Holistic Education: Social Emotional & Whole Person Learning

Given the prevalence of mental health needs and trauma, the case for holistic education is clear. Social emotional and whole person or whole child learning is highly connected to the peace action *Seek Peace Within Yourself And Others*. Whole person, holistic education means just that we meaningfully engage within the needs and gifts of that which makes us human: our physical, mental, emotional, intellectual, creative and social selves. To create conditions for children and adults to thrive, these fundamentals of social emotional learning (SEL) are crucial:

- Development of healthy identities
- A sense of belonging
- Feeling connected in relationships
- The ability to listen to and manage emotions
- Demonstrating empathy and care for others
- Making responsible decisions
- Working toward personal and collective goals
  (Collaborative for Academic, Social, and Emotional Learning, 2021a)

There is ample evidence to demonstrate the need and the long-term positive outcomes associated with SEL such as its positive impact on academics and overall well-being (Collaborative for Academic, Social, and Emotional Learning, 2021b). Many leaders and educators may not yet be confident in guiding children in these areas. As a result, in many schools this leaves SEL as an add-on, an afterthought, occasional practice 'if we have time' or a band-aid response to an outburst or crisis. It is necessary to change how we approach the mental, social and emotional needs that ALL humans have at their core. Know that this book is also designed to engage and support your whole person, holistic learning and wellness!

◎ Pause & Reflect:
- What is your pedagogical philosophy or mindset on deep and intentional integration of social emotional learning?
- Identify a personal goal for deepening your knowledge and application of the peace action: *Seek Peace Within Yourself and Others*; start just as you are!

In Chapter 10, we support you in navigating obstacles and challenges to peace education, but we feel crucial first steps are that considering what limitations and limiting beliefs exist within yourself, colleagues, leadership and families. There is alarm for the way in which we don't truly honor the whole person. This happens at home, in schools, at work, in our communities – and within ourselves.

In order to create cultures of peace in our external world, this inner work (seeking peace within) is imperative to prioritize at all ages and in all spaces!

If we don't focus on the whole person, we will continue to have harm, aggression, violence and suffering. It is important to distinguish that peace education goes beyond SEL to locally and globally address the root causes of violence; to empower positive change; and to promote social justice, human rights, environmental stewardship and global citizenship. Peace education is truly for everyone and as such, should be the thick thread at the heart of homes, organizations, institutions and communities.

Recognizing Limitations & Limiting Beliefs

If we are truly to transform and ultimately evolve to cultures of peace, we can start by recognizing our own limiting beliefs.

◎ **Pause & Reflect:** Take time to deeply think about yourself, your family, classroom and/or school. How much is the whole person really honored, explored and consistently given space and time? Read this list and allow for a quick generally applied *yes or no response*. In my (life, family, classroom, school) we:

- ◆ Learn about and honor all emotions, explore the messages they carry and peacefully release.
- ◆ Have daily practices for seeking and/or allowing internal stillness and going within (i.e., meditation, grounding practices, self-regulation strategies, observation & noticing, mindfulness).
- ◆ Regularly reflect on our challenges, our responses and ideas of ourselves (through the lenses of self-compassion and love).
- ◆ Explore who we are:
  - What's in our heart.
  - How values, needs and wants impact behavior and decisions.
  - Our ideas and internal lessons related to happiness, love, safety, peace and justice.
  - Our ideas and internal lessons related unhappiness, hate, dis-ease and injustice.

◆ Have external support from others who care and help us feel a sense of belonging.
◆ Intentionally foster hope for the future and take small steps to create a just and peaceful world for all life.
◆ Feel empowered that at all stages of life, our ideas, opinions and understandings of ourselves and the world may change or evolve.

Reflect on the trends to your yes/no responses…

How much space and time is really allowed for the whole person?

By now, you have probably also thought of many limitations or barriers to prioritizing seeking peace within yourself and supporting learners in ongoing and meaningful ways in this process. Do any of these sound familiar?

→ There just isn't enough time.
→ I have other priorities (e.g., curriculum, behavior).
→ The academic needs are so high; they are behind.
→ I have too many kids (needs) in my classroom to provide the support everyone needs.
→ There is so much pressure to perform on tests and meet standards, I have to focus there.
→ I don't know what to do because this is new-ish for me too.
→ The master schedule… The budget… The classroom/space…
→ Our __ (district, principal, families), aren't/won't…

The list goes on. We are educators and leaders with over 35 years of combined experience in public school settings … we get it! We extend great empathy and understanding for the challenges, barriers and limitations you're feeling in regard to truly making space and time for the whole person (child) in deeper and more meaningful ways.

We believe there is a beautiful foundation for the implementation of whole-person learning … you! Yes, it can feel overwhelming when we consider how to create sustainable change. Remember, you are not responsible for evolving our entire educational system by yourself. Yet, we need each and every one of us to speak up, take action and keep moving the dial toward creating a more just and peaceful world for all.

Consider this ancient Chinese proverb: *"Limitations are but boundaries created in the mind."* Whatever limitations and barriers that are coming up for you, check-in with the emotions attached with it. Most thoughts are both mental and emotional. We impose limitations, boundaries, barriers and obstacles based on our genetics, beliefs, environment, education and experiences. Though feeling very real and stiff, these *"limitations are but boundaries created in the mind."* They can be released, changed and transmuted with dedicated time, space and action.

Consider what we observe in very young children ... children who have not yet had limiting beliefs imposed or created. Most inherently believe they are capable of anything they want to try. They are curious, creative, passionate, playful, experimenters and unafraid of making mistakes. Our children are models for how we can free ourselves from limitations, to create fearlessly, to explore everything, to discover passions, share joy and to value the lessons and learning in the challenges or mistakes.

◎ **Pause & Reflect:** Though we live in a much different society today, our education systems remain very much the same as the industrial-era.

- ◆ What limiting beliefs do you hold about evolving education to truly make time and space to explore and honor the whole person in ongoing, deep and meaningful ways?
- ◆ Identify an area you feel empowered and inspired to support learners in seeking peace within.
- ◆ What small step can you take today? Tomorrow? What small steps can you take every day?

A child with self-awareness, a connectedness to others and our natural world is one who lives in harmony and embodies peace. Children, if provided the opportunities, can be the largest ripple of change toward sustainable positive peace on Earth.

Start As You Are: Connecting With the Peace Actions

To start implementation of this peace and justice education framework, begin as you are! There are many connections that can be made between the peace actions and your existing curriculum, practices and priorities. We recommend this process to launch your first few months with the core of the framework, the peace actions:

1. On your own, consider your understandings, beliefs, attitudes and questions related to the topics covered in Chapter 1: *What Is Peace Education?*
2. On your own, reflect on what each peace action means to you personally and with learners.

3. With your team, reflect, discuss and record:
   a. What are your ideas and wonderings related to peace and justice education (refer to Chapter 1)?
   b. Go through each peace action – what do you think this means? How does (or might this) look, sound and feel for you? And with children/in your setting?
   c. How do the Five Peace Actions intersect with existing site systems, priorities and goals?
      - For example: mental health and social emotional learning (SEL); diversity, equity, inclusion, belonging and accessibility (DEIBA); Positive School Wide Engagement (PSWE), Positive Behavioral Interventions and Supports (PBIS), restorative practices, Responsive Classroom; Multi-Tiered Systems of Support (MTSS).
   d. What standards, benchmarks and curriculum connect with each peace action?
   e. What practices, lessons, tools and resources are already in place? How do these connect with the peace actions?
   f. What concerns, issues and injustices exist in the community? How might the peace actions inspire and empower short- and long-term solutions?
4. Set a personal intention: How will you take meaningful peace action this month? Share this intention with an 'accountability partner' and check-in with each other regularly.
5. Set a collective intention(s) and take peace action: As a team and in your classroom, how will you connect learners with the peace actions this month? We suggest you start by having learners engage in the above questions (a–f) in developmentally sensitive ways.
6. Gather with parents, caregivers and community partners to share, reflect and gather input from the questions above (a–f).

Here is an example of existing connections with the peace action, *Protect Our Environment*. In Minnesota (U.S.), all grades have standard benchmarks related to understanding the various aspects, impacts and importance of water. It's really important to think about the health of the many freshwater lakes and the surrounding environment. Depending on where you live, you may be thinking about the health of the oceans, rivers, groundwater or other local bodies of water.

This is true for each one of the peace actions; there are some general principles that we can all think about, but the nuances of your particular community are important to consider as a school or organizational community. This is glocalized learning – learning about global problems through local examples and applying sustainable solutions.

Though we suggest this initial process occur over several months, in reality this could be the primary focus of your first year of implementation! That pace would allow you to slowly work through the chapters, discussions, research, guidance, practices and lessons contained in this book. There are so many factors to consider, but based on our knowledge of implementation science, as well as our experience leading school improvement, engagement plans and professional learning, we recommend three to five years to reach full implementation.

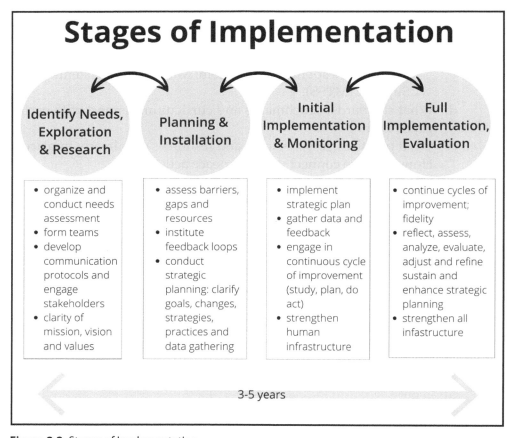

Figure 2.2 Stages of Implementation

Leading for Peace

Peace and justice education is a powerful avenue for school transformation and systemic change that goes on to evolve all levels of humanity. Change takes time and it is crucial that all stakeholders are involved. This includes teachers, students, staff, families, the community and leadership at all levels (school, district, state).

Creating a culture of peace involves stakeholders striving toward and implementing competencies and skills of peace and justice education. This peace action framework and the guidance and practices provide the foundations. Figure 2.2 can help you visualize these stages of implementation. It is essential to gather input and discuss how peace education can support school climate and the overall mission and vision of a school.

In collaboration with stakeholders, leaders can deepen and expand their commitment to creating cultures of peace by becoming a Peace Site. A Peace Site is a more formal declaration of the school or organization's identity, shared understanding and implementation of the Five Peace Actions. Peacelearning becomes internalized and is evidenced by the culture, curriculum and priorities, which are designed from the peace actions. In Chapter 11, we provide further leadership guidance to actualize Peace Sites. Figure 2.3 illustrates the core components of our peacelearning framework.

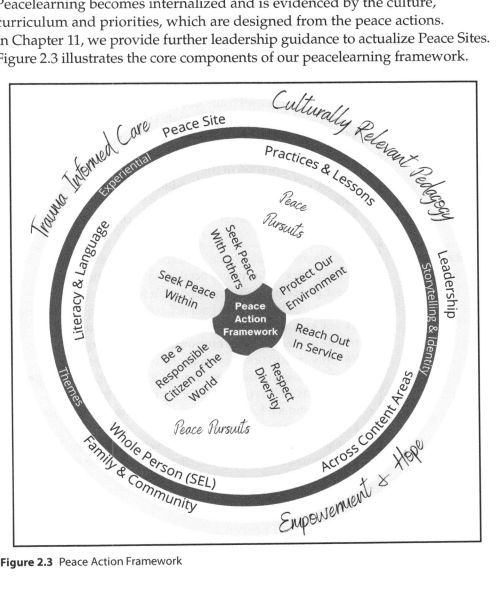

Figure 2.3 Peace Action Framework

Peace Action Framework

The peace actions provide a strong, flexible core for peace and justice education. In addition to trauma informed care, encircling our framework is culturally relevant pedagogies, which is discussed in detail in Chapter 5: *Respect Diversity* and also has a presence throughout this book. Our framework aims to be actionable and to inspire and empower learners, educators, families and community stakeholders in creating inclusive cultures of peace. In the rest of the book, we expand on this action-oriented framework with the following features:

Table 2.2 Core Features & Components of the Peace Action Framework

Framework Feature	Description & Further Context*
Peace Actions	• Throughout the book we engage adult learners in foundational research and opportunities to pause, reflect and make connections with the **peace actions**. • We have a strong emphasis on terminology and **language** designed to deepen your understanding and implementation of the many aspects of each **peace action**, **culturally relevant pedagogy** and **trauma informed care**. • See the Table of Contents for a listing of peace action Chapters 3–8.
Peace Pursuits	• Peacelearning goals (aims, targets) aligned with each of the **peace actions** and occur over space and time. • These **peace pursuits** are applicable for all ages and stages of life, so consider them for yourself, colleagues and community, as well as with learners. Peacelearning is **experiential** in nature and emphasizes **empowerment and hope**. • We provide additional descriptors to deepen your understanding of the meaning and importance of each **peace pursuit**, as well as guidance for putting it into **practice**. • See Appendix B for a cumulative list of the peace actions and aligned pursuits. • Our language choice of **'pursuits'** was inspired by Dr. Gholdy Muhammad's Culturally and Historically Responsive Literacy framework (2020).

(continued)

Table 2.2 Core Features & Components of the Peace Action Framework (continued)

Framework Feature	Description & Further Context
Put It Into Practice Note: beginning on p. 295 is an index of all practices in the book!	• **Practices**, mini-lessons, ideas and guidance for peacelearning, much of which is **experiential** and interwoven with **literacy and language**. • Questions, prompts and guidance **language** are provided for emerging, intermediate and advanced learners. • We weave our own **stories and identities** throughout this book, while also providing **practices** designed to leverage the power of **storytelling**. Our goal is to deepen your and learners' sense of **identity and empowerment** in relation to peacelearning. • **Across content area practices**, connections and ideas by peace action are near the end of Chapters 3–8, 'More Peaceful **Practices**.' • **Culturally relevant pedagogy** and **trauma informed** best **practices** are throughout the book. • *Peacemakers In Practice* are leaders in their field who provide stories and guidance for each peace action chapter.
Lessons & Themes	• Ten comprehensive lesson plans for the theme 'Belonging and Harmony' are also aligned with **literacy and language** Common Core Standards (see Chapter 12). • Many **lessons** (and some **practices**) include recommended anchor texts (read alouds, stories, **storytelling**). • Each **lesson** has questions and **language** prompts for guiding emerging, intermediate and advanced learners. • See Appendix D, p. 288 for a full year of suggested **themes**.
Family & Community Connections	• Many ways to connect and engage parents, caregivers **(families)** and **community** members in peace & justice education and the peace actions are woven throughout the book. • There is also guidance specific to each peace action near the end of Chapters 3–8, 'More Peaceful **Practices**.'
Leadership & Peace Site Implementation	• All stakeholders should be a part of the design, implementation and sustaining work of being a **Peace Site**. In Chapter 11, we discuss these steps in greater detail. • Schools that have challenges (and even violence) can be created cultures of peace; knowing there is always **hope** and the possibility for peace is **empowering**!
* Bolded words are explicitly indicated on the framework graphic.	

The goals of our peacelearning framework and guidance center around creating people and cultures of positive peace. As discussed in Chapter 1, positive peace is just, sustainable and creates lasting peace that opposes the structures and cultures of violence, whereas negative peace is the absence of war and violence (Institute for Economics and Peace, 2018). Positive peace is ultimately more systemic, complex and includes proactive practices and preventative solutions rooted in nonviolence and underpinned by resilience. We deeply believe that the peace action framework, corresponding pursuits, practices and lessons will transform individuals, schools, communities and ultimately nations and our global community toward its evolution of positive peace.

References

American Psychological Association. (2018a, April 19). *APA dictionary of psychology: Burnout*. Apa.org. https://dictionary.apa.org/burnout

American Psychological Association. (2018b, April 19). *APA dictionary of psychology*. Apa.org. https://dictionary.apa.org/trauma

American Psychological Association. (2023). *Posttraumatic stress disorder*. Apa.org. https://www.apa.org/topics/ptsd

Brave Heart, M., Bussey, M., & Wise, J. B. (2007). *Trauma transformed: An empowerment response*. Columbia University Press.

Bylund, L. (2011, December 10). *Gandhi spoke at Montessori London 1931*. Ahimsa Peace Institute Worldwide. https://www.gandhiforchildren.org/gandhi-spoke-montessori-london/

Centers for Disease Control and Prevention. (2022, March 17). *About the CDC-kaiser ACE study*. Cdc.gov. https://www.cdc.gov/violenceprevention/aces/about.html

Centers for Disease Control and Prevention. (2023, June 29). *Adverse childhood experiences: Risk and protective factors*. Cdc.gov. https://www.cdc.gov/violenceprevention/aces/riskprotectivefactors.html

Children's Defense Fund (2023). State of America's children report: Child poverty. Childrensdefense.org. https://www.childrensdefense.org/tools-and-resources/the-state-of-americas-children/soac-child-poverty/

Collaborative for Academic, Social, and Emotional Learning. (2021a, July 1). *Fundamentals of SEL*. CASEL. https://casel.org/fundamentals-of-sel/

Collaborative for Academic, Social, and Emotional Learning. (2021b, August 20). *What does the research say?* CASEL. https://casel.org/fundamentals-of-sel/what-does-the-research-say/

Dubois, M., & Guaspare, C. (2020). From cellular memory to the memory of trauma: Social epigenetics and its public circulation. *Social Sciences Information. Information Sur Les Sciences Sociales, 59*(1), 144–183. https://doi.org/10.1177/0539018419897600

Hanson, M. (2023, September 8). *U.S. public education spending statistics.* Education Data Initiative. https://educationdata.org/public-education-spending-statistics

Institute for Economics and Peace. (2018). *What is positive peace?* Positive Peace. https://positivepeace.org/what-is-positive-peace

Montessori, M. (2019). *Citizen of the world: Key Montessori readings* (Vol. 14). Montessori-Pierson Publishing Company.

Muhammad, G. (2020). *Cultivating genius: An equity framework for culturally and historically responsive literacy.* Scholastic.

National Center for Education Statistics. (2022). Public schools and limitations in schools' efforts to provide mental health services. In *Condition of education.* U.S. Department of Education, Institute of Education Sciences. Retrieved January 5, 2024, from https://nces.ed.gov/programs/coe/indicator/a23

National Human Genome Research Institute. (2023, February 2). *Fact sheet: Human genomic variation.* Genome.gov. https://www.genome.gov/about-genomics/educational-resources/fact-sheets/human-genomic-variation

Noddings, N. (2005). *The challenge to care in schools* (2nd ed.). Teachers College Press.

Substance Abuse and Mental Health Services Administration. (2023, April 24). *Mental health myths and facts.* Samhsa.gov. https://www.samhsa.gov/mental-health/myths-and-facts

U.S. Department of Education. (n.d.). *Raise the bar: Eliminate the educator shortage.* www.ed.gov. Retrieved January 5, 2024, from https://www.ed.gov/raisethebar/educators

World Citizen Peace. (2014). *World citizen peace.* https://worldcitizenpeace.org/

3

Seek Peace Within Yourself

You (and our children) have all that you need inside your imperfectly, perfect self! Lovingly and compassionately accept and celebrate exactly where you are on your peace journey.
~ Julie Lillie and Dr. Carey Seeley Dzierzak

Seeking peace within yourself is a deeply personal journey. This is also a journey we are not on alone, which is one reason this peace action is fully written as *Seek Peace Within Yourself And Others.* We are all both unique individuals and interconnected to one another. How any learner (including you!) views their relationship with themselves is welcomed as part of the exploration that occurs within peacelearning. We invite you into a brave space of curiosity and non-judgment.

In This Chapter:

DOI: 10.4324/9781003449249-4

For most of us, seeking peace within is a lifelong process that is continually changing in response to our limited experience of the world. Our ways of being have been shaped by childhood experiences, ancestral histories, generational trauma, life experiences and depending on your beliefs, our past lives. Though our experiences may feel universal in nature, they are limited by the landscape of our internal world, as well as the influences of our external environment.

◎ **Pause & Reflect:** As you explore your inner world, revisit these questions with loving curiosity:

◆ What makes you, you? Ask yourself, who am I?

If you feel confusion similar to, *'I don't know who I am,'* that is okay. Leave space for your sense of self to shift and flow. The only constant in life is change. Extend self-compassion, grace and connect with others who support and care for you. Lovingly hold space for who you were, are, might be and are becoming!

Peacemaker In Practice

Application of India's Wisdom for Peacebuilding

By Mandar Apte, Executive Director, Cities4Peace

It is known that most violent tendencies we develop, including our judgments, fears and inhibitions, arise from unhealed traumas that are accumulated during our childhood (Wyrick, 2021). Therefore, the knowledge about healing from our trauma and peacebuilding must be provided during these formative years to all relevant stakeholders – the children, parents and educators. We too visualize an elementary school to be the space for individual and community healing and transformation. Educators, especially in violence-affected communities, must learn healthy ways to heal their own trauma so that the education they impart is from a space of compassion, love and peace.

The current approaches to healing trauma and peacebuilding are grounded in Western models and theories that prioritize addressing factors like cultural and structural violence and ensuring institutional solutions like well-functioning civic institutions, low levels of corruption and equitable distribution of resources. Indeed, all these are important 'fixes,' but sustainable peacebuilding also requires that we address the psychological and emotional dimensions of the conflict. If the trauma in individuals and groups affected by violence and conflict is not addressed, then it can build up as frustration and anger and can potentially manifest into violence.

The need for this 'inner development' therefore provides the context and agency for the meaningful integration of India's wisdom of inner peace to deepen the impact of the current conflict resolution and peacebuilding strategies. **According to India's wisdom traditions, peace is the innate nature of all human beings**. Therefore, all Indic wisdom traditions advocate the practice of Yoga, nonviolence, pranayama and meditation to transform negative emotions and develop inner peace. These practices have helped people from all walks of life, across the world, for centuries. Several leaders, like Rev. Dr. Martin Luther King, Jr. (NPR, 2009), Rosa Parks (Ramabadran, 2023) and Steve Jobs (Chouhan, 2011), have acknowledged that exposure to India's culture and wisdom helped them to deepen their leadership purpose, vision and impact.

Leveraging India's wisdom of inner peace and harmonious coexistence, we started the Cities4Peace (https://cities4peace.org/) an initiative to work with educators, community leaders and changemakers to reduce violence and promote peace and social cohesion in the communities impacted by violence across the world. The initiative also works with local, regional and international governmental and non-governmental institutions, educators/ administrators, non-profits and businesses to build the capacity of local leaders and changemakers to design unique solutions to community-specific challenges. This training focuses on building participants' leadership capacity, using yoga and Sudarshan Kriya (SKY™) breathing and meditation practices to assist in managing stress, and empowering participants to heal from trauma and develop greater compassion.

We strive to host our programs in elementary school communities affected by violence, as these hold such potential to be centers for healing. As an example, in Los Angeles, which witnesses approximately 25,000 violent crimes annually, our program was hosted at Budlong Elementary School in the Harvard Park neighborhood. We brought together educators, parents, at-risk youth and other community members along with LAPD police officers in our eight-week Ambassadors of Peace training using SKY™ breath meditation practices to enhance their mental well-being and enable trusted relationships. As shared in her post-video testimonial, the school principal, Ms. Hodo, arranged this training because:

> There is a lot of stress in our district and a lot of stress in our profession… And we live in a violent community. So having this training will help us know how to deal with parents and our students when they are experiencing trauma and it will really assist in the future.
>
> (Cities4Peace & Hodo, 2023, 0:41-1:15)

India's soft power derives not only from its cultural heritage (music, dance, arts etc.) and economic strength but also from its rich history of philosophical and wisdom traditions that have influenced people globally for centuries, to discover healing, solace and transformation and learn to peacefully coexist.

Equanimity (ē-kwə-ˈni-mə-tē)

We all experience stress and uncertainty. How we respond to dis-ease, pain and to those challenging moments is an opportunity – a practice! Imagine you prepared a beautiful lesson and when you delivered it, students were disengaged. Frustrating! But, even when things don't go as we hoped, responding with a calm, kind and an evenness of temper is important. It's not always easy, but modeling, fostering and maintaining mental calmness, also called equanimity, is a best practice of peace guides.

Equanimity is an essential mindset and skill for creating a culture of peace because it supports focus, stress reduction, emotional regulation, resilience and empathy. Equanimity positively influences all forms of intelligence, leading to more peaceful and balanced people and environments. Philosopher and educator, Jiddue Krishnamurti (1963), asserted:

> Most of us think that intelligence is the outcome of acquiring knowledge, information and experience. By having a great deal of knowledge and experience we think we should be able to meet life with intelligence. But life is an extraordinary thing, it is never stationary; like the river, it is constantly flowing, never still. We think that by gathering more experience, more knowledge, more virtue, more wealth, more possessions, we shall be intelligent. (p. 180)

Like the river, life is always changing. We need to be able to navigate through the joys, challenges and traumas of life while within a balanced boat (our inner selves). Imagine you are floating down this river (life) that continually shifts from gentle flows to stressful, raging rapids. What might this experience be like by yourself and with no life vest? What about if you were in an innertube or a boat with a missing rudder? How would this be in a small boat or large yacht? The more stable and balanced our transportation (our grounded selves), the less we will feel the effects of the more challenging and stressful areas of the river of life – and we will navigate the ever changing waves and currents with more ease.

Author's Perspective

In connection with health challenges and developmental trauma, I (Julie) was introduced to and am learning to embody the Buddhist and Zen teachings of equanimity. I used to be swept away in the undertow of my nervous system dysregulation, pain, loss of mobility and independence, as well as the emotional waves connected to it all. Through healing modalities and increased self-awareness, now I recognize needs and give myself permission to respond mindfully. Believe me, I'm not there yet, but I manage triggers, stress and pain with more ease because of this deep inner work and daily nourishing practices. The SKY™ breathwork practice, taught to me by Cities4Peace, has been transformational for enhancing my emotional, physical and mental well-being (see Peacemaker in Practice, p. 49,) ! Whatever you and the children are navigating in life, we all benefit from practices of seeking peace within.

Ongoing mindful practices, like the Pause, Breathe, Notice, Act (PBNA) Strategy (Lesson p. 250), help us live in the present moment and find harmony and balance within – and this is the state of equanimity.

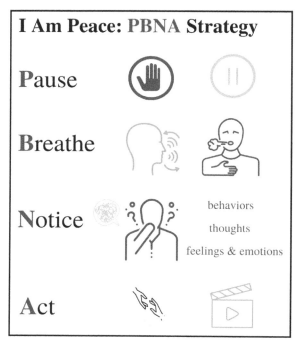

Figure 3.1 I Am Peace: PBNA Strategy

It is important to give ourselves and learners the space to practice calming strategies. When in a regulated or neutral state, we can more easily learn and explore what is/isn't working for us. Even if we feel we don't need 'it' (e.g. breathing or meditation), in that moment, frame it as a practice for internalizing and automaticity. That way, when we are stressed, experiencing uncertainty and heightened emotional states, we can more easily access these self-regulation, grounding and anchoring strategies. When we feel we don't have the time and space for these practices, it is even more important to prioritize it!

Put It Into Practice: The Sound of Equanimity in the Classroom

Routinely utilizing the sound of a bell, singing bowl, rainstick or chime is an invitation to pause, become aware of our breathing and return to peace and calm. The 'bell-ringer' needs to be in a peaceful state and hold still in place before 'ringing' the bell (sound tool). 'Ring' three times. This mindfulness tool helps bring learners into the present moment. They can then more easily adapt to stimulation and distraction, as well as consciously respond, rather than unconsciously react. The sound is also a signal of something beginning, changing or ending like the start/end of the day and transitions. As they listen to the sound, try to hear all of the vibrations until it is totally silent. As attention is concentrated on listening, one can close their eyes and concentrate on the in- and out-breath, letting any thoughts float by like a cloud passing through the sky. Learning to use the breath to find equanimity helps us appreciate and connect with the silent and stillness within.

Self-Awareness Conferring & Interactive Journals

Exploring and understanding our internal world is the basis of our humanity. Seeking peace within truly is a lifelong journey. As you guide learners, emphasize and empower them that as they learn and grow, their ideas, beliefs and understandings of themselves will likely evolve as well.

◎ **Pause & Reflect:** Imagine if all humans, of any age, had an innate capacity to extend love, acceptance and compassion. How might that deepened connection, to the very essence of our being, also positively impact others and our environment?

Throughout the time they are in your care, we highly recommend that you prioritize one-on-one conferring to support learners' exploration of their inner world. When we confer it is very much an individualized conversation that occurs while other students are engaged in self-directed learning that does not require your support (e.g., reading, journaling and projects). **Conferring offers profound opportunities for connection, sharing stories, reflecting and goal setting**. We know conferring is powerful with readers and writers, and the same is true for peace-seekers who gain invaluable insights for personal development. Paired with conferring, the development and maintenance of a self-awareness journal or interactive notebook provides an anchor for this personalized peacelearning. Exploring (and knowing) our evolving inner selves requires a sense of safety, courage and vulnerability.

Put It Into Practice: Conferring to Deepen Self-Awareness

This individualized conversation should be responsive to the student and include a lot of adult listening and observing. General structure:

1. Open-ended check-in and relationship connector.
2. Strategic discussion that holds space for reflection and connects to areas for positive and encouraging feedback (e.g., happenings in the learning space and/or practices from the self-awareness journal or interactive notebook).
3. Responsive discussion to deepen self-awareness, which includes a mini-teaching, suggestion or co-created next step.
4. Student states their next step or take-away from the conference and adds it to their journal/notebook.

The lessons and practices are designed to be introduced in whole or small groups. Have learners add peacelearning to a dedicated self-awareness interactive journal. Then, consistently practice, build upon, reinforce and deepen through discussions, review and conferring with the learner and their interactive journal. Though the lessons and practices can be implemented in a myriad of sequences and styles, here is our implementation recommendation.

1. **I Am Peace: PBNA Strategy** (p. 250): setup and maintain a shared 'peace pad.'
2. Create a dedicated **self-awareness interactive journal**, notebook or portfolio (physical or digital) dedicated to exploring the self; add the PBNA Strategy.
   - **Emotion Explorations** (p. 61): 1–2 emotions at a time; explicit vocabulary instruction, Frayer model (Frayer et al., 1969) and connected processes and experiences.

     – As shared, add entries for lessons, strategies and practices such as breathwork, loving-kindness meditations, questions, reflections and inspired art.

3. **Heart Map: Who Am I** (p. 253)
4. **Matters to Me Map** (p. 57)
5. **Inner Calm** (p. 59):
6. **The Dragons Inside Me** (p. 63)
7. **The Gifts of *'Both/And'*** (p. 66)

The above lessons can be scaffolded with the interactive templates, images, organizers, print/copy materials, key language and labels within the self-awareness journal. You might also use section tabs for easy access. Return organically and often to interact with the content for review, practice, reflection and sharing.

Through the lessons, practices and the conferring process, it is possible that traumas may surface. Trauma can present in many behaviors and ways, as well as be pretty hidden (more on this in Chapter 9). Ultimately as a peace guide and educator, we need to approach all our learners with care, knowing that there is a high likelihood of post-traumatic stress disorder and trauma having a presence. Maybe this is also true in your own life… Peace education is truly for everyone. Given the prevalence of trauma and mental-emotional health needs, why would we not dedicate time and space toward cultivating inner peace? This is especially important in the environments our children spend so much of their time.

Exploring Identity & Core Values

Seeking peace within is a process with many paths that includes ways of knowing and being. Just as knowledge can be acquired in many ways, so too can understanding and experiencing our own existence (ways of being).

As you know, your role is that of a guide and educator, more like a coach – not a therapist. Focus on the strategy, practice or process and follow the learners from there. As you do, have a plan for how you can respond to a child who needs deeper support, such as referring to a therapist, counselor, social worker or school psychologist. If/when trauma arises, follow and stay within your level of training in developmental trauma when you respond. Consider also how you will keep open communication with caregivers. Likely your colleagues' perspectives and feedback are valuable in collaboration, child study, Multi-Tiered Systems of Support, and to continue your learning about lessons, strategies and practices for deepening self-awareness. The key is to flexibly and strategically weave in explorations, processes and experiences to empower learners with their evolving *Seek Peace Within Yourself* toolkits.

Table 3.1 Pursuit: Self-Awareness

Peace Pursuits for: *Seek Peace Within Yourself*	
I have awareness of what makes me, me.	• Observing and knowing the self, as well as reflective expression, creates inner transformation. We can advocate for the best version of ourselves when we know our current wants, needs, values, beliefs, ideas, hopes and goals. • Having awareness of and embracing our gifts, strengths, growth areas and tendencies create self-love. When we love and accept ourselves unconditionally, all things are possible. • Guiding children in exploring their identities (and intersectionalities) is a foundation of culturally relevant teaching practices. • Implement the Lesson **Heart Map: Who Am I** (p. 253) consistently.

To deepen understanding of the many facets and intersections of identity, consider how our values, needs, wants and beliefs impact our behavior and decision-making. As we embrace the beautiful uniqueness within us, there is also an invitation to celebrate our differences. This happens simultaneously to discovering our shared connections with others.

◎ **Pause & Reflect:**

◆ What matters to you most in life? What/who do you value?
◆ How do your values intersect with what you need and want in life?

Table 3.2 Pursuit: Recognize Values, Needs & Wants

Peace Pursuits for: *Seek Peace Within Yourself*	
I recognize how my values, needs and wants impact my behavior and decisions.	• Practice empathy and empathetic communication, listening and perspective-taking, critical thinking, problem-solving and awareness of bias and stereotypes in order to recognize how our behaviors and decisions (may) impact nature and others. • When something is misaligned to our values, it creates conflict. When our needs, wants or rights are not being met, this creates turmoil. Frustration builds up to hostility, aggression and violence. Loving-kindness and giving ourselves and others grace are the antidotes. • Compare and contrast people's needs, wants and values. • Consider the inequalities in how needs and wants are/aren't being met. Recognize any held privilege and take action to help change what is unfair (injustices or oppression).

Table 3.3 Practice: Matters to Me Map

Put It Into Practice: Matters to Me Map		
Emerging	*Intermediate*	*Advanced*
Create a shared visual with each student's voice about what matters to them. Guide the shared writing toward core values, adding key words with sketches/images. The size of the key words might vary based on the number of students who feel that also matters to them.	Extend *emerging* further by having learners create their own art/writing about who and what matters in their lives. Share (build vocabulary) with more sample core values. Then, have students add key words and phrases to connect what matters with values.	Extend *intermediate* further by guiding learners to identify examples of a time they felt conflicted or hurt about something that really mattered to them. Perhaps an experience that was difficult or challenging. Explore how this connects to values. *Example: When my grandpa died I was really sad. I missed him and I felt bad that my mom cried a lot. This experience really mattered to me because I value family.*
Prompts: important people, places, memorable experiences, care – connect those to values. **Example core values:** family, friendship, choice, independence, achievement, faith, fun, creativity, fairness, love, peace, responsibility, learning, community, adventure, kindness, determination, adventure, connection, relationships, belonging		

Self-Regulation & Going Within

It is imperative that we co-create brave spaces for children to explore their identities, beliefs, definitions, values, attitudes, opinions, needs, wants and ways of being; to have awareness of what makes them, them! (More on brave spaces in Chapter 4, p. 81). Learners need to understand their ideas of self may change as they grow, learn and have unique and collective experiences in the world.

All of this requires 'going within,' to notice and listen to the body, thoughts and emotions. To find information, inspiration and guidance in the quiet and stillness. Going within is also an opportunity to release that which is no longer serving our greatest good. Meditation and mindfulness practices offer the space and opportunity for this rest, inner connection, observation and introspection. These types of practices support emotional and neurological regulation, which we go into detail in Chapter 9, p. 194 (regulate). There is a plethora of research about the positive benefits of meditation, mindfulness, grounding strategies and calming practices (Greater Good, n.d.), which include:

◆ Improved self-management, self-regulation and self-control
◆ Management and reduction of stress and anxiety
◆ Improved concentration, attention, focus, performance and retention
◆ Fostering compassion, empathy, kindness and care for self and others
◆ Acceptance and increased resilience
◆ Positive impacts on sleep, mental health and relationships

There are many techniques, but ultimately, meditating is a state of being. It is a settling of the mind and body; it is not doing and doing nothing. The purpose is just to relax and be in the present moment. We all have the instruction within to access this stillness, but it isn't always easy!

Table 3.4 Pursuit: Strategies to Calm

Peace Pursuits for: *Seek Peace Within Yourself*	
I use strategies to calm and ground myself.	• When a human is dysregulated, it is hard for them to listen, comprehend or cope. Regulate first! In Chapter 9, we go into the trauma informed sequence of engagement: regulate, relate, reason. • When co-regulating, get on their level. With body language and minimal words, soothingly communicate safety. Validate feelings and provide a calm and reassuring tone of voice. Engage in peaceful strategies and practices, inviting (not forcing) them to join you or choose their own practice. • **Practices for calming the nervous system:** observing nature, (guided) meditation, body scans, mindful movement, journaling, art, music, awareness and observation of the self, present moment, breath and thoughts in silence, affirmations, being in nature, pets, relaxation and getting support through utilizing tools and trusting relationships. • Weave in and practice the PBNA strategy (Lesson p. 250) and breathwork throughout the day, including in collaboration with families.

Table 3.5 Practice: Inner Calm

Put It Into Practice: Inner Calm		
Support learners in exploring what contributes to, supports or helps them access their inner calm (regulation), as well as causes of dysregulation. See Table 3.4 for a list of practices for calming the nervous system.		
Emerging	*Intermediate*	*Advanced*
When you feel calm, what is happening in your body?	When you feel calm, what is happening in your body, your mind, with emotions?	Extend *intermediate* guidance to include differentiating between 'doing' (talk a walk) and 'being' (meditation) regulation strategies.
What are you doing (not doing) when you are calm?	What might it be/ feel like when dysregulated?	Identify how technology regulates/dysregulates.
When you feel upset, what helps you feel calm?	What do you already do to support your regulation (calm)?	Note that mild dissociation is part of regulation (getting 'lost' in a book, TV, movie, video game or creative project).
Make connections to brain development and nervous systems reactions with the practice 'Neuroplasticity & Resilience' in Chapter 9, p. 208.		

◎ **Pause & Reflect:**

♦ What does (or will) prioritizing your inner peace and creating space every day to 'go within' look and be like for you? Setup support. Staying connected with an encouraging partner, friend or colleague, particularly one on a parallel path, can be highly beneficial.
♦ How will you prioritize ongoing opportunities for learners to 'go within?'

Emotional Intelligence

Emotions are neither inherently bad or good. However, we experience and express emotions with varying degrees of intensity and levels of pleasantness. **Our emotions bring us information and messages, asking us to pay attention, stop, change, communicate, leave, continue, begin or respond**. For example, anger often rises when our boundaries or values are challenged and are in need of protection or restoration. Anger itself isn't a 'bad' emotion, but a messenger to help us speak our truth and lean into vulnerability. It is when anger is expressed violently that it is understandably experienced as a 'bad' emotion.

Emotional intelligence includes our capacity to perceive, interpret and respond to our emotions, as well as navigate interactions with empathy. Because emotional intelligence has been undervalued in recent history, many may struggle with really understanding the language of emotions. In her book *Atlas of the Heart*, educator and researcher, Brené Brown (2021), offered a map of meaningful connection and grounding in language of human experience. She highlighted,

> *Without understanding how our feelings, thoughts, and behaviors work together, it's almost impossible to find our way back to ourselves and each other. When we don't understand how our emotions shape our thoughts and decisions, we become disembodied from our own experiences and disconnected from each other. (p. xx)*

It is important to explore the messages of our emotions and these self-awareness concepts in our life. When we have an internal conflict or parts of ourselves that are not fully integrated or in harmony, it will impact our relationships, health and well-being.

◎ Pause & Reflect:

◆ What emotions have you experienced today?
◆ What messages have your emotions brought forward?
◆ How are emotions honored in your learning space? With family and friends?

Table 3.6 Pursuit: Emotions

Peace Pursuits for: *Seek Peace Within Yourself*	
I identify my emotions and explore their messages.	• Emotions are neither inherently bad or good but are experienced with varying degrees of intensity and levels of pleasantness.
	• Our emotions bring us information and messages and then the energy can be released.
	• Explicit vocabulary instruction of emotions and feelings is an ongoing core lesson.
	• Naming and exploring emotions should occur organically and ongoingly as well. For example, wonder what a book character might be feeling and why or share feelings about an interaction or event.
	• Honor that we can feel multiple emotions at the same time, even when they feel to be opposites.

Table 3.7 Practice: Emotion Exploration

Put It Into Practice: Emotion Explorations		
• Utilize a Frayer model (Frayer et al., 1969) to explicitly teach emotion vocabulary (1–2 per session). Add to self-awareness journals. • Use a tracker to chart emotions throughout the week. How do they show up for you every day? What messages do they bring? • Create art, music and movement inspired by emotions.		
Here are a few core emotions, their messages, gifts and questions to get you started!		
Emotion I Feel…	*Messages & Gifts*	*Ask Yourself (Questions)*
Angry	• Protect your sense of self • Stand up for yourself and others • Set boundaries	• What matters to me? • What do I value? • What needs protecting? • What needs to be reset?
Afraid (Fear)	• Being aware, focused, ready & present • Noticing (instincts, intuition) • Curiosity	• What am I noticing? • What am I sensing? • What am I wondering? • What action should I take?
Shame (Guilt)	• A needed behavior change • Hurt someone else or did something wrong • Doing the right thing	• Who has been hurt or disrespected? • What do I need to do to make it right?
Worried (Anxiety)	• Get ready • Plan & prepare for future • Focus and task-completion	• What is bringing this feeling up? • What needs to be done and when?
Sad (Grief)	• Let go, release • Relax and restore • Grounding • Anchoring to gratitude	• What isn't working for me anymore? • What do I need to let go of? • How can I relax, restore and re-ground? • What am I grateful for?
Bored (Apathy)	• Take a break • Waiting, patience • Accepting what you can't control or influence • Invites in imagination, dreaming, problem-solving	• What is being avoided? • What do you need or want (that is within your control or influence)?
Confused	• Notice overwhelm • Pause, rest the mind, take space • Innocence; navigate newness, change	• Do I need to pause and have some still space? (Yes!) • What do I need? • What action should I take?
Jealous Envious	• Relationships, love, care, connection (jealousy) • Fairness, security, needs, access to resources, injustice, recognition (envy)	• What do I need/want in this relationship? • What needs healing? • What is unfair (injustice)? • What resources do I/others need? • What needs to be made right?

(continued)

Table 3.7 Practice: Emotion Exploration (continued)

Emotion I Feel...	Messages & Gifts	Ask Yourself (Questions)
Happy	• Look forward to fun, playful, amusement • Hope, laughter	• What makes me feel hopeful? • How can I have fun and play?
Joyful	• Celebration • Interconnectedness	• How can I celebrate? • How am I feeling connected?
Calm (Content)	• Pleasure, ease & peaceful • Appreciation & gratitude • Affirming, inner achievement, confidence	• What am I thankful for at this moment? • What am I feeling confident (proud) of?

Adapted from: *The Language of Emotions* and *The Dynamic Emotional Integration Workbook* by Karla McLaren (2010)

Creative Intelligence

Seeking peace within means experiencing the right now, developing and deepening our self-awareness and inner calm. These are the foundations for creative intelligence. Creative intelligence includes connecting in with one's imagination, innovating and bringing a fresh or unique perspective to ideas, experiences and problems. In addition to channeling creativity for expression, one holds a sense of curiosity, wonder and out-of-the-box thinking. This often requires bravery, resilience and embracing failure and mistakes as part of learning and life.

When we know the power within ourselves, through love, we awaken to our true nature as creative beings. As creative beings, we know that our thoughts, words and actions are energy that transforms into our physical world. Often attributed to Mahatma Gandhi, this quote highlights the power of our creative intelligence.

> *Your beliefs become your thoughts,*
> *Your thoughts become your words,*
> *Your words become your actions,*
> *Your actions become your habits,*
> *Your habits become your values,*
> *Your values become your destiny.*
> (Ganguly, 2019)

◎ Pause & Reflect:

◆ Do you view yourself as a creative being? In what ways, explain.
◆ How does this belief/view impact your journey of seeking peace within?

As we engage in our inner work, we learn to notice, release and authentically replace our negative thoughts. If we don't, those negative thoughts will also manifest in our physical world. Notice any negative thoughts and choose (not wish/want) a different thought or path. We all have a range of positive and negative self-talk and thoughts. Our unsupportive self-talk is not to be shamed or hidden. Instead, with a deepened awareness, we are able to consciously and compassionately honor the gifts, messages, lessons and values behind negative self-talk... and can then transform it. As creative beings, we have the opportunity to positively energize our internal and external world through our thoughts, words and actions.

Table 3.8 Practice: The Dragons Inside Me

Put It Into Practice: The Dragons Inside Me		
Introduce the idea that we all have different voices or 'dragons' inside and that our goal is to notice the messages inside. Show a wide variety of dragon images from the scarier fire breathers to the magical and friendly looking. Connect the dragons to normalize that we all have a range of self-talk (voices inside) from negative and seemingly unsupportive (scarier-looking dragons) to the more positive and supportive self-talk (friendly looking). Using your own life examples, create a t-chart to model and visually display positive and negative self-talk (dragon voices).		
Emerging	*Intermediate*	*Advanced*
Scribe students' ideas of negative and friendly dragons. Make a simple shared t-chart. Prompts: • **I am...** • When you are happy with yourself, what do you feel? • When something is hard, what does that sound like? • If you mess up, what does that inner dragon say?	In journals, draw two dragons to represent positive/supportive and negative/unsupportive self-talk. Add labels on each dragon to represent what messages the dragons inside you say. This is a personal process, but you might invite learners to share in trusted partnerships afterwards, which could inspire additions to their own entry. See student sample Figure 3.2 on p. 67. Prompts: • When you are proud of yourself, what types of positive things do you say to yourself? • When something feels really hard, what is your dragon voice saying? • If you make a mistake, what does your negative self-talk say?	Prompts: • When you meet a goal, what supportive voices come from within? • If you are challenged, fail at something or can't do it right away, what does your negative self-talk say?

The 'Both/And'

Seeking peace within yourself is a simple and complex journey. Yes, both simple and complex … at the same time. That's the thing about being human, two seemingly contradictory things (truths, experiences, understandings) can be harmoniously connected and true, at the same time. Sometimes, this truth, which we refer to as the *'both/and,'* can feel conflicting. How can we have two conflicting truths, experiences or understandings?! Many of us get looped into binary, *'either, or'* thinking. *'Either, or'* thinking suggests that there is only one truth or valid option, it is dualistic thinking. Whereas the *'both/and'* invites non-dualistic thinking and the embracing of multiple perspectives, possibilities, qualities and ideas – simultaneously.

We are each having our own limited experience of the world, which often results in this dichotomy being present. Flexibility and widening our perceptions and thinking allow us to embrace the gifts in non-duality.

Author's Perspective

For me (Julie), experiencing and embracing the lessons of the *'both/and'* have been deeply present in my life and integral in developing a sense of inner harmony. An illustration of this is with my unsupportive 'dragon inside,' which I've named *'not enoughness.'* (I'm not good enough; this won't be enough, you can do more/better, etc.) As I gained awareness of this *'not enoughness'* self-talk, I initially shamed myself. I shouldn't say these things to myself; I was flawed and needed to stop internalizing perfectionism. It turned out that my negative self-talk navigation wasn't enough either! I was either enough … or I wasn't … it couldn't be both, right!?

I came to the realization that there are also gifts in what was behind this *'not enoughness.'* The *'not enoughness'* messages invite me to hold high expectations and also to surrender, to let go of outcomes. It helps me to both envision the potential within myself, projects and people and lean into flexibility, patience and acceptance. *'Not enoughness'* has helped me find better alignment with my time and energy. As I gained awareness of and welcomed these gifts, I was able to transmute these *'not enoughness'* internal messages. When we explore the seemingly negative in ourselves and life, along with the seemingly positive, we are embracing the gifts of the *'both/and.'*

In Eastern philosophies, this is the concept of Yin & Yang, two interconnected yet opposite forces interwoven and when in balance create a sense of harmony. In nature, as in the human experience, this interplay of contrasting elements coexists within the interconnectedness of all. Acknowledging and accepting the multifaceted nature of experience and the paradox within supports our journey of seeking peace.

We live in the land of experience through opposites. It is through contrast that we create meaning of our experiences. Be empowered in the nuances of your experience and understand that as you learn, unlearn, experience and grow, your perceptions and personal truths may also shift. Our paths in seeking peace invite flexibility and adaptability in our thinking and ways of being – embrace the '*both/and.*'

◎ **Pause & Reflect:** Think about how the '*both/and*' shows within your life. How can a deeper understanding, acceptance and appreciation of the '*both/and*' support you in seeking peace within? Areas for exploration:

◆ Internal: 'Dragons Inside Me' and identities
◆ Within relationships
◆ In specific situations or experiences
◆ Representations in nature, art, music
◆ Spiritual beliefs

Table 3.9 Pursuit: Empowered in Change

Peace Pursuits for: *Seek Peace Within Yourself*	
I feel empowered that as I learn and grow, my opinions, ideas and understanding of myself and the world may change.	• Highlight that while core aspects of identity may stay relatively similar throughout our life, intersecting aspects can change. • Model peaceful communication, interactions and strategies. When you make a mistake or if harm occurs, address it with honesty and reflectiveness that you too are growing and learning. Mistakes are part of learning! • Normalize that when we receive new information our understanding may change. This is a continual process of having a growth mindset and flexible thinking. • Affirm and lift the power of the mindset word, 'Yet!' Engage in ongoing reflection and transform fixed mindsets (i.e., won't take risks, gets defensive or shuts down with feedback or differing perspectives, won't look at or admit mistakes). • Engage in reflective growth goal-setting processes regularly such as I used to _, but now I __, in the future I might _. • Utilize stories and storytelling to highlight the '*both/and*' in experiences, relationships and in nature. Highlight the balance of opposing forces and the importance of harmony.

Table 3.10 Practice: The Gifts of the *'Both/And'*

Put It Into Practice: The Gifts of the *'Both/And'*		
Emerging	*Intermediate*	*Advanced*
Setup a t-chart for interactive or shared writing. Start with **hot | cold** as an example and add learner ideas about **opposites** in concepts and ideas. You may also need to embed a little language instruction about **and | or** • Bad | Good • Happy | Sad • Fast | Slow • Big | Little • Love | Hate • Hard | Easy (Soft) Point out how we each experience these concepts and ideas uniquely and in shared ways. Highlight that there are many states in-between the opposites as well. *We understand and can name what hot is because of experiencing the cold. Both are important to our understanding. We know what cold feels like because we compare it to its opposite, hot. Hot AND cold.* *Do we all experience hot or cold exactly the same? No, bath water might feel hot to your body, but maybe not so much to me. However if it is really, super hot (boiling) in temperature, we would BOTH agree that this water is hot!* Label the t-chart and name this as the *In-between* or *'Both/And.'* *Sometimes we can have what we can call black or white thinking. But there is a lot in-between!* **In-between** *black and white are many shades of gray. We call this the 'Both/ And.'* (Demonstrate this with paint, or shading) Continually add and build upon this as situations and examples arise organically. *As we learn and grow, it is helpful to have flexible thinking about our experience and to remember the gray, the in-between, the both/and!*	Pose questions for discussion, as well as prompts for role-playing, that provide opportunity for the consideration of multiple perspectives and moving **beyond** *'either/or'* **choices and thinking.** • Are you enough just as you are? And can you also get better? • Can you experience both happiness and sadness at the same time? • Can someone be both caring and hurtful to you? Both a supportive and unsupportive friend? • Can a project be successful and unsuccessful at the same time? **Which is 'right'? Can both be?** • A healthy body is strong. A healthy body is flexible. • You need to work hard. You need to rest. You need to play. • They are a good friend. They hurt my feelings.	Introduce the Eastern philosophy of Yin and Yang by showing images of the symbol. Discuss the idea of contrast, represented by the black and white halves. Connect the symbol to the language *'either/or'* as well as *'both/and.'* Have learners draw and label in their journals to highlight the **contrast** and **interconnectedness** • Quiet | Loud • Calm | Energetic • Sleep | Awake • Summer | Winter • Weak | Strong • Dark | Light • Stillness | Movement Point out that the contrasting dots on the symbol indicate the *'both/and'* – life is not *'either/or.'* Share that the circle of the symbol represents cycles and the continual movement within balance and harmony.

(continued)

Table 3.10 Practice: The Gifts of the '*Both/And*' (continued)

Put It Into Practice: The Gifts of the '*Both/And*'
While conferring with learners, return to their '*Dragons Inside Me*' and uncover what is behind or underneath their positive and negative self-talk. Connect this back to what matters to them (values). Highlight how both our positive and negative self-talk have messages, lessons and gifts. It's not that one is better or worse than the other. *Both* are important to knowing and loving ourselves. *And* that their ideas of themselves might change as they learn and grow! A few samples and connected possible values: • "I can/can't do this" – determination, achievement • "I am loved" – friends, family, safety, connection, relationship, belonging • "I'm better than this" – success, growth, humility • "I am (not) smart" – intelligence, achievement, competence • "I am weird" – belonging, uniqueness, confidence • "Being athletic" – movement, body, competition, belonging

Figure 3.2 Advanced Student Notebook Sample of Practices: Dragon Inside Me and The Gifts of the '*Both/And*'

Happiness & Hope

When parents and caregivers are asked what it is they want for their
children, the most common answers relate to hope and happiness.
Happiness is a subjective, unique experience, as well as a universal idea
and emotional state. Our overall well-being, our perceived pleasure
and enjoyment, along with feeling a sense of purpose, fulfillment and
alignment are part of the picture we paint of our happiness. Though
there can be the idea that happiness ought to be a constant state, it isn't!
Like other emotions or states of being, it is an evolving and dynamic
experience.

◎ **Pause & Reflect:**

- ◆ What brings you happiness?
- ◆ What contributes to learners' overall well-being?

Did you name any people and/or relationships as a contributor to your
sense of happiness? Across multiple longitudinal studies, the Harvard
Study of Adult Development found that the most common indicator and
factor of happiness is good relationships (Waldinger & Schulz, 2023). **When
people are connected and have a sense of belonging, it supports healthy
development and a more positive well-being**.

Social connection has a stronger correlation with happiness than material
possessions and money. However, money and resource access are still
essential for fulfilling our basic needs and sense of security and safety,
which contribute to our overall health and well-being. The United
Nations 17 Sustainable Development Goals (n.d.), which we explore in
Chapter 8, highlight the intersections of sustainability and happiness.
For example, inequalities, poverty, access to food and clean water,
the presence of conflict, violence and war – these all affect a person's
health and well-being and their comparative levels of happiness (or
unhappiness). In addition to our overall sense of peace, happiness is
tied to justice, equity and sustainability of our planet's resources, our
governmental, economic and social systems.

Table 3.11 Pursuit: Happiness, Love & Safety

Peace Pursuits for: *Seek Peace Within Yourself*	

I explore and share ideas about happiness, love and safety.	• Cultivating happiness occurs through an array of sources such as physical health, family, moral values, emotions, social relationships and for some through income, job or careers. When we are generally satisfied with our current situation and have our basic needs met, we also have more of a sense of safety within.
	• Love is our nature – lean into and lift up what is within you.
	• Characteristics to foster: laughing, smiling, movement, meaningful relationships, regulation practices, imagination and creativity.
	• There are so many ways to cultivate and connect with happiness, kindness and love. All the peace actions guide the way!
	  ○ Prioritize relationships, collaboration and positive communication.
	  ○ Be altruistic – voluntarily help another person without expecting anything in return.
	  ○ Promote love, empathy, compassion and happiness through storytelling and story sharing.
	  ○ Practice acceptance of what you can influence/control and that which is outside of your influence/control.
	  ○ Gratitude journaling and expressing appreciation is grounded in love and presence: What did I enjoy today? What am I grateful for today?
	  ○ Write notes, cards, messages and letters and create art, music, movement to express these ideas.

You (and our children) have all that you need inside your imperfectly, perfect self! Lovingly and compassionately accept and celebrate exactly where you are on your peace journey. Hold faith in yourself (and students), just as you hold hope for humanity. We are all having and responding to our limited experience of the world. How we respond to external experiences and internal interpretations is the space in which we seek inner peace.

◎ **Pause & Reflect:** How can you cultivate and honor moments of hope in your life?

Table 3.12 Pursuit: Hope for Future

Peace Pursuits for: *Seek Peace Within Yourself*	
I have a sense of hope for my future and for what the world will be like for those who come after me.	• There will always be hurt, challenges and difficulties in life. How we respond to these issues is our opportunity. As many peacemakers across time have asserted, *"Pain is inevitable. Suffering is optional."* • When one has hope, they also hold compassion, empathy, care, appreciation, resilience and persistence. • Our (and children's) perception of time is a complex subject. In connection with memory formation there is a progression of events, a moving forward, the future. Sharing a timeline of human life can help with understanding that our time on Earth is relatively short, so how can we center happiness, love and hope!? • When feeling doubt or confusion this can be positive, lean on the lessons of the *'both/and'* as it often yields reflections in truth. • Understanding our interconnectedness to others and the natural world motivates us to create the best possible future for all life on this planet. • Celebrate even the seemingly smallest of steps and growth – we all matter to our collective future! • Empowerment is key – we all are a very small part of this world AND we all matter in it. Illustrate this with the ripple of a pebble dropped in water.

Deepening of self-awareness and being helps to *Seek Peace Within Yourself And Others*. When we are more centered, grounded and self-loving, it opens up space for us to examine and act on injustices and to support others. The more stable our sense of inner peace, the more solid we are in our hope and action for co-creating a future grounded in justice and peace for all.

Love is our very nature and has the power to unite us!

More Peaceful Practices: *Seek Peace Within Yourself*

Family & Community Connections

◆ Encourage and support caregivers in their efforts to be present and make space for connection and stillness as a family. For example, group meditation, taking a walk, reflecting or reading a story together and lessening time spent on technology and media.

◆ Host a family night with a 'choose your own peaceful adventure' setup. Have options that mirror lessons and practices at school such as breathwork, meditation, mindful movement, art, self-awareness processes, noticing in nature and gratitude journaling.

◆ Invite community guests to share stories and practices that foster inner peace.

◆ Create space for families to share and learn about their existing mindfulness practices, many of which may be from their cultures and beliefs.

Table 3.13 Content Area Connections: *Seek Peace Within*

Content Area Connections			
Art	**Math**	**Science**	**P.E. (Movement)**
Share examples and cultural background of the intricate and symmetrical geometric designs called mandalas. Mindfully color or create mandalas, emphasizing elements of color, shapes and pattern. Gazing at mandalas is also very meditative.	Create a mindful mathematical practice – allow the mind to deeply contemplate a concept or problem. Explore mathematical puzzles, arts, patterns, symmetries and other creative and visual intersections. Approach content challenges with first anchoring to the breath.	Take a nature walk and ask learners to point out examples of coexistence, the '*both/ and*.' For example: • How sunlight and shade co-exist • Contrasting and complementary colors of flowers • Different textures and symmetries within plants • Life and death – an animal surviving because it eats another	Mindful movement promotes relaxation and the mind-body connection. • Tai chi • Yoga • Qigong • Pilates Aerobic exercise releases endorphins which contribute to feelings of positive well-being. Express emotions through movement, dance and improve.

You Are The Student & The Teacher

As you journey into and around your inner world, be gentle with yourself! Extend compassion, care and grace to yourself just as you would for a loved child. Engage in the practices outlined in this chapter personally (and with trusted colleagues), as this will deepen the outcomes when implementing with learners. Be reminded that everything is in a constant state of change, including you. When you feel stressed, overwhelmed or uncertain, lean on the regulation strategies and practices such as breathwork and meditation. Oftentimes our most challenging times in life are or can become our greatest teachers (the '*both/and*'). Shifting from a place of reaction and suffering to embodying equanimity is possible. Not always easy, but indeed possible!

We would be honored to further support you and children as you *Seek Peace Within Yourself*. We also offer this wisdom, attributed to ancient Chinese philosopher Lao Tzu, "*When the student is ready, the teacher will appear. When the student is truly ready… The teacher will disappear.*"

Ground in love and remember that peace, both begins and ends, within.

References

Brown, B (2021) *Atlas of the heart*. Penguin Random House

Chouhan, S. (2011, October 13). India visit gave a vision to Steve Jobs. *India Today*. https://www.indiatoday.in/world/americas/story/india-visit-gave-a-vision-to-steve-jobs-143292-2011-10-12

Cities4Peace & Hodo, C. (2023, December 22). *Fostering unity: Cities4Peace initiative strengthening bonds in Los Angeles schools.* Youtube @Cities4Peace IAHV. https://www.youtube.com/watch?v=ChqL6nuLbp4

Frayer, D., Frederick, W. C., & Klausmeier, H. J. (1969). *A schema for testing the level of cognitive mastery*. Wisconsin Center for Education Research.

Ganguly, K. K. (2019). Life of M.K. Gandhi: A message to youth of modern India. *The Indian Journal of Medical Research*, *149*(Suppl), S145–S151. https://doi.org/10.4103/0971-5916.251672

Greater Good (n.d.). Studies. *Greater Good Magazine*. Retrieved December 9, 2023, from https://greatergood.berkeley.edu/resources/studies

Krishnamurti, J. (1963). *Life ahead: On learning and the search for meaning*. New World Library.

McLaren, K. (2010). *Language of emotions: What your feelings are trying to tell you*. Sounds True.

NPR. (2009, January 16). Martin Luther King recording found in India. *NPR*. https://www.npr.org/templates/story/story.php?storyId=99480326

Ramabadran, S. (2023, August 28). *Yoga isn't a White activity. Rosa Parks, Angela Davis practised it for inner peace*. Theprint. https://theprint.in/opinion/yoga-isnt-a-white-activity-rosa-parks-angela-davis-practised-it-for-inner-peace/1734421/

United Nations: Department of Economic and Social Affairs. (n.d.). *The 17 goals*. Sdgs.un.org. Retrieved December 9, 2023, from https://sdgs.un.org/goals

Waldinger, R., & Schulz, M. (2023). *The good life: Lessons from the world's longest scientific study of happiness*. Simon & Schuster.

Wyrick, P. (2021, April 29). *Examining the relationship between childhood trauma and involvement in the justice system*. National Institute of Justice. Retrieved December 8, 2023, from https://nij.ojp.gov/topics/articles/examining-relationship-between-childhood-trauma-and-involvement-justice-system#2-0

4

Seek Peace With Others

The source of love is deep in us and we can help others realize a lot of happiness. One word, one action, one thought can reduce another person's suffering and bring that person joy.
~ Thich Nhat Hanh

This peace action is fully written as *Seek Peace Within Yourself and Others*, which helps ground us in the understanding of the connection between our individual and collective paths in creating cultures of peace. As peace activist Hanh (1991) shared, our capacity to enhance the life and happiness of another is immense! There is a well-established correlation between our inner world, feelings of happiness and the presence of positive connections and social relationships (Waldinger & Schulz, 2023). Supportive relationships help reduce stress, enhance emotional resilience and foster a sense of belonging.

DOI: 10.4324/9781003449249-5

Before we launch into the chapter, we invite you to pause and consider your own relationships and how you *Seek Peace With Others*.

◎ **Pause & Reflect:**

- ◆ Call to mind relationships you consider supportive and positive.
- ◆ How do these connections enhance the quality of your life and well-being?
- ◆ Do you ever feel lonely or isolated? If so, why might that be?

Antidote to Loneliness: Social Connection

Loneliness is a subjective feeling that you are alone or your needs are not being met. Loneliness along with social isolation are identified as a significant health issue worldwide (Badcock et al., 2022). Given its many consequences, the Office of the United States Surgeon General (OSG) declared loneliness and isolation an epidemic in 2023.

> *The lack of social connection poses a significant risk for individual health and longevity. Loneliness and social isolation increase the risk for premature death by 26% and 29% respectively. More broadly, lacking social connection can increase the risk for premature death as much as smoking up to 15 cigarettes a day. (p. 4)*

The disconnected feeling impacts mental and physical health and has created a dilemma that we must address. The Office of the Surgeon General (OSG) (2023) outlined why social connection matters so much to our overall health, healing and well-being (p. 10). The report shared three vital components:

- ◆ **Structure:** the number and variety of relationships; the frequency of interactions
- ◆ **Function:** how relationships serve various needs
- ◆ **Quality:** the supportive and unsupportive aspects of relationships and interactions

From a systemic standpoint, the OSG offered some concrete suggestions that teachers, schools and education departments can do to support the healing of communities. These are also cornerstones of this peace education framework.

- *Develop a strategic plan for school connectedness and social skills.*
- *Build a culture of connection; prioritize connection in all policies and actions.*
- *Implement socially based educational techniques.*
- *Create a supportive school environment.*
- *Foster a culture of connection in the broader community.*
- *Reform digital environments to support development of pro-connection technologies.*
- *Deepen and share knowledge through research partnerships and increasing public awareness.*

Schools can serve as a bridge for staff, families and students who need mental and physical health support. Becoming trauma informed is foundational (see Chapter 9).

When it comes to the many benefits of positive connections, it's more about the quality of the relationship(s) than the quantity. When we have an emphasis on building positive relationships and a sense of belonging, schools truly have the capacity to become spaces for community connection and healing. Even when there are differing points of view, a focus on connecting with kindness in our common humanity is crucial.

Table 4.1 Practice: Connection Through Conversation

Put It Into Practice: Connection Through Conversation	
Conversation invites the cultivation of connection and empathy. Every adult can engage deeply with each other and many students daily. Focus on building relationships, deepening connections and increasing the amount of positive interactions through sharing and conversation. With more reluctant communicators, you might start with sharing a little about yourself and then invite in their experience. Here are some questions to get you started!	
Emerging	*Intermediate & Advanced*
• What makes you smile? • What do you enjoy doing with your family? • What is your favorite thing to do with a friend? • Tell me about the best and worst parts of your day (high, low).	• What is one of the best things to ever happen to you? • If you had any superpower, what would it be and why? • Where is a special place for you? Why? • What are you really proud of right now? • What qualities do you look for in a friend? Why? • Who is someone you admire? Why? • What kind of person do you want to be as an adult? Why?

We can come together to build positive social interactions, deepen resilience and create connections in our classrooms and across all levels of humanity. Being able to *Seek Peace With Others* limits the feelings of social disconnection and isolation. We must be dedicated to positive social interaction and in supporting one another as a community; both locally and globally!

◎ **Pause & Reflect:**

   ◆   What is a goal that you have personally related to social connections (i.e. less cell phone use, more social interactions and family game night)?
   ◆   Think about a recent conflict. What was the impact within yourself and other(s)?

Practicing Empathy

As we navigate relationships, it's important to be empathetic and ground ourselves in hope and love. We show up as our full selves daily; with our stress, worry, joy, love, despair and challenges. Be as conscious as possible of your actions and interactions.

Before you send the email, say the harsh remark, pause and think about your impact. Are you reacting or responding? Is this taking a stance of empathy? As psychotherapist and doctor Alfred Adler offered, *"Empathy is seeing with the eyes of another, listening with the ears of another and feeling with the heart of another"* (Clark, 2016). You never know what someone is going through, so be thoughtful and kind. Are you assuming positive intent? This is also important when on the receiving end of feedback or criticism from others.

◎ **Pause & Reflect:**

   ◆   How do you respond to constructive criticism and/or critical feedback?
   ◆   Consider how your response varies when feedback is from people with different perspectives than your own. How can you hold empathy in this scenario?

When humans *Seek Peace Within* (inner peace), it opens a way of being that honors and facilitates the sustained creation of peace with others and the environment. From these foundations, extend compassion and empathy to all. Empathy softens our hearts and allows for deeper connection and understanding.

Table 4.2 Pursuit: Listening, Empathy & Compassion

Peace Pursuits for: *Seek Peace With Others*	
I practice active listening, empathy and compassion.	• Seek out, consider and value the points of view, perspectives and experiences of others. Create opportunities for students to listen with empathy, seek to understand and/or be accepting of divergent perspectives. • Practice listening deeply by inviting reflection or paraphrasing back what was said. Lean in with curiosity and openness in response. ○ Make it a routine to ask learners to partner and paraphrase their next steps and ask questions after directions are given. • Model empathy journaling, which can be added to learner's self-awareness journals (see Chapter 3, p. 53). Have students write or draw about a situation trying to 'be in the other person's shoes.' Journal about when they felt empathy or experienced it from others. Occasionally discuss common noticings and experiences, further fostering empathetic ways of being. • Implement Peace Circles Lesson, p. 259.

Scarcity Mindset & Competition

To *Seek Peace With Others* includes awareness of internal and external conflict. A scarcity mindset and competition are common sources of conflict for all ages. This mindset is problematic because it promotes fear instead of cooperation, collaboration and empathy. If we live in a space of wishing and wanting more, the ego is in a constant state of gathering, accumulating and competing. This results in not being fully present. Instead of a sense of abundance, there is a feeling of '*not enoughness.*' This fuels competition for resources and opportunity and invites a binary win-lose view. There is an '*us vs. them*' mentality that often exists, which contributes to and reinforces biases, stereotypes and discrimination (more on this in Chapter 8, p. 163). These mindsets are barriers to collaboration and peacebuilding.

◎ **Pause & Reflect:**

◆ Identify an example of a scarcity mindset or '*not enoughness*' in your life or work.
◆ How does this mindset impact you? And others?

In classrooms, especially with high student-to-adult ratios, some children may be disruptive, act out or demonstrate needy behaviors to receive more adult attention. Behavior may be influenced by existing developmental trauma, perceived or real scarcity of adult engagement and support, as well as other social emotional and mental health needs. Attention-seeking behaviors, especially when they are harmful, are highly effective at getting adults to engage. Children, both consciously and unconsciously, are competing for a sense of connection and belonging.

In society, and therefore also in schools, there is often a division of winners and losers, of haves and have-nots. Peace education thinks critically about why this may exist. Consider how divisions impact our ability to evolve to spaces that do not reinforce the idea that there are not enough awards or resources for everyone. *'Not everyone can be a winner'* mentality promotes that you need to take whatever you can get, when you can get it. Though certainly, we have to learn to experience loss (or not winning); this mindset impacts our beliefs and behavior when positioning an individual against the collective.

◎ Pause & Reflect:

- ◆ Identify an example of what you would describe as unhealthy competition in your life and/or work. What characteristics make this competition feel unhealthy?
- ◆ Repeat this process identifying healthy competition and characteristics.

Competition is not inherently bad or problematic. Friendly competition can feel fun and motivating (e.g., gamification of learning, sports, clubs, academics). There is research to support that some competition positively influences effort, attention, motivation and learning (DiMenichi & Tricomi, 2015). Healthy competition plays a role in developing or deepening resilience and perseverance, enhancing problem-solving skills and fostering cooperative relationships. Competition can provide an opportunity for children to make mistakes, fail and celebrate the successes and gifts of others.

Conversely, aggressive and/or stressful competition can negatively impact emotional well-being and resilience. If there are no or minimal parameters and mutual understandings, it can lead to frustration, anxiety and aggression. Friendships and peer relationships can be fractured when there is big pressure to win, achieve or outperform one another. Concerns related to competition and its impact that are worth considering more deeply include:

- ◆ Supporting that in order to 'get ahead' it sometimes requires harm, aggression and even violence

◆ Pinning people against each other – winner vs. loser; haves vs. have-nots; success vs. failure

◆ Reinforcing *'either, or'* thinking

◆ Emphasizing more on individual accomplishments and less on collective goals

◆ Competition, winning or being right becomes more important than consensus, compromise and/or collaboration

◆ Perpetuating the myth that if someone doesn't succeed, they only have themselves to blame

◆ Contributing to frustration, anxiety and aggression

For primary learners (PreK-3rd), in particular, competition should be used minimally or not at all. After all, our focus (really for all learners) should be on building resilience through effort, curiosity and growing through learning and mistakes.

Table 4.3 Practice: Competition

Put It Into Practice: Competition	
Instead of this...	**Shift to this...**
• Grading on curves • Giving individual grades based on how well a group or team performed • Overemphasizing tests and grades	• Equitable grading practices • Emphasize the learning process and growing (including making mistakes) • Effort, participation and growth are valued
• Creating rivalries in academic or sports achievement • Winning is highly important	• Having fun, keep it friendly • Winning is a lower level of importance and participation emphasized
• High-stakes goals and rewards • Labeling as failing if not meeting set achievement benchmarks or standards 'now'	• Goals and rewards are not highly valuable, real or low stakes • Anchoring to the power of the word 'yet' – emphasizing it's okay not to have met the goal 'yet'; building perseverance and resilience
• Showing favoritism • Comparing students to each other • Shaming or criticizing individuals publicly	• Be intentionally inclusive and consistent • Constructive feedback delivered privately
Note: Informed by Shindler (2010).	

Co-Creating Democratic Spaces

Peace educators co-create democratic spaces with learners. This means shared power such as a fair process for making class-wide decisions, being mindful about representation and participation from all students. Democratic spaces have a high degree of student agency, ideas, and contributions. Successful peace education leans on culturally relevant pedagogy, where students have a voice and choice. Peacemakers Harris and Morrison (2013) shared:

> A peaceful classroom…is an open environment where each student has an equal chance to learn, and the welfare of each individual is maximized. Students and teachers learn to interact with each other in constructive ways. Everybody contributes his or her perspectives on reality, and students and teachers together set limits for behavior. (p. 169)

Teaching and management approaches that are not co-created typically result in power struggles, implicit/explicit bias and underlying conflicts. We believe that all spaces are best co-created: classrooms, after-school programs, school-wide and even within families! Doing so creates a deeper sense of connection, belonging and engagement.

Table 4.4 Pursuit: Belonging

Peace Pursuits for: *Seek Peace With Others*	
I belong to a community. **With others I:** • **learn** • **connect** • **show respect**	• The identities of the whole person are supported and celebrated. • There is a common thread of understanding about loneliness, belonging and the importance of social connection. • Reaching out, being kind, empathetic, supportive and valuing the contributions of others is the shared climate. • A mindset of giving yourself and others grace includes seeking to understand, opening to acceptance and finding forgiveness. • Practicing flexible thinking and ways of doing/being that honor individual and collective experiences. • Implement foundational Lessons: The Great Peacemakers (Seminar Circle), p. 255 and How Do I Belong (Writing Process), p. 276.

Put It Into Practice: Opening & Closing Circles

Holding space for a daily opening and closing circle are excellent ways to prioritize social interactions, community connection, fun, engagement and reflection.

There are multiple resources about Responsive Classrooms morning meetings, but one we like is *The Morning Meeting Book*, 4th edition (Poplawski, 2014). This book walks educators through features and structures of setting up a morning meeting, including:

1. **Morning Message:** invite students to respond to a letter/note
2. **Greeting:** get into a circle and greet one another by name.
3. **Share:** invite a few students to share
4. **Activity/Game:** play an engaging learning game or activity

Closing circles provide an opportunity for reflection from the day and setting intentions for the following day. Once children understand the routines, they can rotate leading and/or choosing greetings, shares, games and reflections. Provide intermediate and advanced students with scaffolded materials so they can plan these circles!

Co-Creating Brave Spaces

Safe spaces are intended to eliminate any ideas, actions or dialogue that could be perceived as threatening or create conflict. Safe spaces are also meant to be bias free. However, being inclusive of all voices and engaging in critical dialogue may not always feel comfortable (safe). We must co-create spaces that center compassion, empathy and critical thinking. Brave spaces allow us to engage in conversations about social issues with honesty and sensitivity. Through vulnerability and storytelling, we listen to the lived experiences of others and become connected through our shared humanity.

Table 4.5 Safe vs. Brave Spaces

Safe Spaces	Brave Spaces
Let's agree to disagree	Curiosity, wonder
Don't take it personally	Focus on systems, structures
Assume positive intentions	Know your intention & honor your impact
Keep 'comfortable'	Invite vulnerability lived experiences: truths
Individualism	Connect to shared humanity
Note: Our interpretation of Safe & brave Spaces is informed by: Hawthorne, B. (2022), Sylvain, D. (2020) and Meeks, A. (2017).	

Take a stand and prioritize co-creating brave spaces that honor all identities and allow for developmentally sensitive conversations about harm, structural violence, systematic oppression and the exploration of peaceful alternatives and solutions. Our students' voices and experiences are integral to this work.

How will you raise up the voices and stories of children and provide opportunities for constructive and critical feedback?

All forms of oppression, marginalization, racism, sexism, classism, ableism, agism, heterosexism, anti-semitism, microaggressions, bias, prejudices, stereotyping and discrimination can and should be explored in developmentally sensitive ways. Peacelearners need these brave spaces for exploring questions, ideas and solutions, to give feedback and to share their hopes and dreams in creating a just and peaceful world.

◎ **Pause & Reflect:**

- ◆ Are you engaging in conversations about systemic and structural violence, oppression, racism, White supremacy, social justice and the complexities of justice and peace? Are learners in developmentally sensitive ways?
- ◆ Whose stories, ideas and opinions are centered? Whose voices are missing or silenced?
- ◆ What actions will you take to co-create brave spaces with students, staff and colleagues moving forward?
- ◆ How will you know if others feel that this is a brave space?

Leadership coach and inspiring creator Didier Sylvain (2020) offered the acronym C.A.R.E. in service of creating brave spaces for conversations. In addition to the foundational Class Charter and Peace Circles (Lesson, p. 259), we recommend using this as a launching point for democratically co-creating brave spaces, as a site, with colleagues (teams) and with learners.

Table 4.6 Practice: C.A.R.E to Co-Create Brave Spaces

Put It Into Practice: C.A.R.E to Co-Create Brave Spaces		
C	Center	Seeking peace within, being present within ourselves and our bodies, utilizing practices like breathwork for grounding and listening to the messages of emotions
A	Align	Co-create agreements or guidelines; speak your own truth and experiences and own your impact; avoid assumptions and judgments; wonder and lean into curiosity
R	Reflect	Model vulnerability, demonstrate compassion, empathy and peacefulness; challenge with respect; honor your impact and emotions
E	Experiment	Try out new things, explore different ideas and approaches, be humble, make changes, avoid limiting, either-or thinking or linear-only thinking; share what are you noticing and learning
Adapted from: Didier Sylvain (2020), YouTube: *Creating Brave Spaces*. More at https://www.didiersylvain.com		

We envision the co-creation of spaces that allow children to courageously step into their light, explore shadows, empathetically listen to varying and diverse perspectives and lean in with vulnerability and compassionate curiosity. It is in brave spaces, which may at times feel uncomfortable, that people can fully engage in all aspects of peacelearning.

Conflict & Approaches to Peace

One of the most important aspects of peace education is seeking peace with others, even when you have differing beliefs, ideas or opinions. Conflict or disagreement is inevitable, but responses of aggression and violence need not be. Dig into the causes of why a conflict may be occurring, it may be due to differing thoughts, values, communication styles and/or goals. Conflict also occurs when someone's needs or wants are not being met. When there is competition (or perceived competition) for resources and a scarcity mindset is present, disagreement and even aggression or violence may arise. As researchers Harris and Morrison (2013) outlined,

> *For an individual to live peacefully, he or she must be able to satisfy basic needs and resolve conflicts within friendships, work places, families, and communities in a way that promotes the well-being of all. (p. 15)*

Whatever the reason for conflict, our emotional state is usually a part of how we interpret and respond. Conflict actually begins within ourselves and then is expressed outwardly. This is why seeking peace within yourself is the foundation for peace in the world.

Peacebuilding is a long-term process encouraging reparations, repairing relationships and resolving conflict. If peacebuilding is going to last, everyone impacted by a destructive conflict must be involved in the process. This takes commitment and brave spaces. It's not always the easiest way to handle situations, but it's essential if we are to find peace. Let's go deeper into some key approaches to peace, including guidance for putting it into practice.

◎ <u>**Pause & Reflect:**</u>

◆ Look at the top of Table 4.7. Which is your 'go to' conflict resolution style?

Table 4.7 Practice: Approaches to Peace

Put It Into Practice: Approaches to Peace		
Term	**Definition**	**Guidance**
Conflict Resolution Styles	Style is based on the situation and determined by the level of concern for others (cooperative/ uncooperative) and the concern for self (assertive/unassertive). a. **Competing:** dominating, asserting power to make their point known and 'win' b. **Avoiding:** being unassertive and withdrawing c. **Accommodating:** letting go of your concerns or needs d. **Compromising:** finding the mutually agreed upon middle ground e. **Collaborating:** working together to find the solution that is most advantageous for both (Thomas, 1979)	Questions and considerations for reflection: a. **Competing:** Is making my point and 'winning' more important than the relationship and a mutual outcome? b. **Avoiding:** Use with caution as it can create resentment or aggravate the issue as it ultimately doesn't resolve the conflict. c. **Accommodating:** What are my needs and concerns? How can I balance letting go and honoring them? d. **Compromising:** How can we meet in the middle? What are our goals, needs and values? e. **Collaborating:** What is compatible and/or can be changed to find the best solution for us both?

(continued)

Table 4.7 Practice: Approaches to Peace (continued)

Put It Into Practice: Approaches to Peace		
Term	**Definition**	**Guidance**
Peacemaking Conflict Management	Usually short-term, peacemaking is an immediate response to end active aggression, violence and/or conflict. (Miller, 2005, p. 56–57) Techniques and strategies: • De-escalation • Separation (short-term avoidance) • Diffusion • Mediation • Bargaining • Negotiation • Compromise	Conflict management involves communication, persuasion, dialogue, promoting empathy and reconciliation. Chapter 9, p. 195 goes deeper into de-escalation techniques. Pausing and breathing can help diffuse a situation, calm emotions and invite in mindful responses like compromise and collaboration. (see Lesson: PBNA Strategy, p. 250)
Peacebuilding Conflict Transformation	Supporting people to prevent or end conflict and violence includes addressing the root causes and underlying injustices. A longer-term, structural approach that promotes nonviolence and works toward sustainable positive peace. (Miller, 2005, p 56–57)	Restorative practices such as peace circles allow you to get to the root of the conflict (see p. 259). The *Five Peace Actions*, which anchor social justice, are foundations of peacebuilding!
Peacekeeping	Coordinated efforts for public security, stability, services and ceasefire agreements in war and conflict zones. Typically these troops, police and civilians are under the authority of the United Nations and viewed as impartial. (Miller, 2005, p 61–62)	Protecting human rights is key. Children and adults in conflict zones may be able to support mental-emotional needs, as well as delivery and distribution of humanitarian aid.
Peace Enforcement	Enforcement of 'the rule of law in peace' is usually negative peace, absence of violence through threat or force. (Miller, 2005, p. 29)	School Resource Officers can result in criminalizing methods, especially harmful for students with historical and multigenerational trauma related to policing.
Third-Party Approaches	A third-party is anyone who isn't directly involved in the conflict; neutral or trusted on both sides. (Miller, 2005, p. 21)	The third-party listens to both sides' feelings, experience and hopes. They help to compromise, manage and/or resolve the conflict. Teachers, coaches, administrators and other adults often fill this role, but peers do too. We highly recommend setting up Peacemaker Leaders or a peer mediation program (below, p. 88).

◎ **Pause & Reflect:**

   ◆ As you review Table 4.7, what peacemaking approaches are you comfortable applying?
   ◆ Set an intention. What is one approach that would most benefit your class and/or school? What is the next step for putting this into action?

It's important to be able to face our problems and handle them in peaceful and timely ways. This eases both parties' angst, holding on to the issue and potentially internalizing and exacerbating the situation. Understanding a variety of peace approaches is important because situations can be nuanced. Being able to resolve and transform conflicts are highly important skills for creating a just and peaceful world.

Author's Perspectives

As cisgender women, **we feel that raising the voices and ideas of diverse women is essential.** Across time, geographies and cultures, women have held unique and important perspectives as providers, caretakers and leaders in their community. They are also disproportionately impacted by conflict and violence (during and in the aftermath), such as forced migration, economic insecurity and unraveled cultural and social supports (Miller, 2005, p. 58). Women should be upheld for their wisdom and strength for their key roles in conflict prevention, resolution, education and peacebuilding within family and community structures.

◎ **Pause & Reflect:**

   ◆ Are there women in your life and community that inspire you?
   ◆ How can you honor their efforts in creating cultures of peace?

Peaceful Communication & Restorative Practices

Creating peaceful people takes in-depth modeling and practice. Despite all of the strategies we share with students, conflicts are a daily occurrence and it can feel like a long or repetitive process! It's important to offer creative and varying approaches, but with consistency of implementation. Adults can also be reactionary, so share with students when you need a breath in order to reestablish calm and composure. Students may appreciate the demonstrated honesty and integrity of modeling vulnerability and a peaceful strategy.

◎ **Pause & Reflect:**

- ◆ What are some root causes of conflicts that frequently occur in your community/school (see Chapter 1, p. 14)?
- ◆ How do you typically de-escalate and help resolve student conflict? (See Chapter 9, p. 195 for guidance on de-escalation.)
- ◆ What skills and strategies do students have and need to resolve conflict peacefully without adult intervention?

To create peacemakers and peacebuilders, actively include children in the development and practice of these skills. For example, peer meditation and peace circles are grounded in democratic practices that center all students. First Nations and Indigenous peoples have long used circles as a process for conflict resolution, making decisions, seeking support, sharing and healing. Peace circles invite connection, community, individual and collective accountability and change (Downwind-Bald Eagle, 2014–2021).

Robert Yazzie, a retired Chief Justice of 18 years on the Navajo Nation Supreme Court, shared an emphasis on peacemaking circles. Explaining the difference between vertical (Western) and horizontal justice systems, Yazzie (1994) said, *"In a circle there is no right or left, nor is there a beginning or an end; every point (or person) on the line of a circle looks to the same center as the focus."*

In a 2004 opinion, Chief Yazzie offered this further distinction, *"The western law way is to punish you, so that you don't repeat the behavior. But the Navajo way is to focus on the individual. You separate the action from the person"* (Mirsky, 2004).

Chief Yazzie went on to discuss peacemaking as a process that can help restore dignity with one another. Both parties can come to a responsible and accountable resolution. Peace circles are much more effective and peaceful in the long-term.

Restorative justice practices give voice to all who are involved in a conflict. We encourage you to implement peace circles with your own conflicts, as well with students. Build your level of comfort as a mediator and also step back and allow children to facilitate. Don't wait to feel you've perfected this process. Learn from observing and doing, which can sometimes be a bit messy!

Table 4.8 Pursuit: Peaceful Communication

Peace Pursuits for: *Seek Peace With Others*	
I practice peaceful (nonviolent) communication and actions when: • **I disagree with someone** • **I feel hurt or wronged** • **My needs or wants are not being met**	• Sharing peaceful strategies about how to engage in constructive conversations when you don't agree, feel hurt or wronged by someone is a skill children will use their whole life. • Many children view/experience models of violent communication and actions through the prevalence of bullying, trauma, local crime and media consumption. Counternarratives and experiences rooted in nonviolence offer peaceful alternatives. • Ongoingly model and practice communication and non-verbal strategies to avoid aggressive or violent conflict. • Restorative justice practices (and peer meditation) allow for peaceful dialogue to repair harm and invite reconciliation. If we simply try to end the conflict without addressing the root of it, we miss the opportunity for growth and sustained positive peace. See Lesson: Class Charter and Peace Circles (p. 259). • Conflict transformation is more systemic and means trying to understand the causes of the conflict(s) and then transforming the underlying structures and relationships. This is an aim of peace and justice education!

Put It Into Practice: Peacemaker Leaders

At one school, students were asked to be Peacemaker Leaders. This group of upper elementary-age learners met twice a month to focus on being friendship coaches, helping younger students, ensuring inclusion, making safe choices and modeling leadership. For peer mediation programs like this, students were also trained to help peers resolve conflict. As the principal, I (Carey) set this up as our student government, though it could also be set up by rotating in new peacemakers.

Here are some examples of leadership opportunities throughout the course of the school year:

➢ Role-playing and helping younger students at recess with peaceful turn taking
➢ Building inclusion among younger students and with peers such as how to play and join games
➢ Researching and sharing ideas (speakers) at whole school peace rallies
➢ Being leaders at peace rallies by helping younger students in the audience, singing peace and friendship songs etc.
➢ Conflict resolution, bullying prevention, peacemaking and peacebuilding approaches

These students built peacemaking skills and really embraced different aspects of the role. When asked what had been most rewarding about this role, students shared:

> ➤ "I loved being able to help the younger students."
> ➤ "I taught some of the second graders how to play GaGa Ball; when I first saw them playing they didn't really know how to play it."
> ➤ "A few of the first graders were arguing about whose turn it was on the swings, I helped them work out a system."

Being Peacemaker Leaders was a fulfilling job that was important to our whole school community!

When it comes to peacemaking, peacekeeping and peacebuilding, systems and structures should be set up to ensure learners take the lead to navigate, resolve and transform conflicts. Seek out, listen to and embrace students' ideas. This is embodying democratic and culturally relevant teaching practices. It is important to recognize that restorative justice practices are not a 'quick fix,' rather, it's a deeper process and moving to forgiveness can take time. As Harris and Morrison (2013) pointed out,

> Reconciliation is a long process, not a one-time event, even though a one-time meeting between the victim and offender can facilitate the process of reconciliation. Reconciliation in this sense implies bringing the wounds to the surface so that others may empathize with the suffering of those who have been wounded. It is a healing process, not a typical justice process that seeks retribution. (p. 150)

Deep empathetic listening, a hope to make amends and/or accepting and forgiving are all ways that children (and adults) become skilled peacemakers and peacebuilders.

Importance of Acceptance & Forgiveness

> *To forgive is not just to be altruistic. It is the best form of self-interest.*
> ~ Bishop Desmond Tutu

To *Seek Peace With Others* following conflict, we need to find our way to accept and forgive. Being altruistic and caring for others is just as important as attending to your well-being through these actions. Pause and cultivate empathy by looking at another person's perspective and experiences. Some issues are deep and accepting and forgiving may be challenging. Forgiveness doesn't mean that we aren't hurt or that there isn't accountability, but that we ultimately accept what's happened, apply the lesson learned and reclaim our energy.

◎ Pause & Reflect:

- ◆ What are tools or methods you use to process emotions, conflict and forgive others?
- ◆ How does forgiveness impact your overall well-being? What about resentment?

Accepting people and situations as they are is critical and freeing. From our personal experience, holding on to blame, anger, guilt, resentment and other negative feelings ultimately impacts our mental and physical health and well-being. Finding forgiveness, as Desmond Tutu (2000) said, is very much in our self-interest!

Put It Into Practice: Finding Forgiveness

Forgiveness moves us toward a healthier mind and way of being. These strategies can aid you and students toward a state of acceptance, understanding and peace.

- ➢ Look at the situation through a lens of empathy; try to accept their perspective.
- ➢ Be curious and seek to understand. Ask why the person made that decision. Consider that perhaps you may have acted the same way if faced similar circumstances.
- ➢ Think about times when people forgave you and how that felt.
- ➢ Process, accept and release by writing in a journal, drawing a picture, going for a walk, engaging in a guided meditation and/or talking to a friend, counselor, teacher or loved one.
- ➢ Forgiveness is a process and making amends can be challenging, give it space and time.

Utilize Peace Circles (Lesson, p. 259), for processing and reconciling conflict.

We encourage you to think about how you approach situations, pause and respond mindfully instead of reacting. Listen to the messages in emotions, regulate and ultimately choose peace and love over hate! **Forgiveness is an act of grace.** It's the path toward peace and ultimately a more harmonious environment.

Even in the midst of tragedy, trauma and despair, anchoring to hope allows for acceptance and healing. Consider this inspiring story and message.

Peacemaker In Practice

By Moses Abolade
Peacebuilding Consultant and Peace Ambassador (PEPNET Nigeria)

In fragile realms where chaos seeks its place,
Peace educators stand with steadfast grace;

At risk,
they sow the seeds of harmony and light,
In lands where darkness often takes its flight;

We teach at risk.
Through strife and turmoil, we hold the flame,
Teaching love and empathy, we aim.
Resilient souls, in peace, we firmly believe,
Our work in fragile contexts, a gift we weave.

I wrote this poem in 2019, after reading the news of some peacebuilders kidnapped and killed by an insurgent group in Northern Nigeria. Titled **"Peace Educators at Risk,"** I wanted to acknowledge the effort and resilience of peace educators and peacebuilders across the globe. This poem reminds me of the journey that I, Moses Abolade, have personally traversed; a path I am committed to treading and a commitment to risk it all for the cause of peace.

....

My odyssey as a peacemaker commenced in the heart of Ajah, Lagos, Nigeria, while teaching Civic Education to a group of students marked by their propensity for bullying, chaos and violence. As a social master, I delved into the core of their actions, seeking the underlying reasons for their behavior. Over time, I came to a profound realization – my role as an educator extended far beyond textbooks and exams. It was about shaping values and character, molding the very essence of these students. The classroom, I discovered, was not just a realm for academic learning; it was a fertile ground for planting the seeds of peace, empathy and mutual understanding.

This epiphany spurred me to embark on a journey of self-improvement and further education. I enrolled in the Institute of Peace and Strategic Studies at the University of Ibadan, Nigeria, to gain deeper insights into peace education. My experiences, training and development laid the foundation for what would become the Peace Education and Practice Network (PEPNET). PEPNET was established with the noble mission of enhancing access to peace education by creating content, conducting capacity-building workshops and implementing peacebuilding programs. Our aim was clear – to equip young people, vulnerable groups, peace educators and policymakers with the tools needed to foster peace. We envisioned a ripple effect where the youth, who were already shaping the future, would carry the torch of peace education into their classrooms and communities.

In our quest to understand the root causes of violence among students and young people in Nigeria, we discerned a disturbing pattern. Much of their violent behavior could be attributed to the violent content they were exposed to through media, including television, radio and social platforms. In response, PEPNET embarked on a bold initiative to design peacebuilding content and programs in the media with the intention of disrupting this cycle of violence. This journey redirected my focus toward the realm of peace media, particularly as a peacebuilding journalist.

As a peacebuilding journalist, my role has evolved to include investigating and capturing stories related to peacebuilding, humanitarian efforts and development. The power of storytelling, when aligned with the cause of peace, is immeasurable. I have the privilege of shedding light on the positive endeavors of individuals and communities dedicated to peace. I amplify the voices of teachers and peacebuilders who, in their unique ways, are architects of peace.

To all teachers and peacebuilders, know that your roles extend beyond the confines of the classroom. You are the peacemakers in practice, shaping the destiny of nations. For those starting their journey as early career peace educators, understand that there is ample room for you to practice your craft. If traditional teaching doesn't resonate with you, consider creating content for peace. If program design feels challenging, advocate through various media and platforms, or embark on peace media projects. Volunteering or collaborating with peacebuilding organizations that aligns with your abilities and interests to make relevant, meaningful and sustainable impact.

Remember, you wield the power of education to nurture peace in the hearts of young minds. The knowledge, skills and attitudes you cultivate can create a positive ripple effect that reaches those in need. Embrace this power and continue to be the changemakers who shape the future through the practice of peace. Your influence is immeasurable, and your dedication is a beacon of hope in a world that often yearns for harmony.

Hope After Despair

We all feel moments of despair in our lives at some point; death, divorce, trauma, health issues, relationships or friendships that falter or break, losing a job, financial or emotional strain. Despite these challenges, it's important to pause and recognize that change is possible and that this period of despair will pass. In this emotional state and condition, it is hard to feel hopeful. Feelings of despair may point to something (an idea or behavior) that must stop or can no longer be tolerated. Perhaps realizing that despite all of the challenges one is facing, you have the resiliency to overcome, to make change, to move past or to surrender to the present.

If you are in the midst of despair or notice this within someone you care for (such as students), seek out support from friends, family and professionals. Be an empathetic listener and meet the person (child) just as they are. Take one little step at a time. There is always hope for the next day, stage or chapter in life.

◎ **Pause & Reflect:**

- ◆ How do you find hope in the midst of despair?
- ◆ How can (do) you support others who are experiencing despair, pain and trauma?

In healing from despair one can develop a renewed appreciation for life (more on this [post-traumatic wisdom] in Chapter 9, p. 209).

Cooperation, Collaboration & Problem-Solving

That feeling of hope, trust, optimism and security can be fostered through cooperation, collaboration and problem-solving. Working together, instead of competing or being isolated, enhances relationships, motivation, learning, thinking and problem-solving skills. Cooperative learning methods increase academic achievement and provide long-term readiness skills (Johnson et al., 2000).

Table 4.9 Pursuit: Cooperation & Collaboration

Peace Pursuits for: *Seek Peace With Others*	
I practice cooperation and collaboration with others (problem-solving)	• Class climate improves when all learners feel they are valued contributors to tasks and learning goals. • Equal participation and individual accountability increase engagement and learning. • Class and team building activities create a sense of belonging and collective caring. • Cooperation and collaboration structures and strategies should go beyond one content area or isolated experiences and ultimately be how learning regularly occurs. • Learners develop social skills as they share, listen and appreciate the varied ideas, perspectives and points of view of others.

At the beginning of my teaching career, I (Julie) received extensive training in cooperative structures and every subsequent year of implementation demonstrated positive outcomes of harmonious and highly engaged learners! Cooperative learning structures should always include clear goals, equally accountable individual and group interactions and positive interdependence.

To ensure there is positive interdependence in cooperative learning structures, author and psychologist Dr. Spencer Kagan (2007) recommended ensuring students are on the same side by asking yourself: *"Is a contribution by one helpful to others? Is it necessary?"* Another key to collaborative learning is engaging a maximum amount of students in speaking/responding simultaneously. If you often have just one learner responding at a time, this is an indicator of lower engagement. Enhance your practice and stimulate more thinking and conversation by shifting to collaborative and cooperative structures.

Put It Into Practice: Cooperative Structures

These cooperative structures, named by and adapted from Dr. Kagan (1992, 1995), are some favorites! The name of the structure outlines the basic directions. Begin by making intentional plans for which engagement structures you will do and when. With practice, this embedding implementation becomes automatic. Start by modeling and practicing the structure with low-stakes content and/or sharing. Add a new structure once relative proficiency is demonstrated.

➢ **Stand Up, Hand Up, Pair Up: Or SUHUPU!** A fun way to get learners up and moving before finding a partner for discussion.
➢ **Think Pair Share; Timed Pair Share**

> **Numbered Heads Together:** Assign each student in the group a number. Pose a question (open-ended are great here) and then provide time for learners to put their heads together to discuss and problem solve. Randomly call a number to hear a summary from each group.

> **Rally Coach:** A great option for math, working with partners, one student coaches (step by step or evaluates the work) and the other solves and then they switch roles.

> **Jigsaw:** Each student in a group is numbered and assigned to independently work on a different part of the project, reading or researching. All of the learners with the same number/topic meet to share/discuss and then they return to their original group to process the whole scope of the work/learning.

Reflection

Relationships, navigating conflicts and collaborating aren't always easy, but they are so rewarding to our sense of hope and belonging. Connection enhances our overall well-being. Be kind and gentle with yourself and others. Understanding and transforming our self and ways of being in relationship is core to peace and justice education. This combined action, *Seek Peace Within Yourself and Others*, truly lays the foundation for our evolution toward sustained positive peace.

More Peaceful Practices: *Seek Peace With Others*

Family & Community Connections

◆ Bridge students, families and community members by inviting them to share oral stories or read aloud books that highlight social connection, hope, happiness, peacemaking and peacebuilding.

◆ Hold circles for sharing and discussing peacekeeping techniques used at home and school. Include dialogue about experiences, beliefs and values related to disciplining children and managing conflicts. Invite in community learning.

◆ Model and practice effective communication and conflict resolution skills in partnership with families and community organizations.

◆ Advance efforts to *Seek Peace Within Yourself and Others* by including family and community members in feedback and decision-making.

◆ Celebrate and connect through special events, invitations and informal gatherings. Create a sense of belonging for all!

Table 4.10 Content Area Connections: *Seek Peace With Others*

Content Area Connections			
Literacy	**Social Studies**	**Music**	**Art**
Discuss and co-create a Y-chart about how peace may look, sound and feel different to other people, and that that is okay! Compose a class book, with each learner contributing a page. Resource: *What Does Peace Feel Like?* by Vladimir Radunsky (2004).	For intermediate and advanced learners: Discuss the history of World War II and the decision to deploy atomic bombs. Learn about the aftermath and discuss how we can avoid using this type of force in the future. Resource: *A Bowl Full of Peace: A True Story* by Caren Stelson (2020).	Explore songs with themes of peace, belonging and connection. Highlight how making music together is an act of being in a peaceful community.	A wonderful way to bring people of any age together is through art. Create a mural or other interconnected art piece. Create a tree with students' handprints as leaves to represent belonging and community.

References

Badcock, J. C., Holt-Lunstad, J., Bombaci, P., Garcia, E., & Lim, M. H. (2022). *Position statement: Addressing social isolation and loneliness and the power of human connection.* Global Initiative on Loneliness and Connection (GILC).

Clark, A. J. (2016). Empathy and Alfred Adler: An integral perspective. *Journal of Individual Psychology*, 72(4), 237–253. https://doi.org/10.1353/jip.2016.0020

DiMenichi, B. C., & Tricomi, E. (2015). The power of competition: Effects of social motivation on attention, sustained physical effort, and learning. *Frontiers in Psychology*, 6. https://doi.org/10.3389/fpsyg.2015.01282

Downwind-Bald Eagle, I. (2014–2021). Leech Lake Anishinaabe, Minnesota, personal communication.

Hanh, T. N., (1991). *Peace is every step: The path of mindfulness in every day*, edited by Kotler, A. Bantam Doubleday Dell Publishing Group.

Harris, I. M., & Morrison, M. L. (2013). *Peace education* (3rd ed.). McFarland & Company, Inc. Publishers.

Hawthorne, B. (2022). *Raising antiracist children: A practical parenting guide.* Simon & Schuster.

Johnson, D. W., Johnson, T., & Stanne, M. B. (2000). *Cooperative learning methods: A meta-analysis.* Retrieved from https://www.researchgate.net/publication/220040324_Cooperative_learning_methods_A_meta-analysis

Kagan, S. (1992, 1995). *Kagan cooperative learning*. Kagan Publishing.

Kagan, S. (2007). *The two dimensions of positive interdependence*. Kagan Publishing. Kagan Online Magazine. Retrieved December 1, 2023, from www.kaganonline.com

Meeks, A. (2017, November 14). *Cultivating courage in our professions and communities (w/Brave Spaces)*. Thoughts On. Retrieved from https://outspokinandbookish.wordpress.com/2017/11/14/cultivating-courage-in-our-professions-and-communities-w-brave-spaces/

Miller, C. E. (2005). *A glossary of terms and concepts in peace and conflict studies* (2nd ed.). University for Peace. Africa Programme. Retrieved from https://maryking.info/wp-content/glossaryv2.pdf

Mirsky, L. (2004). *Restorative justice practices of Native American, First Nation and other Indigenous people of North America*. International Institute for Restorative Practices. Retrieved from https://www.iirp.edu/news/restorative-justice-practices-of-native-american-first-nation-and-other-indigenous-people-of-north-america-part-one

Office of the Surgeon General (OSG) (2023). *Our epidemic of loneliness and isolation: The U.S. surgeon general's advisory on the healing effects of social connection and community*. US Department of Health and Human Services.

Poplawski, K. (2014). *Morning meeting* (4th ed.). Responsive Classroom. Retrieved from https://www.responsiveclassroom.org/product/morning-meeting-4th-edition/

Radunsky, V. (2004). *What does peace feel like?* Simon & Schuster Children's.

Shindler, J. (2010). *Transformative classroom management: Positive strategies to engage all students and promote a psychology of success* (1st ed.). Jossey Bass Wiley.

Stelson, C. (2020). *A bowl full of peace: A true story*. Carolrhoda.

Sylvain, D. [@didiersylvain3986]. (2020, June 23). *Creating brave space*. YouTube. https://www.youtube.com/watch?v=83rYV5SDqzY

Thomas, K. W. (1979). *Organizational conflict*. In S. Kerr (Ed.), *Organizational behavior*. Grid.

Tutu, D. (2000). *No future without forgiveness: A personal overview of South Africa's truth and reconciliation commission*. Bantam Doubleday Dell.

Waldinger, R., & Schulz, M. (2023). *The good life: Lessons from the world's longest scientific study of happiness*. Simon & Schuster.

Yazzie, R. (1994). *Life comes from it: Navajo justice concepts, 24 N.M.L. Rev. 175, 177*. The Navajo Nation Court System.

5

Respect Diversity

*Students need spaces to name and critique injustice to help
them ultimately develop the agency to build a better world.
As long as oppression is present in the world, young people
need pedagogy that nurtures criticality.*
~ Dr. Gholdy Muhammad

For peacemakers and peacebuilders, the action *Respect Diversity* is
essential! We believe diversity is a gift, an asset to a community. We
learn so much from people of differing backgrounds and believe we all
thrive in diverse environments. In alignment with Dr. Muhammad (2020,
p. 12) in our leading quote, we have a responsibility to co-create brave
spaces that nurture criticality in order for learners to explore injustices.
This happens through culturally relevant pedagogy. We strive to create
spaces for the whole school community to feel seen, heard, valued and
recognized. This develops agency and empowers us to build a better
world for all life.

Diversity is a strength and benefit to our communities – an opportunity
to learn from people, genders and cultures of all backgrounds. A global
approach invites us to celebrate diversity.

◎ Pause & Reflect:

  ◆   What does *Respect Diversity* mean to you?

DOI: 10.4324/9781003449249-6

In This Chapter:

Author's Perspective

Growing up, my (Carey's) older brother, Krishna, originally from India, shaped my life in amazing ways. We always had diverse friends and family gatherings, which enhanced my life and helped me see the world from a global perspective. Equity is a core value of mine. I see how important this is for our communities, including our students, families and school systems. I focused my dissertation and now my leadership on culturally relevant teaching and creating systems of equity. I coined the term **culturally affirming systems** (2021) to expand and sustain systemic changes in school culture, curriculum, professional learning and the inclusivity of diverse perspectives and cultures. We encourage you to continue your own personal equity journey; ask questions, push back, learn from others and determine how you can support and create culturally affirming systems. In Chapter 11, we offer further leadership guidance for this work.

Human Rights & Equity

Human rights education empowers the attitude, advocacy and action for respect, equality and dignity of all people in the world. The Universal Declaration of Human Rights (United Nations, 1948) highlights the true meaning of the peace action, *Respect Diversity.* Almost every article of this declaration is important to equitable peacelearning, and the first is crucial.

Article 1:

> *All human beings are born free and equal in dignity and rights. They are endowed with reason and conscience and should act towards one another in a spirit of brotherhood.*

◎ **Pause & Reflect:**

- ◆ What words stand out to you in Article 1?
- ◆ How does this resonate with your beliefs and actions?

We recognize globally this is still a goal and not a reality. It is so important that we lift up universal human rights and the inherent dignity of all people. Equity means there is fair and just access to opportunities, resources, rights and privileges. Our goal is to support near-future generations in fulfilling this declaration and living in peace. As Harris and Morrison (2013) stated,

> *Peace, a concept that motivates the imagination, connotes more than no violence. It implies human beings working together to resolve conflicts, respect standards of justice, satisfy basic needs and honor human rights. Peace involves a respect for life and for the dignity of each human being without discrimination or prejudice. (p. 14)*

By ensuring equity in meeting basic needs, upholding justice and honoring the rights and dignity of all life, we uphold the meaning of *Respect Diversity.*

Framing Through Language & Terminology

Let's ground in some terminology important in our approach to this peace action. We acknowledge this (Table 5.1) is a limited set of terms and language is ever-evolving, yet this vocabulary will support your peacelearning implementation.

Table 5.1 *Respect Diversity* Key Terminology

Term	Definition & Context
Diversity	Our Peacemaker in Practice for this Chapter, Dr. Taylor defined diversity as *"A term that refers to the presence of individuals with a wide range of identities, backgrounds, and perspectives within a particular group or community. Diversity encompasses the various aspects that make individuals unique, such as their race, ethnicity, culture, gender, and more"* (p. 102).
Global Majority People of the Global Majority (PGM)	This collective term includes people who have been racialized as minorities (Black, Indigenous, Asian, Brown, Biracial etc.), but in actuality represent about 80% of the worldwide population. The majority of people live in the global south and are of African, Asian, Latin American and Arab descent. This is important when talking about race and diversity because it distinguishes that globally Whiteness is not the norm (American Psychological Association, 2023, p. 5).
Multiculturalism	This term is used to describe diversity in specific populations and therefore is influenced geographically in its meaning and interpretation. Generally, it considers the social and cultural diversity present in the community, state or nation (i.e., ethnic, racial, cultural, religious groups).
Social Justice	Social justice has many meanings, which vary based on context, geographic and personal background. In general, it is a *"Commitment to creating fairness and equity in resources, rights, institutions, and systems and in the treatment of marginalized individuals and groups of people who do not share equal power in society"* (American Psychological Association, 2023, p. 8).
Tolerance	Being tolerant of others' way of living, being and beliefs has been seen as a condition for a functioning society. *"Tolerance is considered a critical and adequate response to the challenge of how conflicting ways of life can freely express themselves and peacefully coexist with each other. A society that is culturally, religiously, and ideologically plural implies diversity of substantive worldviews and lifestyles"* (Verkuyten & Kollar, 2021). However, we must go beyond tolerance, which means valuing, respecting and embracing diversity, as well as critiquing injustice and/or intolerant words and actions.
White-Centered White-Centering	*"White centering is the centering of white people, white values, white norms and white feelings over everything and everything else"* (Saad, 2020). This terminology can lead to defensiveness around race and culture for some people. It is not meant to 'call out' Whiteness in only a negative way, but to acknowledge the privilege and status that Whiteness can provide.

We see these terms primarily in education settings, yet diversity is all around us, in our day-to-day lives, our workplaces and businesses as well as our family and community. Considering this peace action from a global majority view connects us to culturally relevant and responsive practices. These practices include recognizing and incorporating strengths and assets as well as making sure content is relevant. Consider this story and guidance from our Peacemaker in Practice as a foundation for understanding characteristics of culture and bringing this peace action into practice.

Peacemaker In Practice

I Am, We Are, A Community of Learners

By Dr. Naomi Rae Taylor, Founder, Pleasant Spirit Consulting
https://www.pleasantspiritconsulting.com/

What is diversity? "Diversity" is a term that refers to the presence of individuals with a wide range of identities, backgrounds and perspectives within a particular group or community. Diversity encompasses the various aspects that make individuals unique, such as their race, ethnicity, culture, gender and more. *Respect Diversity* is one of the peace actions that centers the individual's identity within the community context.

Imagine a 13-year-old multiracial girl in junior high school trying to find her way and who she is in this world. A peer asks her in the girl's locker room one day: *"What are you?"* Defensively, the young girl says, *"What do you mean? What are you?"* Perplexed, the peer walks away while the 13-year-old girl walks past the blurred locker mirror and wonders- *"Who am I?"*

Fast-forward ten years, this young girl is now a first-year teacher in a large public school district. Her inkling is to parallel how her veteran teachers teach. Yet, her instinct tells her to embrace diversity, live it by introducing a pluralistic curriculum and reach every student in her classroom. Not having the language or framework of culturally responsive pedagogy, she centers on race and learns about the identity of her students to celebrate their differences and share their commonalities. Community was no longer a thought; it was a reality of learning about who you are as an individual to understand cultures different from your own. One example is to bring folks together, young and old, to share cultural practices and identity stories. The **Culture Wheel Activity** (Figure 5.1) expands and encompasses a practical approach to bridging diversity, equity, inclusion and belonging interactively and engagingly.

This story highlighted the transformation of a young girl into a culturally responsive teacher, signifying her commitment to understanding and celebrating the differences among her students, creating a sense of belonging for everyone in her classroom where everyone thrives. Respecting diversity as one of the *Five Peace Actions* aims to foster justice and peace while respecting the dignity of every human being and acknowledging that staying in the community means never disregarding others' humanity.

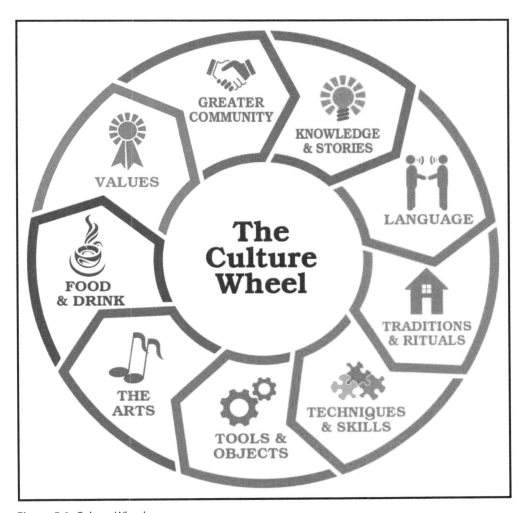

Figure 5.1 Culture Wheel

> **Put It Into Practice: Culture Wheel Activity**
>
> The Culture Wheel Card Game was created by Social Designs (2023) "… *to share cultural practices and identity stories with each other in an interactive way. This game is diversity, inclusion and belonging in ACTION.*" We highly recommend purchasing the game, wonderful for people of all ages. https://culturewheelcardgame.com/
>
> Here are some Culture Wheel prompts to get you started! Check out Figure 5.1 for the many sharing categories. Start by explaining what culture is and then invite participants to be concise and descriptive in their sharing.
>
> > ➤ Cultural or traditional actions or remedies for your health.
> > ➤ Describe your home (where you live): sounds, smells, things you see.
> > ➤ The ethnicity you identify with (a social group with common cultural or national tradition).
> > ➤ Religion/Spirituality that you do (or do not) identify with.
> > ➤ Traditional dish, receipt, snack or drink.
> > ➤ Ritual, heritage event, custom and/or belief passed from generation to generation.
>
> ◎ **Pause & Reflect:** After sharing, debrief and process.
>
> > ◆ How did the activity make you feel? (Like, dislike, comfortable, uncomfortable)
> > ◆ Did you have anything in common with fellow players? If so, what?
> > ◆ How does this activity relate to the peace action, *Respect Diversity*?

Our Epistemology

Though we are all interconnected, people have differing identities, cultures, backgrounds, beliefs, histories and philosophies. Cultural differences are an asset, bringing new perspectives, creativity, solutions and skills to work, school and communities. Respecting diversity is crucial in creating systems of inclusion and peace worldwide.

Recall from Chapter 3, that seeking peace within yourself is a lifelong process that continually changes in response to our limited experience of the world. Individuals have a limited lens, their reality sits amongst multiple realities to grapple with the world. Researcher and educational leader, Muhammad Khalifa (2021), referred to this as a person's epistemology (p. 11). Each person, regardless of their race, culture or background, has a unique epistemology, which is their understanding of knowledge, lived experiences and upbringing.

A person's epistemology cannot be changed, but one's ability to unlearn or relearn from biases is possible. One can pause, reflect and reconsider when biases are coming up and move in a different direction, hopefully to one of openness and acceptance. Khalifa (2021) explained,

> *Epistemology is concerned with anything that informs or influences us in how we learn and understand what we believe is real. For educators engaged in anti bias work, this is deeply important. This is partly why people can have different realities for the same topic or phenomenon. One person's (or groups') truth is often not the truth for others.* (p. 11)

Khalifa also encouraged educators and leaders to strongly align with their communities. Highlighting the disconnect that often happens between a school-centric community and a community-centric focus, he argued that the latter is more culturally responsive. Likewise, we encourage school leaders and staff to authentically connect with students and families, not just asking the community to 'bend' to school culture. This is how sustainable culturally affirming systems are established and sustained.

Rather than coming into education with a school-centric mindset, schools and educational communities can work in partnership to learn from their communities. Through this model, schools can become culturally affirming environments in which students, staff, families and community members feel welcomed, seen, heard and valued.

> *To push back on education as a school-centric enterprise – which re-colonizes communities of color in dynamic, iterative ways – school leaders must find ways to engage communities without merely reinscribing school-centric perspectives, but with the added claim that schools are "involving" or, even worse, "training" the community.*
>
> (Khalifa, 2021, p. 27)

Authentic, inclusive involvement from the entire community is integral for creating sustained cultures of peace. Keep in mind that many people have had poor experiences with schooling (or historical trauma), so it can take time to establish trust. It's worth it, there is so much wisdom in the collective! Through our differences, we can learn from one another, gain richer understandings and embrace our world as a whole, rather than as factions. Exploring intersections of identities and epistemologies grows an understanding of what binds us as living beings on this planet.

◎ **Pause & Reflect:**

- ◆ What is your epistemology? How does this show up in your life?
- ◆ Consider your biases – what are they? This may be based on race, gender or other characteristics you may not consider overtly.
- ◆ What is the relationship between your epistemology and biases? What have you been (or have you considered) unlearning/relearning?

Table 5.2 Pursuit: Unique Experiences

Peace Pursuits for: *Respect Diversity*	
I understand that every person uniquely experiences the world.	• Appreciate that each person has their epistemology (personal knowledge, experience and upbringing) that guides their perspective in life. • When in disagreement with another's point of view, lean in with curiosity, vulnerability and acknowledge their 'truth.' • Storytelling and stories are an opportunity to listen and learn from people's perspectives, knowledge systems and ways of being. • Upholding this peace pursuit shows students that they are accepted and appreciated. This creates a brave environment for community connection and expression.

Table 5.3 Practice: Celebrating Diversity Through Art

Put It Into Practice: Celebrating Diversity Through Art		
Art is a great way to share diverse ideas, identities and perspectives. Honoring student epistemologies, lived experiences and their backgrounds through art enhances learning.		
Set up students to create a piece that represents their unique selves. Incorporate the pointillism technique, which uses distinct dots to form a larger image. Great way to practice fine motor skills, too!		
Emerging	*Intermediate*	*Advanced*
Use large dot markers or have children use paint on the tip of their finger to create large dots.	Use Q-tips or pencils with paint on the tip to create their piece. Once created, add a short artist statement that explains what the piece shared about their unique selves.	
Celebrate the uniqueness of the artist and their creation through a gallery walk. Invite each learner to share how their piece represents them. Discuss similarities and differences of their paintings, as well as their connected self-stories.		
Extension: Students can create almost any design using pointillism and this fosters unique points of view, as well as perspectives in what they sketch for their pieces.		

Intersections Between Culturally Relevant Pedagogy & Peace Education

Respect Diversity should not be focused on tolerance, rather it should be an active stance of learning and unlearning. We urge you (and students, families) to engage with humility and awareness of your epistemology and sense of self and to be open to learning and exploring varying cultures, experiences and knowledge systems. Upholding cultural identities and developing critical perspectives is what culturally relevant pedagogy is all about! This encircles our framework because it is essential for creating just cultures of peace.

In learning about and implementing culturally relevant pedagogy, there is a variety of related terminology to consider. We lean on these definitions (see Table 5.4) and use them throughout our approach to peacelearning. We appreciate the nuances from different scholars and build from their work to put into practice sustainable, culturally affirming systems. Respecting diversity and culturally relevant teaching practices go hand in hand. It really is a mindset, not just a set of terms, research or a stagnant pedagogy.

Table 5.4 Culturally Relevant Pedagogy Terminology

Term	Definition & Context
Culturally Responsive Teaching	*"Using the cultural characteristics, experiences, and perspectives of ethnically diverse students as conduits for teaching them more effectively"* (Gay, 2002, p. 106).
Culturally Relevant Teaching	*"Culturally relevant teaching/pedagogy rests on three criteria or propositions: a. Students must experience academic success; b. students must develop and/or maintain cultural competence; and, c. students must develop a critical consciousness through which they challenge the status quo of the current social order"* (Ladson-Billings, 1995, p. 160).
Culturally Sustaining Pedagogy	*"Culturally sustaining pedagogy seeks to perpetuate and foster – to sustain – linguistic, literate, and cultural pluralism as part of the democratic project of schooling. In the face of current policies and practices that have the explicit goal of creating a monocultural and monolingual society, research and practice need equally explicit resistances that embrace cultural pluralism and cultural equality"* (Paris, 2012, p. 93). As discussed in Chapter 4, p. 81, co-creating democratic and brave spaces is crucial to developing critical consciousness.

(Continued)

Table 5.4 Culturally Relevant Pedagogy Terminology (Continued)

Term	Definition & Context
Culturally Affirming Systems	*"Culturally affirming systems are inclusive of school culture, professional development for teachers, diverse curriculum; windows and mirrors[1] for students and an opportunity for student voices and cultures. A culturally affirming system is a learning-centered structure that sees diverse perspectives as an asset versus a deficit for students, families and staff"* (Seeley Dzierzak, 2021, p. 162).
Cultural Proficiency	Cultural Proficiency focuses on educating all students and using their assets based on their backgrounds. This includes culture, language, learning style and considering the context of teaching. This notion also assumes that a student has their own set of assumptions and beliefs (Nuri Robins et al., 2012). We feel that a person doesn't 'arrive' at proficiency; rather, they can have a level of understanding and humility about various cultures.
Cultural Humility	Cultural humility is *"a lifelong commitment to self-evaluation and critique, to redressing power imbalances... and to developing mutually beneficial and non-paternalistic partnerships with communities on behalf of individuals and defined populations"* (Tervalon & Murray-García, 1998, p. 123). This connects with the peace pursuit of feeling empowered that as we learn and grow our opinions and ideas of the world may change.

◎ **Pause & Reflect:**

◆ As you review Table 5.4, what resonates with you?
◆ What elements or characteristics of culturally relevant pedagogy are present within your teaching?

As you can see from the definitions above, culturally relevant and culturally responsive are very similar terms. **We use the framing of culturally relevant in our work because of the emphasized partnership between the educator and students.** Though nuanced, we also feel culturally relevant is more proactive, versus reactive. Culturally relevant pedagogy keeps the children at the center of peacelearning and honors their voice and choice more clearly. There are many scholars who have done important work on these topics, but we feel the particular leaders we highlight in the remainder of this chapter embody the connections between culturally relevant pedagogy and peace education. We are grateful to learn from these scholars and to grow and expand on the genius that has come before us! Through this short literature review, our goal is also to present the core research, elements and practices for creating culturally affirming systems.

Essential Elements of Culturally Responsive Teaching: Dr. Geneva Gay

Culturally relevant and responsive teaching practices uphold and celebrate diverse cultures and perspectives. The essential elements of these practices are important beyond the educational setting. For example, as adults, we make choices every day about how we interact, view and respond to other people, businesses and our environment based on our values, beliefs, past experiences and hopes.

Professor Emerita, Dr. Geneva Gay (2002), defined culturally responsive teaching as, *"using the cultural characteristics, experiences, and perspectives of ethnically diverse students as conduits for teaching them more effectively"* (p. 106). Dr. Gay outlined five essential elements that have strong links to our peace action framework. As we explore these, think about how each area supports living in alignment with *Respect Diversity*.

Table 5.5 Five Essential Elements To Culturally Responsive Teaching & Links To Peace Action Framework

Five Essential Elements of Culturally Responsive Teaching*	Links to the Peace Action Framework
Developing a knowledge base about cultural diversity.	Through research, stories and storytelling, seek out and include multiple voices and cultures.
Including ethnic and cultural diversity content in the curriculum.	Include a balance of people and cultures that respect and celebrate diversity. Be mindful to decenter Whiteness and/or your own culture and epistemology.
Demonstrating caring and building communities.	Peace education values caring, peaceful communities that honors all life. Becoming trauma informed is an important foundation (see Chapter 9).
Communicating with ethnically diverse students.	Peacelearning places a high importance on being inclusive of all peoples and members of a school community. Communication & conflict resolution practices and lessons are particularly supportive practices (see Chapter 4).
Responding to ethnic diversity in the delivery of instruction.	Practices and lessons throughout the book include intentional opportunities for student identities to be shared and honored through multiple modalities.
* (Gay, 2002, p. 4)	

◎ **Pause & Reflect:** As you consider the Five Essential Elements (Table 5.5):

- ◆ Identify an area for continued personal and professional development.
- ◆ Set an intention to actively engage, learn from and with people who are ethnically, racially and/or culturally diverse from you.

Think about all the interactions you have with other people; at work, school, while shopping, traveling, through media and communicating with your family and community. Respecting diversity through your actions, choices and communication is an important part of creating a more peaceful and just world.

Culturally Relevant Pedagogy: Dr. Gloria Ladson-Billings

Dr. Ladson-Billings is a professor, researcher and teacher educator whose research on culturally relevant pedagogy guided our teaching and is critical to our core beliefs for this peacelearning framework. Dr. Ladson-Billings (2009) defined cultural relevance as moving beyond language to include the culture of the student and school. *"Thus culturally relevant teaching uses student culture in order to maintain it and to transcend the negative effects of the dominant culture"* (p. 19). Empowerment, paired with cultural connection in all areas of living, being and learning, is foundational.

Dr. Ladson-Billings (2009), also emphasized the importance of teaching practice (pedagogy). She highlighted *"It is the way we teach that profoundly affects the way that students perceive the content of that curriculum"* (p. 15). She broke down five key areas of culturally relevant teaching for engaging, motivating and growing learners across all instruction and content areas.

1. *When students are treated as competent, they are likely to demonstrate competence.*
2. *When teachers provide instructional "scaffolding," students can move from what they know to what they need to know.*
3. *The focus of the classroom must be instructional.*
4. *Real education is about extending students' thinking and abilities.*
5. *Effective teaching involves in-depth knowledge of both the students and the subject matter* (2009, p. 135–136).

We appreciate the emphasis that educators are not 'tellers' of knowledge but partners in learning. A key facet in how we teach is truly getting to know children and making learning relevant and engaging. It's always been important to meet students halfway as both learners and people. We encourage educators to first consider your students and make adaptations as needed to the peacelearning practices and lessons.

◎ **Pause & Reflect:**

- ◆ What stands out to you as you review Dr. Ladson-Billings suggestions for culturally relevant teaching?
- ◆ Which of these key areas do you feel makes the greatest difference in your student's learning?

Our goal is to accelerate student learning by building an inclusive and welcoming culture of peace. We want educators and students to feel empowered to shape their school with their own stories, experiences and cultures. The growing or deepening of critical consciousness is crucial to peacelearning (and justice). Following Dr. Ladson-Billing's guidance (1995), culturally relevant teaching is a *"pedagogy of opposition not unlike critical pedagogy but specifically committed to collective not merely individual empowerment"* (p. 160).

> **We don't want to simply observe or acknowledge the problems in education, our systems and world; rather, we want to offer some concrete and powerful tools to empower teachers and students.**

We seek to create a culture of equity through peace and justice education. Students come to school with many gifts and it's up to us as educators to uphold their cultures, honor voices and support them in cultivating or deepening the values, beliefs and attitudes for peace. Empowerment extends beyond individual situations and students to embracing and considering the perspectives of others, cultures, situations and contexts.

Embracing Similarities & Differences

Being committed to collective empowerment means embracing *both* similarities *and* differences in people. This is an ongoing process that requires authentic relationship building. Getting to know children and creating ample opportunities for them to get to know each other are essential culturally relevant strategies.

Table 5.6 Pursuit: Similarities & Differences

Peace Pursuits for: *Respect Diversity*	
I describe similarities and differences between myself and people with different experiences, histories or cultures from my own.	• When exploring similarities, we build bridges of connection and understanding. • Affirm our interconnectedness, as well as unique perspectives, experiences, histories and cultures. • Value and validate the identities of students and families to create a community of belonging and acceptance. • Explore identities and what matters to individuals and as a collective (see practices in Chapter 3). Ask: What are your hopes and dreams? How are they similar and different from others – and why might this be?

Put It Into Practice: Class Collage

Facilitate the sharing of different cultures and backgrounds by creating a class collage. Think BIG – create a quilt-sized collage that can take up a large space in a hallway or classroom.

Provide each student the opportunity to decorate their "quilt square" with a photo of themselves. (Do this at school for equitable access to a standard size and quality photo of each student.) Invite learners to decorate their squares with images of their culture and upbringing such as food, clothing, holidays, religion and family members that are important to them. Consider adding a "frame" around the quilt that has a class mantra such as, *"we are all equal parts of our classroom community"* or something that resonates with the group.

Through the class collage, explore similarities and differences of individuals and as a collective.

Just as adults do, learners need brave spaces and opportunities to listen to the perspectives and 'truths' of others, even (and especially) if it challenges their worldview. Explicit modeling and providing support for critical conversations and peer interactions fosters a more inclusive learning environment. Listening to other perspectives, ideas and opinions in an authentic way offers students the opportunity to develop strong social emotional skills. Support students through a variety of peer learning structures such as partnerships, small and whole groups (see Chapter 4, p. 93 for more cooperation and collaboration guidance).

Table 5.7 Pursuit: Honoring Ideas & Perspectives

Peace Pursuits for: *Respect Diversity*	
I listen to and consider others' ideas or opinions. **I honor the ideas, views or perspectives ('truth') of others, even if it is different from mine.**	• Create opportunities to learn from cultures and perspectives that reflect and challenge their worldview. • Truly listen and seek to understand and value other cultures (asset approach). • Provide voice and choice in how learners explore and receive the ideas, feedback and opinions of others. • Co-create brave spaces (see Chapter 4, p. 81) and utilize peace circles (Lesson, p. 259) for sharing and listening.

Put It Into Practice: Exploring Perspectives

Share books, articles, videos, art and other 'texts' that highlight differing perspectives on the same topic or subject. A seminar circle structure (Lesson, p. 255) works great for this purpose.

Questions to explore:

➤ What is this person(s) 'truth'?
➤ How is it similar to yours? Different?
➤ How can you disagree with someone else's perspective?
➤ Are perspectives that are different from ours a gift or a challenge? (Ultimately emphasize the *'both/and'* here!)
➤ Why is it important to consider and embrace diverse perspectives?
➤ How can we honor other's ideas or views?

Curriculum: Windows, Mirrors, Sliding Glass Doors & Curtains

The books, materials, visuals and other media we share are influential for students. Mindful choices of curriculum and culturally relevant teaching methods allow learners to explore the perspectives, 'truths' and ideas within themselves as well as of others. We espouse the theory that half of your curriculum walks through the door each day. We learn as much from our students as they learn from us as educators. They deserve voice, choice and the opportunity to create a classroom and school culture based on their own unique backgrounds and learning styles. Let us always empower children!

Inspire children by providing opportunities to learn from cultures and perspectives around the world. Distinguished scholar and researcher,

Dr. Rudine Sims Bishop (1990), used the analogy *"windows, mirrors and sliding glass doors"* to discuss the importance of diversity in books and the authors who write them. **Students need to see themselves reflected (mirrors), and books or media can also be windows to other people, perspectives, cultures or even worlds.** Sliding glass doors means that this goes both ways and shares all people with a sense of equality. We encourage you to consistently go through your classroom and school library to make sure that there are *"windows, mirrors and sliding glass doors."*

Debbie Reese, a Nambé Pueblo Native scholar and activist, added curtains to Dr. Sims Bishop's analogy of windows, mirrors and sliding glass doors. She shared that many Native Americans felt the need to put up curtains to shield White authors from 'peeking' into their culture and writing about Native cultures and customs in an authoritative way that may be inaccurate and ultimately damaging. Reese (2016) explained that:

> *Curtains have gone up as a form of protection or a shield to protect their cultural identities and ways of being. That curtain is there because we've had hundreds of years of white people looking in our windows and not understanding what we were doing, and then writing about what they saw in an authoritative way...and used as a weapon that was used over us, over and over again. (3:10)*

In learning from and interacting with Native American people, educators and students, this really resonates and we appreciate the addition to the analogy. There has been so much generational trauma from colonization, boarding schools and (attempted) erasure of culture, that indeed sensitivity is required. This consideration should be applied to all curriculum and teaching choices; be thoughtful to find primary sources, first-person perspectives and not to appropriate other cultures.

◎ Pause & Reflect:

- ◆ How do you include diverse voices, ideas and perspectives in your curriculum (text, media)?
- ◆ What resonates with you about windows, mirrors, sliding glass doors and curtains?
- ◆ Where do you see the line of appreciation and appropriation of other cultures?

Table 5.8 Pursuit: Inspiring Peacemakers

Peace Pursuits for *Respect Diversity*	
I view and am inspired by stories of peaceful people from around the world.	• Stories help us be empathetic, to problem-solve, imagine and be empowered to create change. • Gain inspiration by learning about the histories, experiences and contributions of peacemakers and leaders (of all sizes) through stories and storytelling. • Provide a rich perspective, as well as windows, mirrors and sliding glass doors into the histories, cultures and perspectives of others. • See www.thepeacepad.org for a list of peacemakers!

Table 5.9 Practice: Compare & Contrast Peace Heroes

Put It Into Practice: Compare & Contrast Peace Heroes	
Use a modified t-chart or Venn diagram to explore similarities and differences between two or more peaceful people. These might be students, adults in the community, characters in a book you've already read together or through highlighting specific peace heroes.	

Check out Global Peace Heroes (2020) story-based resources to empower students at: https://globalpeaceheroes.org/

Guide discussion and reflections: A seminar circle structure (Lesson, p. 255) works great for this purpose.

• What is special about this person?
• What makes them a peace hero?
• How did they make a positive impact on the world?
• What barriers or challenges did this peacemaker have to overcome?
• What did you learn from this person?
• How were their experiences, culture and histories similar to each other? Different?
• How does this compare/contrast to your 'truth,' ideas or perspective?

Emerging	*Intermediate & Advanced*
Ask students to show their understanding by: • Drawing a picture and possibly labeling it with key words or the peace heroes' name. • Using one of the discussion prompts as a sentence frame and fill in the rest with their response.	Guide students to compose a reflective essay, research writing and/or create a multimedia presentation showing their understanding and ideas about the peace hero(s). Connect to the questions above.

Celebrate the peace heroes with a gallery walk or other sharing opportunity. Ensure equity by providing any materials and support for preparing presentations at school.

A word of caution, steer clear from "wax museum" projects where students dress up as real people. It creates the possibility of showing up in offensive ways (unintentionally) and/or may be a form of cultural appropriation. An alternative is creating an artifact, object or symbol representation of the person.

◎ **Pause & Reflect:**

- ◆ How will you learn from past and present peacemakers?
- ◆ What steps need to be taken to create windows, mirrors, sliding glass doors and potentially curtains for (with) your students and curriculum?

The Next Step in Culturally Relevant Pedagogy: Zaretta Hammond

It is essential to give students voice and choice in their academic, justice and peace pursuits. By honoring student identity, a core practice of culturally relevant pedagogy, we motivate and engage learners. Teacher educator Zaretta Hammond (2015) created the Ready for Rigor framework and we agree that *"More than a motivational tool, culturally responsive teaching is a serious and powerful tool for accelerating student learning"* (p. 3). Like the Ready for Rigor framework, our peace action framework puts students at the center of the classroom environment.

Leaning on brain research, Hammond (2015) shared that it is important to move students from dependent to independent learners:

> *It is not just a matter of grit or mindset. Grit and mindset are necessary but not sufficient by themselves. We have to help dependent students develop new cognitive skills and habits of mind that will actually increase their brain power. Students with increased brainpower can accelerate their own learning, meaning they know how to learn new content and improve their weak skills on their own. (p. 15)*

Hammond (2015) broke down the Ready for Rigor Framework into four quadrants with a focus prompt in the center, *"Students are ready for rigor and independent learning"* (p. 17–19). We incorporate these learnings throughout our peace education framework. The four quadrants are as follows:

- ◆ *Awareness*: of cultural lens, interpretations and triggers; how the brain learns
- ◆ *Learning Partnerships*: relationships in balance; being empowered
- ◆ *Information Processing*: honoring neurodiversity and multiple modalities
- ◆ *Community of Learners and Learning Environment*: rituals and routines; brave spaces; restorative justice; voice and agency

Creating awareness of multiple perspectives, allowing for information to be processed in a variety of ways and becoming a community of learners and partnerships who feel supported and valued are foundational to peacelearning.

Author's Perspective

A great way to support students to be ready for rigorous independent learning is by helping them discover their assets and gifts. I (Carey) have used multiple formats, such as poems, narratives and memoirs to highlight students' strengths. For example, with a group of fifth graders, we used the book *The Best Part of Me* (Ewald, 2002) as a mentor text. Some students wrote about their beautiful brains, some about their hands, others their eyes and one student wrote about her self-control. This piece was moving, as she explained that when she gets older, she has *"big responsibilities"* … and will need her self-control to make good choices. All of these students wrote from the heart, and we also took photos to "zoom" in on the best parts of themselves. Look for joy and raise awareness in the community of learners!

Cultivating Genius & Joy: Dr. Gholdy Muhammad

As former school literacy leaders, we have been greatly inspired by the scholarship of Dr. Gholnescar (Gholdy) Muhammad, who presented a teaching and learning model based on the histories of African American literary societies. In 2020, Dr. Muhammad offered a four-layered equity framework for culturally and historically responsive literacy (p. 12):

1. *Identity Development*
2. *Skill Development*
3. *Intellectual Development*
4. *Criticality*

Dr. Muhammad broke down this framework into various goals for **Literary Presence in the Classroom** (p. 28):

1. Opportunities to create contexts for students to add voice and choice in their literacy work.
2. Create a collection of texts that highlight multiple identities.
3. Provide multiple ways for students to share their thinking beyond just reading and writing (voice-text, spoken word, art etc.).

As with peacelearning, these pursuits for reading, discussing, thinking and debating have the power to engage the individual and extend to the classroom, school and throughout systems.

Literary pursuits were enacted simultaneously so as literary society members were reading, they were also thinking through the text, writing about related topics, and then debating these subjects. These literary pursuits were collaborative, embodied a chain-like effect, and encouraged others to participate. (p. 29)

Motivation, connection and empowerment through literacy is a goal we believe to be core to enacting the *Five Peace Actions*. As we noted in Chapter 2, our language choice of 'peace pursuits' was inspired by Dr. Muhammad (2020), who shared these **Literary Pursuits in the Classroom**:

1. *Engage students with texts that create social action and cause them to think differently as a result of what they read.*
2. *Create an environment that affords students the opportunity to shape their own ideas through acts of literacy.*
3. *Structure opportunities for critiquing and evaluating what students read and write about within their instruction. (p. 30)*

Peacelearning through literacy pursuits such as these is inspiring and empowering to students. It gives them a voice and the agency to form their own ideas and make their own choices. As learners explore themselves and others, they can discover inner peace and work toward a just culture of world peace. In addition to many of the practices throughout the book, the language and literacy-based unit of lessons in Chapter 12: Belonging & Harmony (p. 245) support educators in creating culturally relevant, empowering peacelearning opportunities that center students.

◎ **Pause & Reflect:**

   ◆ How do (could) you utilize various forms of literacy in your classroom as a means to understanding identities and/or creating social action?
   ◆ Are you providing multiple ways for students to express themselves and have their voices honored?

Put It Into Practice: Identity Writing

As a teacher and leader, I (Carey) have had some powerful experiences using diverse texts and helping students share their voices and identities. For example, in collaboration with a non-profit reading organization that I *Reach Out In Service* with, we created an opportunity for students to tell their stories and share what makes them unique. We encouraged students to express themselves in a mode that suited them, such as:

> ➢ Personal Narrative
> ➢ Memoir
> ➢ Interview
> ➢ Spoken Word
> ➢ Poetry
> ➢ Other – we invited students to be creative!

We have had some amazing writing pieces emerge from this project over the past few years. Students have written about the best part of themselves, shared their stories through memoirs, held interviews with important family members and conducted research projects on leaders that have inspired them.

Dr. Muhammad's framework can expand this project by helping educators plan and consider multiple entry points for students to share their stories. This is what excites me about culturally relevant teaching practices. It brings students to the center of learning by making it relevant, empowering and joyful!

◎ **Pause & Reflect:**

   ◆   How do you bring joy into your life and work?
   ◆   How do you light up the joy within children?

In her book *Unearthing Joy: A Guide to Culturally Responsive Teaching and Learning* (2023), Dr. Muhammad added joy to her equity framework for culturally and historically responsive literacy. We are in deep agreement that the focus on joy is essential for student learning, teacher preparation and collective mindsets. Dr. Muhammad made a strong case for the importance and beauty of joy in our classrooms:

Joy is the practice of loving self and humanity; caring for and helping humanity and earth; recognizing truth, beauty and aesthetics, art, and wonder; and working to solve social problems of the world. Joy is also about advancing happiness by elevating beauty in humanity, as well as truthful narratives and representations of our studenst. (p. 77)

The focus on joy is an excellent connection with the goals and pursuits of peace education. Prioritizing joy in school helps the whole community find their center as they *Seek Peace Within Yourself and Others.* Utilizing Dr. Muhammad's framework and including a focus on the *Five Peace Actions* will help students access both the what and the how of peacelearning – and to put it into practice in their schools, homes and communities.

Table 5.10 Practice: Culturally & Historically Responsive Peacelearning

Put It Into Practice: Culturally & Historically Responsive Peacelearning		
Dr. Muhammad's Framework	**In Action**	**Curriculum Review** (texts, media, resources, lessons) *Ask: Does the curriculum…*
Identity	Help students understand who they are and learn about the diverse lives and identities of others.	Support students to learn something about themselves and/or others? Inspire connection and exploration of identities?
Skills	Support students in their development and proficiency of content areas and learning standards.	Respond to or build upon students' peacebuilding skills? Deepen understanding of peace actions and pursuits?
Intellect	Encourage students to gain new knowledge that connects to the context of the world where they can apply their skills.	Build upon and deepen students' knowledge and understanding of peace and justice? What are they learning?
Criticality	Have students name, understand, question and disrupt oppression (hurt, pain) in the world and within the self. Foster empowerment to make the world a better place.	Inspire students' understanding and encourage them to act on power, harm and injustices?
Joy	Create spaces for all life to live in peace and harmony.	Foster hope and empowerment within students?
Adapted from: *Cultivating Genius: An Equity Framework For Culturally and Historically Responsive Literacy* (p. 150) (Muhammad, 2020)		

Culturally Affirming Systems

There are many different entry points and levels of engagement in working toward cultural relevance, yet we advocate for a system-wide approach. Culturally affirming systems mean that culturally relevant pedagogy is embedded into all levels of a learning organization. For a school district, this means including ongoing professional development and practice for teachers, support staff, district leadership and at the school board level. There are many ways to actualize culturally affirming systems and the foundation is building relationships with students and families.

As you review Figure 5.2, notice the interconnected layering of how culturally relevant pedagogy (Ladson-Billings, 1995, p. 160) and culturally sustaining pedagogy (Paris, 2012, p. 1) support the implementation of culturally affirming systems (Seeley Dzierzak, 2021, p. 163).

Note: we provide further support for putting culturally affirming systems into practice in Chapter 11.

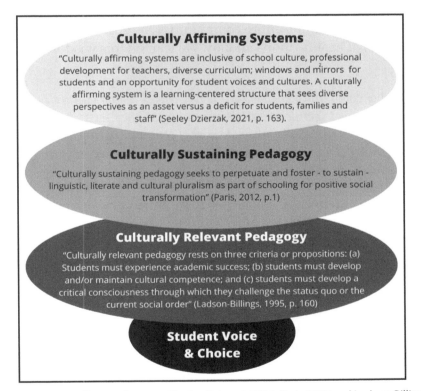

Figure 5.2 Culturally Affirming Systems (Seeley Dzierzak 2021, Paris 2012 and Ladson-Billings 1995)

◎ Pause & Reflect:

◆ Synthesize your understanding of Figure 5.2: What is the relationship between culturally relevant pedagogy, culturally sustaining pedagogy and culturally affirming systems?

This peace action, *Respect Diversity*, is immensely important to peacelearning. Without it, there are many missed opportunities and injustices. Peace and justice education have the power to transform and evolve schools and our communities. This work is not easy, but it is necessary. Our communities deserve our bravery, compassion and advocacy!

More Peaceful Practices: *Respect Diversity*

Family & Community Connections

Creating an environment grounded in culturally relevant and responsive learning will empower the entire community. Our goal is for schools to truly become places of healing, hope and joy. We lean on this wisdom shared by Khalifa (2021):

> *One goal of community engagement is for schools to find culturally responsive ways to connect with the communities they serve, but this focus remains school centric. The ultimate goal of community empowerment, however, is for communities to become healthy, whole, free from oppression, and positioned to craft and live out their own vision. (p. 21)*

For schools to actualize this vision, there must be consistent steps in making authentic connections and fostering leadership with families. School leaders and teams can support the planning and implementation of:

- ◆ Site leadership councils
- ◆ Parent Teacher Association (PTA) or Organizations (PTO)
- ◆ Utilizing parent/community school leadership platforms
- ◆ Ongoing feedback loops with a variety of possible engagement methods (online, video, in person, email, newsletter etc.)

Providing meaningful, varied and frequent opportunities for parents and caregivers to have voice, choice and ownership in the school decisions creates an inclusive community. Culturally relevant leadership broadens the scope so that schools provide not just school-centric identities, but a community-centric focus.

Table 5.11 Content Area Connections: *Respect Diversity*

Content Area Connections			
Social Studies	**Art**	**Science**	**Math**
Critically analyze the history presented in various texts, as well as current events. Prompts: Whose voice is (not) present? Who benefits? Who is harmed?	Create a collage of peace heroes studied. Create a portrait of a peacemaker whom you know. Collaboratively create a mandala with the words *Respect Diversity* in the center of the circle. Have students take turns adding to a ring around the mandala, capturing in symbols their ideas and interpretation of the peace action.	What are science-related issues in your neighborhood? What are students grappling with? Create a list of topics that students are curious about and engage in research. Invite local scientists from diverse backgrounds to share how they arrived in the field and what inspired or empowered them.	Apply math skills to a 'real world' topic relevant to learners. Example: We need to build an addition to our school. What would this look like? What are the measurements? What do you need to turn the plan into reality?

Note

1. From: Bishop, R. S. (1990). *Mirrors, windows, and sliding glass doors*. Perspectives: Choosing and using books from the classroom, *6*(3), ix–xi.

References

American Psychological Association. (2023). *Inclusive language guide* (2nd ed.). Apa.org. http://www.apa.org/about/apa/equity-diversity-inclusion/language-guidelines

Bishop, R. S. (1990). *Mirrors, windows, and sliding glass doors*. Perspectives: Choosing and using books from the classroom, *6*(3), ix–xi.

Ewald, W. (2002). *The best part of me: Children talk about their bodies in pictures and words*. Little, Brown & Company.

Gay, G. (2002). Preparing for culturally responsive teaching. *Journal of Teacher Education*, *53*(2), 106–116. https://doi.org/10.1177/0022487102053002003

Global Peace Heroes. (2020). *Empowering students to be proactive peacemakers – peace heroes*. Peace Heroes – We Let Peace Tell the Story. https://globalpeaceheroes.org/

Hammond, Z. (2015). *Culturally responsive teaching and the brain: Promoting authentic engagement and rigor among culturally and linguistically diverse students*. Corwin/Sage.

Harris, I. M., & Morrison, M. L. (2013). *Peace education* (3rd ed.). McFarland.

Khalifa, M. (2021). *Culturally responsive school leadership* (H. R. Milner, Ed.). Harvard Educational Publishing Group.

Ladson-Billings, G. (1995). Toward a theory of culturally relevant pedagogy. *American Educational Research Journal, 32*(3), 465–491. Retrieved from https://doi.org/10.2307/1163320

Ladson-Billings, G. (2009). *The dreamkeepers: Successful teachers of African American children* (2nd ed.). Jossey-Bass.

Muhammad, G. (2020). *Cultivating genius: An equity framework for culturally and historically responsive literacy*. Scholastic.

Muhammad, G. (2023). *Unearthing joy: A guide to culturally and historically responsive curriculum and instruction*. Scholastic Professional.

Nuri Robins, K. J., Lindsey, R. B., & Terrell, R. D. (Eds.). (2012). *Cultural proficiency: A manual for school leaders* (3rd eds.). Corwin Press.

Paris, D. (2012). Culturally sustaining pedagogy: A needed change in stance, terminology, and practice. *Educational Researcher* (Washington, DC.: 1972), *41*(3), 93–97. https://doi.org/10.3102/0013189x12441244

Reese, D. (2016, October 12). *Mirrors, windows, sliding glass doors, and curtains, from: Writing Native American characters*. Writing the Other. https://www.youtube.com/watch?v=ctOJtK-ONgo

Saad, L. (2020). *Me and White supremacy: Combat racism, change the world, and become a good ancestor*. Sourcebooks.

Seeley Dzierzak, C. (2021). *The case for culturally affirming systems of education: Exploring how professional development impacts culturally relevant and critical literacy teaching practices* [Hamline University]. School of Education and Leadership Student Capstone Theses and Dissertations. 4516. https://digitalcommons.hamline.edu/hse_all/4516

Social Designs. (2023). *The culture wheel card game*. The Culture Wheel Card Game. https://culturewheelcardgame.com/

Tervalon, M., & Murray-García, J. (1998). Cultural humility versus cultural competence: A critical distinction in defining physician training outcomes in multicultural education. *Journal of Health Care for the Poor and Underserved, 9*, 117–125. Crossref. PubMed. ISI.

United Nations. (1948). *Universal declaration of human rights | United Nations*. https://www.un.org/en/about-us/universal-declaration-of-human-rights

Verkuyten, M., & Kollar, R. (2021). *Tolerance and intolerance: Cultural meanings and discursive usage. Culture & Psychology, 27*(1), 172–186. https://doi.org/10.1177/1354067X20984356

6

Protect Our Environment

Mother Earth cannot heal herself alone. She needs our help.
~ Ed McGaa (Eagle Man)

To *Protect Our Environment* means that human life is in balance and living in harmony with nature and its resources, which in return provides for sustainable life on this planet. Earth has the resources to provide for and nourish all beings and nature knows how to restore its inherent harmony. As Eagle Man (1990) shared, Earth also needs our help. We humans have the teachings, knowledge, technology, ingenuity, inventiveness, creativity and skills to protect, restore and rejuvenate our planet and all who inhabit it. It is imperative that we take deep and decisive actions at all levels of humanity: as individuals, communities, institutions, nationally and globally, in order to protect our planet and its resources.

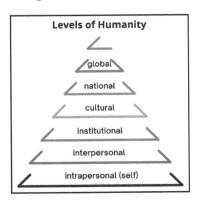

Figure 6.1 Levels of Humanity

In This Chapter:
- ➢ Our Teachers: Indigenous Worldviews – p. 126
- ➢ Water Is Life – p. 129
- ➢ Who Is 'All Life?' – p. 131
- ➢ Peacemaker in Practice: Helen Thomas, Hunkpapa Lakota Educator – p. 134
- ➢ Planetary Concerns – p. 137
- ➢ More Peaceful Practices – p. 139

DOI: 10.4324/9781003449249-7

◎ **Pause & Reflect:** How any learner (including you!) views their relationship with our environment is welcomed as part of the exploration that occurs within peacelearning.

- ◆ How did your upbringing influence your current view and relationship with nature?
- ◆ How do you support learners in caring for our environment?

Author's Perspective

Growing up, I (Julie) lived in the rural midwest. I spent much of my time outside, playing and exploring in the woods, by the creek, up and down the rolling hills and at the nearby farms. I've always loved and appreciated animals and the peace I find being in nature. My parents were conscientious about water, as we had our own pristine well. As nature tends to do when we share the same environment, we had many animal visitors near our house. My father would treat it like he was going to war when, for example, a raccoon would attempt to explore the contents of a trash can or flower pot. Irritated, he would say, *"we are constantly under attack here!,"* and plan an aggressive and sometimes violent response. There was often this sense that the animals had *"invaded his territory"*. This view, of needing to dominate the environment, also laid aside his appreciation for the beauty and bounty in the nature around us. However, the dominant, aggressive and war-like views always unsettled me and I felt a knowing that I (would) explore, hold and share a differing relationship with nature … one that is reciprocal.

Our Teachers: Indigenous Worldviews

We offer an exploration of this peace action, *Protect Our Environment*, which supports and aligns with global human rights education and a decolonized view of peace education. Let's begin by centering knowledge, practices and ways of being of traditional American Indians, Native Americans, Hawaiians, Alaskan Natives, First Nations, Inuit, Metis and Indigenous peoples around the world. Indigenous worldviews offer some of our greatest assets, leaders, stewards and teachers toward living sustainably and in harmony with all life.

We extend our gratitude to the Indigenous peoples and knowledges that guide humans in thriving on the land. According to the United Nations

Permanent Forum on Indigenous Issues (United Nations Environment Programme [UNEP], 2020),

> *When land is owned, managed or occupied in a traditional way, the word "traditional" refers to a knowledge that stems from centuries-old observation and interaction with nature. This knowledge is often embedded in a cosmology that reveres the **one-ness** of life, considers nature as sacred and acknowledges humanity as a part of it. And it encompasses practical ways to ensure the balance of the environment in which they live, so it may continue to provide services such as water, fertile soil, food, shelter and medicines.*

Revering the one-ness of life means understanding that all of Earth is alive, of equal importance and that this balance keeps us alive. This is not just metaphorical or philosophical; this is the science and cosmology of life on this planet. Environmental liaison, Jan Hartke (1990), wrote,

> *A person depends every moment of every day upon Mother Earth. We breathe her air into our lungs, we drink her waters, we eat her nutrients. Our cells are dying and are constantly being replaced. The flow between nature and ourselves is always in process. We degenerate and regenerate with nature's help. (p. xvi)*

Therefore, this flow or circle of life means that any act which ultimately harms the planet is also harmful to ourselves. In order to more deeply experience the interconnectedness of all life and for solutions to *Protect Our Environment* today and for the future, peace-centered people, schools and organizations should respectfully listen to, engage with and seek to act in accordance with the traditional and practical knowledge of Native and Indigenous peoples in their community. Oglala lawyer, writer and lecturer, Ed McGaa (Eagle Man) (1990), is one of many voices who offered guidance toward realizing this peace action.

> *Mother Earth cannot heal herself alone. She needs our help. We two-leggeds must all come together and form a commonality of realization, a realization of potentially fatal calamities. Most of our remedies will be to see, or drastically curtail what we have been doing. Rising temperatures, vanishing rainforest, overpopulation, pollution of water, and acid rain can be, and will have to be, addressed by abrupt remedies. Some solutions will be reached through **having** nations sharing and helping **have no** nations. Other solutions will require convincing major corporations that they can no longer pollute and that they too, are related to all things. (p. 19)*

We share concern for our environment and, like Eagle Man, are also optimistic that humans are evolving (and returning) to universal models of sharing, generosity, empathy and caring, including with our environment. We are appreciative that there are (and have been) many peacemakers, philosophers, scientists, activists, leaders, teachers and beings across the planet, who, like us, hold some understanding, as well as awe, of the interconnectedness of life. Sustainability education also offers sound, researched and creative solutions to environmental issues and models for a shared, just and fair global economy. United globally, we can help heal the environment and ultimately protect and nourish all life.

◎ **Pause & Reflect:**

   ◆   Are you familiar with Indigenous worldviews, which honors the one-ness of life and that humanity is an interconnected and a reciprocal part of nature?
   ◆   How does this compare with your view and relationship with our environment?

Table 6.1 Pursuit: Interconnectedness

Peace Pursuits for: *Protect Our Environment*	
I learn about the interconnectedness between myself, others and the environment.	• Cycles of life, connections between life cycles, human beings and environmental cycles (i.e., water cycle), food chains and webs are important to critically learn about, explore, observe and experience. • Like us (our cells), nature is in a constant state of change, of death and rebirth. Observe and embrace this. • When nature is harmed, (ultimately) so are humans. Support learners in their understanding of this interconnectedness and cause – effect, cyclical and reciprocal relationships. Extend this through ongoing opportunities in nature and in utilizing technology to visit environments around the world. • Additional science and environmental lessons should always allow for analysis and processing related to this pursuit, as this supports the development of a planetary consciousness.

Put It Into Practice: Be Outside!

Accessibility to natural environments is an equity consideration for all communities. There is great benefit in getting outside, playing, exploring and engaging deeply with the natural world. Research indicates positive outdoor experiences more strongly predict subsequent actions of stewardship and later inclinations toward environmental activism than when only learning about environmental issues (Chawla, 2015). As much as possible, let's get children outside! Outdoor classrooms and natural spaces for reading, music, drama, art, science, physical education and really any subject area are powerfully important. Here are some more outdoor activities that support cognitive development, overall well-being and connection with our natural world. These are also great options to invite families to participate in or support!

➤ Events: field day, science fairs, read-a-thons, games and sports, guest speakers, picnics or meals, field trips, scavenger hunts
➤ Nature walks and discussions about local habitats, flora, fauna
➤ Play! Play! Play!
➤ Observation and journaling (see Lesson: Noticing Nature, p. 270)
➤ Environmental projects – planting trees, gardening, litter clean-ups, fallen leaf collections
➤ Yoga, meditation, breathing practices
➤ Collaborative projects and experiments

Water Is Life

Let's explore a natural resource that is key to health and sustainability for all on planet Earth – water. The Standing Rock Water Protectors remind us of the facts, *"Mni Wiconi,"* which means *"Water is Life."* This declaration, *"Water is Life,"* became well-known internationally when in 2015, The Standing Rock Sioux Tribe, a sovereign nation, passed a resolution against the construction of the Dakota Access Pipeline. From there, many Native Nations and non-Native allies joined the water protector movement in protesting the pipeline on the grounds that an oil spill would threaten the nation's water supply and cultural resources. Oceti Sakowin youth also planned and carried out a 2,000-mile run from North Dakota to Washington D.C, U.S. (Smithsonian National Museum of the American Indian, n.d.). These are great examples of the contemporary efforts and advocacy of Indigenous peoples in leading folks in taking peace action to *Protect Our Environment*.

A well-cared-for, reciprocal relationship with water is essential for human society. Water access and sanitation are human rights and yet there are some very concerning water-related issues in front of us. The World Water Development Report (UNESCO, 2023) warns, *"Globally, 2 billion people (26% of the population) do not have safe drinking water and 3.6 billion (46%) lack access to safely managed sanitation."*

While we know that humans rely on clean freshwater for our basic survival, our actions (and inactions) often do not align with this key fact. All peoples and nations must demonstrate cooperation and care for this most precious resource.

◎ **Pause & Reflect:**

- ◆ How many ways do you rely on water in your community? Consider the various usages such as personal, business, agricultural and industrial.
- ◆ What does water conservation and protection mean to you and your community?
- ◆ What are the biggest concerns for water and sanitation in your community? How can learners explore this and potential solutions?

When teaching and learning about water and our environment, at first keep the focus with the habitats and ecosystems near the school and community. **Use local examples to teach about global problems – this process is called glocalizing** (Abrom, 2020).

Table 6.2 Pursuit: Community Habitat(s)

Peace Pursuits for: *Protect Our Environment*	
I describe the habitat(s) near my community and explain why it is important.	• Create a sense of belonging and empowerment by anchoring to place (place-based education), which is also a culturally relevant practice. Learning and inquiry begins at the home, classroom and school environments, then expands to other levels of humanity. • Through (virtual, in person) place-based holistic thinking and exploration of local habitats, watersheds and food sources, learners develop an appreciation for the interconnectedness and importance of healthy environments. • Learner-centered, hands-on and inquiry-based learning allows for interdisciplinary and holistic learning. • Empower learners in creative thinking and problem-solving to make a positive impact in local environments. Connect to real-world needs, issues, concerns, observations, curiosities, wonders and solutions. • Make ongoing connections between the local habitat(s) and ecosystem and how this impacts the food, water, soil, weather, plants, animals and human health & society.

> **Put It Into Practice: Water Is Life**
>
> Engage learners in key water issues in their community/area. Explore existing and creatively possible sustainable and scalable solutions. Make connections to other communities, states and nations. Highlight the link between water sources and the health of all life on our planet. Engagement strategies include:
>
> ➤ Personal and community connections
> ➤ Multidisciplinary and cross-curricular approaches
> ➤ Guest speakers – highlight differing cultures and views of water management
> ➤ Interactive discussions (seminar circle)
> ➤ Real-life stories and inquiry processes
> ➤ Critical analysis of media, policy and practices
> ➤ Simulations and role-playing
> ➤ Art, music and movement
> ➤ Service learning (*Reach Out In Service*)
> ➤ Research projects
> ➤ Implement Lesson: We Are Protectors, p. 267

Peacelearners explore short- and long-term solutions to protect water and take action (personally, locally, nationally and globally) to *Protect Our Environment*. Through peace education, we are called upon to increase awareness and understanding of the link water has to all life.

Who Is 'All Life?'

While water is a precious resource for life, the balancing and respect for all life are of equal importance to the ecology of the planet, of which all life is interconnected. The definition and understanding of 'all life' are of significant consideration in peacelearning. Quantum, nuclear and particle physics, chemistry, biology, geology, astrology, cosmology and many scientific disciplines guide many understanding of the commonalities of all life. At an elementary level, we explore the science of cycles and webs and share the many beautiful stories that aid in our understanding that we are all one and that all life is in a constant state of change. We learn to categorize living and nonliving and/or dead, alive, never alive.

Many people, like us, believe that the definition of all life includes that which can take life and/or give life. For example, rock can take life. Change is a constant for beings, for all life. **Learning to practice unconditional love for animals, plants, water, air, rock, soil and minerals – all life – allows us to live within peace.** Centering from a place of gratitude and reciprocity with our environment and natural resources means taking into consideration that anything ultimately harming the planet, environment and nature is also harmful to ourselves.

◎ Pause & Reflect:

- ◆ We consume animals and/or plants for our survival. When we do so, do we honor and acknowledge that life? (The life that sustains us.)
- ◆ If the Earth sustains us, do we have a responsibility to sustain the Earth in return? What does this mean for you?

A reciprocal, caring and mindful relationship with nature shows respect for the diversity of all beings, organisms and ecosystems. Beyond sustainment of our physical bodies, nature offers profound and simple lessons of balance, cycles, life/death and interdependence. It is of crucial importance that we recognize our role in this symbiotic relationship. We are called upon to nurture, adapt, restore and revere the many gifts we live upon and within. Our well-being, as well as that of our future generations, requires protection of our environment.

Author's Perspective

While an educator and coach in a large urban midwest school district, I (Julie) had the wonderful opportunities for ongoing, deep relational, philosophical, and hands-on learning and unlearning with colleagues in our Indian Education Department.

Turtle Mountain descendant and author James Vukelich Kaagegaabaw often spoke of how **language is culture and the culture is in the language.** I recommend his book *Seven Generations and the Seven Grandfather Teachings* (2023), which guides us toward living "the good life."

My mentor, Leech Lake Anishinaabe Elder and Healer, Ida Downwind-Bald Eagle opened, expanded and immersed me in Indigenous ways of knowing and being (2014–2021). Our relationship began through storytelling, listening and sharing food. At first, I didn't even realize how much wisdom, best practice, knowledge and gifts were being shared with me, as the cyclical and holistic learning styles were different from the linear progressions of my school and home experiences. There is so much to be learned from long-standing Indigenous knowledges and practices!

Potawatomi botanist and author, Robin Wall Kimmerer (2015), shared a wondrous perspective about the grammar of animacy and how this impacts our view of the natural world. The language of animacy refers to a semantic or grammar feature that exists in some languages to express the aliveness or how sentient a noun is. For example, in most Indigenous and Native languages (cultures), when one speaks of a rock, the meaning is to be or being a rock, indicating rock is animate, full of life and our relative, just as another human. Rock is a teacher, full of wisdom, a friend and a being worthy of respect. Kimmerer (2015) remarked,

> English doesn't give us many tools for incorporating respect for animacy.
> In English, you are either a human or a thing. Our grammar boxes us in by
> the choice of reducing a nonhuman being to an it, or it must be gendered,
> inappropriately, as a he or a she. Where are our words for the simple
> existence of another living being? (2:20)

Language embeds messages. Take for example that World Citizen Peace (2014), the lovely organization who created the Five Peace Actions, writes this as 'Protect the Environment.' Though our change of this action to *Protect Our Environment* may seem inconsequential upon first glance, we made a very conscientious decision to make this change in order to highlight our deep reciprocity with nature. We are not separate from *the* environment. We are interconnected and one with all of *our* environment. As you consider your understanding and implementation of this peace action and pursuits, these questions will be of great value to explore:

◆ How do you view your relationship with rock (and bird, insect, tree, animal, water, wind, etc.)? In what ways do you build and foster that relationship?

◆ When nature (i.e., rock) is communicated as an inanimate thing, how does this impact human views and relationships with nature? How about when a rock is communicated with animacy, what is or may be the impact?

◆ Anthropomorphism is when human characteristics are ascribed to an object or species (something avoided in scientific studies, writing and terminology in order to maintain objectivity). What is problematic about seeing others only through the lens of human experience? What are some potential benefits to anthropomorphizing nonhuman beings?

◆ How do you feel about gendering nature? Do you consider Earth your Mother? In what ways is the gendering of nature harmful and/or helpful? How might patriarchal systems impact how Mother Earth is viewed & treated?

◆ In the English language, being human is the only way to be animate. What explicit and implicit messages, beliefs and values does this communicate (e.g., hierarchies)?
  – Keep in mind that some humans (i.e., women, enslaved peoples) were (are) communicated and considered less than human.

◆ How can we build more equitable and reciprocal relationships with people and places? What role does language play in that cultural shift?
  – For example, Kimmerer (2017), offered a suggestion for a shift in language by utilizing the word *"ki,"* pronounced 'kee,' just like the word chi that describes that energy of all beings or our vital life force. The pronoun *kin* (them, multiple, plural) could also support our evolving recognition of personhood and justice for nature.

◆ What language do (and will) you personally use in your communication of nature and our (the) environment? How about with students?
  – For example, instead of learning about *"the Mississippi River,"* you can learn about *"Mississippi River."* Instead of *"the apple is …"*, *"Apple is …."*

Peacemaker In Practice

Protecting All Our Relations: Learning from Indigenous Peoples

By Helen Thomas, Hunkpapa Lakota Educator

Those familiar with Indigenous worldviews and cultures know that relationships play a crucial role in our knowing, being and learning as Indigenous peoples. Throughout life we are taught, through modeling and demonstration, that these relationships, which extend beyond our human relatives to the lands and beings we share them with, are accompanied by responsibilities. From a young age, I often heard the phrase *"mitakuye oyasin"* being used in cultural and community contexts. Roughly translated to *"we are all related"* or *"all my relatives"*, this phrase reflects the belief we as Lakota people, as well as other Indigenous communities, hold around interconnectedness and relationality. As this phrase has been shared widely and appropriated often, I find it important to note I have been taught these words are akin to a prayer and are not to be used lightly. I have seen this belief around interconnectedness expressed through daily interactions my whole life. For example, whenever I am introduced to someone new in my community, my relatives make a point to acknowledge how we are related to them, whether through blood or some other form of connection. Whatsmore, I often see my mother, my first and greatest teacher, embodying the sense of responsibility that accompanies this understanding of interconnectedness through her actions of compassion and commitment to the well-being of not only our family members but our entire Standing Rock Sioux tribal nation and our homelands. My mother currently serves as the Chairwoman of our tribe and is continuing the fight for the protection of our lands and waters through her leadership.

These values and beliefs have greatly informed my practice as an educator. Beyond prioritizing strong relationships and community within classrooms, I strive to foster an understanding among learners that these relationships extend beyond ourselves and include our environment as well. For example, when I taught a culturally responsive after school STEAM program for Native American elementary students in an urban school district. One of our lessons focused on our relationships with water. After reflecting on the various ways we depend on water in our daily lives and how the well-being of our water also depends on our own actions, we learned more about the long-standing relationships Indigenous peoples in our local area have had with water. In our community, this included learning about the intricate canal systems built by the ancestors of the Akimel O'Odham peoples in what is now known as Phoenix. Importantly, I intentionally exposed students to the continued existence and resilience of the Salt River Pima Maricopa Indian Community, a tribal nation to which many Akimel O'odham people belong. Lastly, we acknowledged and expressed gratitude for the Indigenous contributions that allow us to live and thrive on these lands today and wrote about how we can take action in protecting our community's water. I share this example to encourage all peace educators to consider how you can foster understandings of interconnectedness among your students in a way that honors and affirms Indigenous peoples and worldviews.

Deepening our respect for and understanding of relationships with all life is crucial peacelearning. When we look to the beginning of human history, overall we have lived more so in harmony with the natural world. There was a stewardship of the natural world, a respect for needed limits and an intergenerational perspective that we must not compromise the needs of future generations. Histories of colonization have shifted many toward a world view of dominion, linguistic imperialism, human exceptionalism and/or a more adversarial relationship with nature. Indigenous peoples have always resisted this and continue to be our greatest protectors, sustainers and teachers. For us, just as in many Indigenous cultures, references to and considerations of all life are inclusive of nature beings, elements and landforms such as rock, river, mountain, soil, wind, microorganisms, minerals, etc. Nature beings have a crucial role in maintaining the balance of our bodies, environments and world. How all life works, from its simplicities to complexities, is truly amazing!

Table 6.3 Pursuit: Respect All Life

Peace Pursuits for: *Protect Our Environment*	
I respect all forms of life.	• Holding respect for all life positions us to advocate and take action in protecting our environment, all creatures and forms of life. • Being outside and experiences in/with nature (throughout the seasons) are highly encouraged. Even a small patch of soil or grass holds an entire ecosystem to observe and cherish. Utilize technology to explore nature and environments around the world. • Exploring what binds life together, the commonalities, similarities and interdependence builds appreciation and motivation to protect the beautiful diversity on Earth. • What language and pronouns are used in reference to nature? The grammar of animacy is an important consideration. • Humans tend to position themselves as different, superior or smarter than nature. However, when we mindfully consider the knowledge and teachings from nature and the environment, one moves from thinking mostly about me, to we.

Table 6.4 Practice: Who Is All Life?

Put It Into Practice: Who Is All Life?		
Begin by reading books, viewing nature videos, discussing and studying a particular habitat or ecosystem.		
Emerging	*Intermediate*	*Advanced*
Setup a role-playing game where each child takes the role of different animals, plants and natural elements (nature beings such as water, rock, soil, air). Support the narrative to simulate interconnectedness and how humans are part of this as well.	Create and label chains, webs or circles of life that demonstrate how various organisms, elements and nature beings are interconnected, interact, are reciprocal and dependent on one another. Highlight the transfer of food, energy and nutrients.	Use microscopes (or video models) to study soil samples and compare them to the human gut or micro-biome (microbial cultures). Compare the two, highlighting the diversity in microorganisms that is present in both. Make connections to soil health (farming practices), our food and a balanced and healthy gut biome.

Planetary Concerns

Environmental and planetary concerns are important to be explored at all ages of peacelearning. **Concerns include: increased global temperatures, food waste, species extinction, plastic waste, deforestation, air pollution, ocean acidification, freshwater quality and access, greenhouse gas emissions and top-soil erosion.** When we truly understand that destroying or polluting anything is destroying ourselves, then we will be mindful of harms to our environment.

We need to also be mindful of the pollution of our consciousness (harm, aggression, violence, anger, anxiety, fear). In complete agreement with peace activist and monk Thich Nhat Hanh (1966), *"We need to protect the ecology of the Earth and the ecology of the mind, or this kind of violence and recklessness will spill over into even more areas of life."*

It can sometimes feel discouraging to be increasingly aware of the hurt, suffering and significant consequences of decisions and inactions that negatively impact life on planet Earth. We surmise that we are not alone in feeling powerless at times or frustrated at the slow pace of change to globally healthy and sustainable practices. Knowing this, it is also important to intentionally foster hope and empowerment as we enliven the peace action, *Protect Our Environment.* Children, our agents of change, then develop personal and community-based solutions (and beyond!) and take actions that ultimately positively impact all life.

Through peace education, we grow in understanding and appreciation of the gifts shared by nature and move into a generative way of being that is balanced, sustainable and reciprocal with our natural world. The development of a planetary consciousness and global identity begins with individual choices and actions.

◎ **Pause & Reflect:** We invite you to:

1. Choose an environmental concern or issue that is close to your heart or community.
2. Consider how your individual choices impact this environmental concern.
3. Set a personal short-term and long-term goal that helps protect the environment from this issue.
4. Engage learners in a similar process, setting individual and collective goals.

Table 6.5 Pursuit: Impact of Choices

Peace Pursuits for: *Protect Our Environment*	
I consider the impact my choices have on the (our) environment.	• Help students explore their choices and reflect on how they impact the environment and world around them. Be aware of opportunities to guide & prompt children to consider their impact. For example, if a child breaks a branch off a tree on the playground, how might that impact the tree, the animals, other people etc. • Development of a planetary consciousness and global identity begins with individual choices and actions. Guide children in considering both short-term and long-term impacts and possible harmonizing solutions. • Start locally, analyzing needs, barriers, strengths, setting goals and implementing actions as an individual and a classroom. Then move to the school, community, nation and world.

Table 6.6 Practice: Inquiry Process & Stories

Put It Into Practice: Inquiry Process & Stories		
The inquiry process and using stories to deepen learning really bring this peace action to life. 1. Take an environmental subject or concern and invite learners to share what they think they know and to also ask questions about what they want to learn and discover. 2. Share and discuss stories about the topic that offer varied and diverse perspectives. 3. Create opportunities for experiential and hands-on learning. 4. Integrate and deepen the learning by setting up for rich discussions and processing through discussing, writing, creating and taking action! When provided the opportunity, children are eager to learn about needs and how to help *Protect Our Environment*.		
Emerging	*Intermediate*	*Advanced*
• What do you think you know? • What do you want to learn? • Who is telling this story? • Whose voice or ideas are not being shared in this story? • How might this issue get better (improve)? • What do you hope for? • What do/can you do to help?	• What do you think you know? How do you know it? • What questions do you have? What are you curious about? • Whose voice, point of view or experience is being shared? • Who is missing? • What are possible solutions? • What action can/will you take to help? Make a plan.	• What do you think you know? • What are the gaps, questions, possibilities or wonders? • What do you want to discover? • Whose perspectives, experiences or ideas are being shared? • Who (what) is unheard, undervalued or ignored? • What solutions exist? What solutions might you create or envision? • How can/do you advocate and take action? Make a plan personally and collectively.

Be a Protector

Being a protector and reaching out in service of nature's well-being is an important role we have as humans. Our health is intertwined with that of our planet and all life. Some of our best guides for how to live in harmony with our environment are folks who hold Indigenous knowledges. Everyone can learn (unlearn, relearn) from these long-standing worldviews and practices that help us understand how to live and reciprocate within the intricate balance of all life. Our natural world is full of wonder! Let us be immersed in this awe and empowered in taking peace action to *Protect Our Environment*.

More Peaceful Practices: *Protect Our Environment*

Green Team(s)

A way to take this peace action even further is by establishing a fun and empowering 'Green Team' program. Often, the Green Team supports other students and staff with learning about planetary concerns and actively implementing practices that reduce waste, reuse, recycle, compost, reduce pollution and conserve energy. For example, it could be a small group of committed students who take initiative with limited adult support to raise awareness about school and community-based environmental needs. Or a Green Team could ultimately involve all students on a rotating schedule for supporting waste reduction and sorting efforts. Perhaps it is a club that meets after school and then brings information and projects back to their classes and community through service learning. There are many ways a Green Team could be setup and structured and we recommend first determining what your site's greatest needs are, as well as the capacity of staff and community/family volunteers to support the initiative. Keep a look-out for financial support and implementation resources that are often available through the district, city, county, local and national organizations. Here are some examples of projects a Green Team might implement to *Protect Our Environment*:

◆ Meeting with custodians, administration and Parent Teacher Association or Organization (PTA/O) to explore school & community-based environmental concerns, needs and to set and monitor goals.
◆ *Reach Out In Service*: organize a trash clean-up of the playground, park or community.

- ◆ Do an audit of the amount of waste in a typical day or week and use this as a starting point for setting waste reduction goals and taking action. For example, begin sorting waste, reduce single-use plastic from the cafeteria or transition to compostable or reusable plates and wares.
- ◆ Sort waste (landfill, organics, recycling) in clearly marked bins in all areas: the cafeteria, classrooms and common spaces. Green Team members take the lead in teaching the basics and why it's important, as well as monitoring sorting.
- ◆ Conduct energy efficiency audits, set goals and take action to reduce energy consumption or transition to renewable energy.
- ◆ Special events: Earth Day celebrations, science fairs, reuse swaps, upcycled projects, walk/bike to school, zero waste challenge.
- ◆ Field trips: environmental landmarks, waste and energy facilities, gardens.
- ◆ Setup composting bins; worm farm; donate and arrange for pickup of food waste (e.g., pig farm) or add-in compost to the garden space or use for classroom or take-home projects such as seed plantings.
- ◆ Awareness activities for zero waste or waste reduction, environmental and energy issues, pollution, sustainability, clean-ups, food waste reduction, water conservation etc. This might be creating videos, art, presentations, signs, posters, newsletters, announcements, pledges and modeling.

Family & Community Connections

- ◆ Supporting Green Team efforts (e.g., volunteering in the lunchroom to support organics, recycling, trash sorting).
- ◆ Presentations from caregivers and community members who have environmental jobs or *Reach Out In Service* of nature.
- ◆ Hands-on learning with Indigenous folks, tribal members and Native-run organizations.
- ◆ Storytelling and talks by Indigenous caregivers, community members and environmentally conscious families about how the health of the Earth is a part of and essential for all of us.
- ◆ Re-imagine carnivals or events: use a former event to become an Earth Day celebration with educational experiences, booths and tables about the environment.
- ◆ Create a school garden or greenhouse and have parents, staff and students care for all aspects of the life cycle. (Be sure to create a sustainable plan – who tends to the garden over the summer, during breaks?)

Table 6.7 Content Area Connections: *Protect Our Environment*

Content Area Connections			
Any science topics will be easy to connect with this peace action!			
Art	**Math**	**Social Emotional Learning**	**Media**
Create art related to the natural environment with messages of protection. For example, a peace garden with painted rocks messages. Use natural materials for collective art projects such as murals and collages.	Investigate patterns in nature such as symmetry, different geometric shapes and spirals. Math/science connections about environmental education, architecture and engineering plans. Explore environmental building designs and how mathematicians support this.	A class animal or plants are a great opportunity to learn about how to care for another. Setup routines that ultimately puts all learners at the center of the care for the environment. Empower students in caring for their indoor classroom and school environments and connect it to this peace action. Be out in nature as a way to support mental health and SEL (mindful walks, focus on the five senses while out in nature).	Display and promote books about the environment and animals. Research projects about the environment and planetary concerns. Create a mini-news show about local nature, needs and ways to *Protect Our Environment*.

References

Abrom, A. (2020, October 17). *Glocalizing: Teaching global problems through local examples*. United Nations Association of the United States of America. https://unausa.org/glocalizing-teaching-global-problems-through-local-examples/

Chawla, L. (2015). Benefits of nature contact for children. *Journal of Planning Literature, 30*(4), 433–452. https://doi.org/10.1177/0885412215595441

Downwind-Bald Eagle, I. (2014–2021). Leech Lake Anishinaabe, Minnesota, personal communication

Hanh, T. N. (1966). The sun my heart. In A. Kotler (Ed.), *Engaged Buddhist reader* (pp. 162–170). Parallax Press.

Hartke, J. (1990). Introduction. In McGaa, E. *Mother earth spirituality: Native American paths to healing ourselves*. HarperOne.

Kimmerer, R. W. (2015). *Braiding sweetgrass: Indigenous wisdom, scientific knowledge and the teachings of plants* (R. Kimmerer, Narr.) [Audiobook]. Tantor Media.

Kimmerer, R. (2017, June 12). *Speaking of nature*. Orion Magazine. https://orionmagazine.org/article/speaking-of-nature/

McGaa, E. 'Eagle Man'. (1990). *Mother earth spirituality: Native American paths to healing ourselves*. HarperOne.

Smithsonian National Museum of the American Indian. (n.d.). *Treaties still matter: Standing rock Sioux and Dakota access pipeline*. Americanindian.si.edu. Retrieved December 9, 2023, from https://americanindian.si.edu/nk360/plains-treaties/dapl

UNESCO. (2023, May 3). *Imminent risk of a global water crisis, warns the UN World Water Development Report 2023*. Unesco.org. https://www.unesco.org/en/articles/imminent-risk-global-water-crisis-warns-un-world-water-development-report-2023

United Nations Environment Programme (UNEP). (2020, June 8). *Indigenous peoples and the nature they protect*. UNEP. https://www.unep.org/news-and-stories/story/indigenous-peoples-and-nature-they-protect

Vukelich, J. (2023). *The seven generations and the seven grandfather teachings*. James Vukelich.

World Citizen Peace. (2014). World Citizen Peace. https://worldcitizenpeace.org/

7

Reach Out In Service

*What you do makes a difference, and you have to decide
what kind of difference you want to make.*
~ Dr. Jane Goodall

As renowned primatologist and conservationist Dr. Goodall (2021) shared, we each can make a difference in the world. Being in service of others and our environment is a powerful way to give back and contribute to positive change. As educators, the crux of our role is to *Reach Out In Service*. This makes self-care and caring for our teammates and colleagues essential. How are you providing this spirit of care for yourself? How are you fostering a sense of care among colleagues? Before reaching out in service, we encourage you to 'fill your own cup.' Meaning, prioritize your needs and sense of well-being. Sometimes this may require setting and upholding boundaries, yet well-being may also be enhanced through reaching out in service! From a more balanced self, we can make a positive impact by reaching out and caring for teammates, colleagues, learners, community and our environment.

◎ **Pause & Reflect:**

◆ How do you prioritize your physical and emotional health and well-being? Others?
◆ When you think about making a difference, what inspires you or brings you joy?

DOI: 10.4324/9781003449249-8

In This Chapter:

What Is Service Learning?

Service learning is an approach where students can learn and be active participants in the community. The power of service learning is that it's a way to directly participate, connect with and give back to the community. In the United States, the term *"service-learning"* was defined in the 101st Congress (1990) as the National and Community Service Act, which was amended and reauthorized in 2009. It is a method that:

◆ Meets the needs of a community
◆ Connects and coordinates school-based learning with the community
◆ Promotes service of others and weaves with the academic curriculum
◆ Offers opportunities for students to reflect on their learning

Rich in relationships and collaboration, service learning is a transformational method that provides students and participants a richer experience versus transactional rote tasks, checking a box or completing work outside of its real-world application.

Why Service Learning?

Peace and justice education has strong ties to service and teaching children to support others and engage with their community. Ultimately it is our choices and actions that demonstrate care and respect for all life, so it's important to offer students an opportunity to *Reach Out In Service* for issues that matter to them. **Children need real-world opportunities to put into practice the Five Peace Actions.** Through experiential learning, students are empowered and engaged in learning, both at school and in the community.

Philosopher and educator John Dewey (1897) understood that *"education must begin with a psychological insight into the child's capacities, interest and habits."* Through democratically co-created environments we foster the power behind what interests and motivates children. An emphasis on the process of living in the present can *"be translated into terms of their social equivalents - into terms of what they are capable of in the way of social service"* (Dewey, 1897, p. 77). This is an important concept to remember in peace education, as it's a dynamic juxtaposition of creating opportunities and allowing students to guide the learning environment and their service goals.

An example of empowering culturally relevant practices, hands-on service learning gives students voice and choice. There are many ways to brainstorm and share ideas about reaching out in service based on students' interests and hopes for their school, community and world. When students are connected to learning and feel a sense of investment and ownership, at its essence this is culturally relevant teaching. All students can participate in and benefit from various types of service.

◎ **Pause & Reflect:** Think about a time your students reached out in service or helped others.

- ◆ What did you observe in your students?
- ◆ Were students empowered? Engaged?

Helping others and our environment is a common thread that propels learners. The Five Peace Actions go hand in hand, and being able to *Reach Out In Service* provides a tangible way for people to enact their beliefs, care and passions. It also bridges to the culminating peace action, *Be A Responsible Citizen Of The World.* The many benefits of service learning include:

- ◆ Feelings of connectedness, value, pride and responsibility
- ◆ Strengthened social skills, cooperation, collaboration and problem-solving
- ◆ Deepened relationships with peers, service recipients, the community and environment
- ◆ Increased engagement, motivation and improved academic outcomes
    (Youth.gov, n.d.)

Table 7.1 Pursuit: Respect & Act for All Life

Peace Pursuits for *Reach Out In Service*	
I respect all forms of life and show this through my actions.	• Foster inclusivity, empathy and compassion through direct interaction with others and our environment. • A sense of responsibility for the well-being of others is core to ethical decision-making, civic engagement and global citizenship. • Through literature, media, dialogue and action, discuss what it means to respect all forms of life and the world around us. • Demonstrate and reflect on how students' actions make a difference in their classroom, school, community and the world.

Getting Started With Service Learning

We recommend starting small with service learning. Organize one project at a time and expand from there. From your students, learn what they are interested in doing and follow their lead. Here are a few examples of how this could look at your site:

◆ Have students help clean up the school campus and explain why this is important. Hopefully, students will think twice about littering if they have been part of a clean-up effort!

◆ If students are enthusiastic about cleaning up the playground/campus, consider having this become a weekly effort with your class or a rotating group of students. This can be followed up with caring for other environments such as the lunchroom, classrooms and common spaces.

◆ Set up weekly or bi-weekly mentorship opportunities by pairing up different classrooms and/or grade levels. For example, peers can support and empower each other through a supportive buddy room. Or reading or math buddies are a wonderful way to build leadership and support friendships for both older and younger students.

Author's Perspective

A group of 5th grade students noticed there was a lot of waste during their school lunch. Students were throwing away uneaten bags of crackers, untouched bananas and many other sources of food. They were upset by not only the waste and the environmental impact but also that there were people who could benefit from this food that was simply being thrown away.

As their school principal, these students worked with me (Carey) and teachers to ask for support from the school community through signing a petition to make a change. Then, they wrote a letter to the director of food service illuminating the issue and asked to put the packaged and untouched food onto a 'share table,' where students could use this food at another time in the day or share it with a local shelter. It took some time for this to happen, due to the guidelines of the district and state food policies, but eventually, this became a reality.

Not only did these students feel empowered to make change, but they also made a real impact on the environment and food resources at their school and in their community. These students shared their process with classmates by doing a short segment on their school news that explained their steps and how they were empowered to make a positive impact on their school and community.

Enhancing Intrinsic Motivation

Intrinsic motivation is that sense of purpose that leaves us feeling fulfilled. Unlike extrinsic, which creates motivation by external rewards, intrinsic motivation comes from within and allows for a deeper, more connected learning process. Culturally relevant teaching practices enhance intrinsic motivation. For example:

- Allowing learners to have autonomy and agency
- Feeling connected and mutually cared for
- Holding high expectations, yet scaffolding from within the learner's zone of proximal development
- Encouraging play, curiosity and wonder
- Emphasizing the process in growing and developing
- Engaging in feedback and reflection cycles

When learners are intrinsically motivated to *Reach Out In Service*, this develops characteristics that empower young people in becoming leaders and helping others as their way of being. Start by supporting students in determining what is important to them and what they want to change or improve upon in their school or community.

Passion Project Opportunities
Some schools call this 'genius hour,' in which students learn about a topic and then share about it with classmates. This can inspire others to learn more about this topic or take action themselves. This is an excellent

opportunity for students to dig into their passions and explore things they are curious and excited about. By following the child, educators are embracing culturally relevant teaching. As learners discover and share their passions, support them in making the connection for how they will take peace action and *Reach Out In Service*.

◎ **Pause & Reflect:**

- ◆ What is important to your students and community?
- ◆ How will you find out more about students' passions, interests and how they are motivated to help?

Project-Based Learning

Project-based learning is an excellent way to foster student voice, choice and engagement. It's a way to organize multiple interdisciplinary standards, go deeper into topics and allow students to bring a project to fruition. Project-based learning enhances intrinsic motivation because it is designed to address real-world needs and issues. Through inquiry, curiosity and collaboration, learners engage in active and meaningful learning. Longer-term projects develop perseverance in staying committed to seeing the project to completion, even as challenges arise.

When students set goals and put them into action, it creates a strong sense of independence and autonomy. This creates empowerment and ultimately encourages students to find new and additional ways to *Reach Out In Service*. Look to help students find intrinsic power within themselves. Guiding learners to discover what they care about is an essential first step.

Table 7.2 Pursuit: Stand Up for Needs & Rights

Peace Pursuits for *Reach Out In Service*	
I ask questions and stand up for the needs and rights of myself, others and the planet (empowerment, justice).	• Engage in inquiry processes to identify needs and injustices that impact your community and environment. • Empower students to speak up for themselves and others to make a positive impact. • Seek out and listen to multiple perspectives, allowing different voices, cultures and ideas to be seen, heard and valued. • Lean in with curiosity and wonder about how to be in service to the world. • Respond to injustice and needs through project-based service learning.

Table 7.3 Practice: Project-Based Service Learning

Put It Into Practice: Project-Based Service Learning

Project-based learning typically takes place over several weeks at minimum.

1. Brainstorm thought-provoking topics connected to students' community. This includes identifying injustices, needs and rights of others and the environment. What is needed in your community?
2. Guide students to ask questions, inquire and research several topics that address ideas or concerns they have an interest in pursuing more deeply.
3. Identify and plan for links and connections to academic standards.
4. Facilitate and scaffold learning to ensure student ownership of the project. This may be independent or in collaboration in small groups. Students' voices and choices lead the way!
5. Implement the project, likely in partnership with the community (see ideas by level below). Include opportunities for feedback from project recipients.
6. Reflect on the process and the outcome of the project.
7. Share the learning and results with an audience or in celebration with project recipients.

Many of these projects would be great for family and community events or for volunteers to support. Consider setting up a service station or space in your classroom to encourage ongoing service!

Emerging	Intermediate	Advanced
• Take care of plants and/or animals (stuffed or real). • Write/draw cards for seniors and elders in hospitals or care homes in your community. • Create pet toys for animals at the local humane society. • Volunteer at a local animal shelter.	• Create bracelets or write/draw cards for children in hospitals. • Organize a food drive for homeless shelters; collect non-perishable goods. • Organize a neighborhood, park or school trash clean-up. • Create a biking/walking club to decrease environmental pollution. • Build a pollinator garden.	• Visit folks in local nursing or care homes and increase social interactions through craft/art activities, singing and playing games. • Put together kits for children in crisis or foster care (toothbrushes, blankets, stuffed animals, change of clothing etc.). • Start a tutoring or buddy reading/math program. • Organize a book swap or a book drive to share gently used books with other students and the community.

Student Leadership Opportunities

One essential aspect to encouraging service in a school setting is to create opportunities for students to become and see themselves as leaders. This helps increase their sense of efficacy and provides a greater sense of emotional safety, a sense of belonging and a strengthened self-worth. There is a special magic that happens when students become empowered! Empowerment is important to all students, and for students of the global majority, this is especially important because of the histories of oppression, exclusion, segregation and other injustices that have limited leadership. As we build personal confidence, autonomy and agency, this inspires collective action and social change.

Lean on Leaders From the Past & Present

Learning about other peacemaker leaders can inspire students in how they can make a difference in their communities and the world. Provide children with examples from the community and throughout the world. Leaning on leaders past and present can inspire students to create change, *Reach Out In Service*, and make a positive impact on the world.

Create Leaders & Foster Teaching Opportunities

Students thrive on sharing their learning and being in a leadership, teaching or support role. In addition to feeling empowered, they gain the knowledge and capacity to create change. However, students should not be expected to be 'helpers' just because they are advanced. It should be a choice that they make. Similarly, students should not be expected to consistently translate for others; they should be able to focus on their own learning. Ensure there is autonomy and provide options for students to share their time and talent in service of their community.

Table 7.4 Practice: Leadership Service Roles

Put It Into Practice: Leadership Service Roles		
Invite students to journal about their core values (see 'What Matters to Me' in Chapter 3, p. 57). Take themes from their core values and make a plan for a class or team-oriented goals for service and leadership.		
Discuss ideas that are important to you and learners; make a plan to put these ideas into action. Leadership service can look like taking care of the various people and environments around the school. Ensure all students have an opportunity to participate in leadership roles.		
Emerging	*Intermediate*	*Advanced*
• Hallway and room cleaners • Line leader • Classroom library organizer • Paper passer • Recycling leader • Coat & boots helper (helping others who need help with buttoning, boots, snow pants etc.) • Playground clean-up	• Playground organizer: equipment care, ensuring fairness • Classroom table leader • Lunch table leader • Classroom librarian • Junior bus patrol or school safety patrol • Student government representative • Media center helper: organizing books, shelving, supporting librarian/clerk	• Student government; representing student voices in making school-wide decisions. • Green Team: organizing the recycling, organics and trash reduction efforts • School news crew: creating newsletter and/or digital news to share with the school (including school updates, weather, lunch and passion projects)

If they are enlivened about a topic or issue, children will be motivated to *Reach Out In Service* to help make a change, put new steps into action and truly make a difference in their school and community. This sense of care and advocacy develops a sense of self-confidence and social responsibility that are vital to life! We share the sentiment from our Peacemaker In Practice (below) who said, *"We are producing leaders, I want them to be better!"*

Peacemaker In Practice
The Power of 'We over Me'

Omar McMillan has been an elementary teacher for over 23 years and was a finalist for the Minnesota Teacher of the Year award (in 2020). He is the Richfield boy's head basketball coach and a statewide basketball community leader.

I (Carey) was honored to interview him about his amazing community service work!

In his teaching, McMillan offered 'shoe talks,' where he shared life lessons, connecting with students. In one example, he shared that one student came to his class and was withdrawn and introverted. This student wore a hoodie with the hood up every day. Instead of saying the expected response, *"take off your hood,"* McMillan started wearing a hoodie as he taught. The student shared that he was having trouble hearing and seeing him. McMillan responded, *"I want to see and hear you too."* This made a dramatic shift in the student, and McMillan is still in touch with this student and his mother. This is the heart of culturally relevant teaching and the peace action, *Respect Diversity.*

"It's about relationships. You have to be willing to adjust to your students."

McMillan's strength is building relationships and a sense of community in sports and in the classroom. As head Basketball coach, McMillan and other coaches have adopted a mantra, **"We over Me."**

McMillan shared, *"I'm strong in my faith, God first, family second and then everything else."* When asked about his other community service, McMillan spoke about being a leader in the basketball community. He serves on the board of the Minnesota Coaches Basketball Association and then founded the Minnesota Black Coaches Association with some colleagues, where he serves as the vice president; through his work, more Black coaches have joined the association.

We talked about the retention of not only African American coaches but also teachers.

McMillan says, *"At a lot of round table discussions, that question comes up— mentorship and providing resources."* We discussed the importance of having mentors, resources and support for both teachers and coaches who are African American.

In reflecting on his career of service, he shared that it's the impact he has had on students and athletes over the years that means the most to him.

"When I can genuinely say that I have made an impact on them, that's what matters…I'm not going to be a millionaire, but when there is joy for a student or athlete, that is my success!"

McMillan spoke fondly of his mother and mentor, Iris Nichols. *"My motto and philosophy comes from my Mom. She was an evangelist, throughout the community; in hospitals and nursing homes. I have modeled after her service; as a teacher and coach…Whether you want to or not, you are a leader in these roles. Students are looking at you, it's about building relationships."*

Sharing a writing assignment in 6th grade with his mom who called her his hero, she said, *"I don't really want you to write about me…I'm overjoyed… but… we live in the projects, and I never went to college. If you think I'm your hero, be better than me, do better than me!"*

McMillan said, *"We are producing leaders, I want them to be better! I want to teach these students to be better than the daily lesson."*

In closing, he said, *"The big thing is to be a great leader; because you don't know who is watching! It's those educators and coaches who have that extra something who will make a difference!"* McMillan embodies the peace action, *Reach Out In Service* with his dedication to education and coaching.

Navigating Service-Related Challenges

When it comes to being in service within the school or greater community, challenges may arise. In new spaces and within the excitement that can come with service, children's behavior may sometimes be inappropriate. The best practices outlined in Chapter 9 will be supportive in navigating behaviors. As a baseline, support regulation before anything else. For some, differing or new environments and people can be stressful until relationships and routines are established. Here are a few tips to consider (Youth.gov, n.d.):

- ◆ Ensure learners understand the meaning behind their service learning. If they are an integral part of the process and the service is developmentally appropriate, they will be more invested and engaged.
- ◆ If going off-site, know in advance the rules and expectations of the people and service site and communicate that with learners.
- ◆ Model, demonstrate and set clear expectations for behavior and communication.
- ◆ Communicate calmly, respectfully and positively, even when redirecting.

When it comes to project-based service learning or larger, longer service projects, it can sometimes feel like a lot to oversee, support and implement. Collaborate with other educators, organizations, families and community members for support. School leaders should provide adequate resources, planning/reflection time and professional learning opportunities to support students and staff as they *Reach Out In Service*. Good planning, preparation, supported action and reflection go a long way to ensuring service is a rewarding experience for all involved.

Put It Into Practice: Service Learning Action Steps

1. **Research:** Do some research in your community and determine how you want to provide service/give back to your community. Research the topic. Identify related academic standards. What are you hoping to accomplish?
2. **Planning and preparation:** Once you have established your service project, co-create a plan and prepare for putting it into action. What supplies and steps are needed? This likely requires collaboration and communication with others!
3. **Action:** Once the action plan is put together, (co)train students and begin the project or ongoing service.
4. **Reflection:** After service, pause and reflect on how it's going. Are there adjustments to make? Are the people you are supporting/serving getting their needs met? Do you have enough support to accomplish your goals?
5. **Celebrate:** Acknowledge accomplishments and the impact of service. Consider demonstrating or sharing your work with other groups.

A Culture of Kindness

Encouraging random acts of kindness is a wonderful way to connect to the spirit of service, as well as foster empathy and care. When reaching out in kindness, there is no expectation of anything in return. Kindness has a ripple effect that encourages generosity and compassion of all life. Practicing kindness as a school culture creates a sense of connection and belonging. All of which improve the mental and emotional well-being of everyone in the environment. There is already so much negativity in the world; promoting understanding and kindness demonstrates that even the smallest, everyday actions can have a positive and profound impact on others.

Put It Into Practice: Random Acts of Kindness

As students experience and engage in random acts of kindness, they will learn and foster a culture of kindness. A few examples:

➤ Opening and holding the door open
➤ Helping someone clean up a mess
➤ Picking something up that was dropped
➤ Smiling at a visitor
➤ Draw/write a thank you note
➤ Celebrate someone's growth
➤ Reach out to someone who seems sad or lonely

Be an Upstander

By creating a culture of kindness and being in service to others, students are likely to speak up against bullying and other demeaning or harmful communication, actions and behavior. A culture of kind upstanders means students stand up, speak out and make responsible choices to support the well-being of others. Encourage students to be advocates and champions for their friends, classmates and the environment. At the end of the day, being a leader means doing the right thing, even when nobody's watching!

Unpack what it means to be an upstander and advocate for others. This conversation is also an opportunity to connect back to your class charter (Lesson, p. 259), about what is important to the class and school community regarding needs, rights and a sense of psychological safety. As you review the class charter, discuss the challenges of creating and maintaining a just and peaceful learning environment for everyone. What is the role of an 'upstander' in supporting the community charter? It's important to understand that a bystander just watches passively, but if you encourage students to stand up for one another, a bystander can become an upstander.

Table 7.5 Pursuit: Help Others

Peace Pursuits for *Reach Out In Service*	
I try to help others in need (advocacy, justice, kindness).	• Engage in inquiry about needs and injustices in the community. Brainstorm and enact solutions. • Inspire advocacy through selected stories and mentor texts that highlight peacemakers, storytellers and peace leaders. • Put into action two random acts of kindness every day – one for yourself and one for another. • Learn what it means to advocate, be an 'upstander', and practice these skills: identify a cause, investigate the facts, set clear objectives, respectfully communicate & listen, be persistent and resilient in your approach. • Anchor to the power of cooperative learning (Chapter 4, p. 93) and foster community engagement.

Table 7.6 Practice: Be An Upstander

Put It Into Practice: Be An Upstander		
Discuss: How can (does) everyone in the community care for themselves, others and the environment? Connect back to the Class Charter Lesson, p. 259.		
Emerging	*Intermediate*	*Advanced*

• What happens when you see someone who feels sad, left out or picked on?
• How can you be a helper?
• When has someone helped you? How did it feel?
	• Discuss what it means to be an upstander. How is this the same or different from being an advocate?
	• What are examples of being an advocate or upstander in your own classroom community or school/community?
		• As a class, discuss a topic where someone has been wronged or taken advantage of.
		• Role play how this could go differently.
		• Have students take turns acting out the following roles:
		  ○ Bystander
		  ○ Victim
		  ○ Advocate or upstander
		  ○ Witness

Prepare learners to be upstanders through role-playing or scenarios about ways to stand up when they see or hear something that is hurtful or makes them/others uncomfortable. Collaboratively brainstorm scenarios that happen on the playground, in the classroom, on the bus or in other places where students can practice being upstanders.		

Reaching Out After Traumatic Events

When there is a traumatic event, serious accident or natural disaster, people often want to help those impacted. Sometimes the darkest times in a community can also be the moment that people light each other up with a sense of collective love, care and belonging. This social support is valuable and as much as possible should be coordinated with those impacted and/or community-led. **To be trauma informed and culturally affirming when reaching out in service, especially with individuals and communities also coping within oppressive systems,** *do and be with* **instead of doing** *to* **or** *for* **those impacted.**

Schools are often important community centers for service and resource coordination. Educators and staff support affected caregivers and children while offering a sense of routine, comfort and opportunities for processing. However, schools can also be sites of traumatic events. Be aware that there will be a range of physical, emotional, behavioral and cognitive responses and impacts related to the traumatic event and that these may shift and change over time. How people respond and cope from trauma is also layered upon other complexities such as systemic racism, socio political and economic factors that were present before the event. Consider your positioning, are you in a privileged position that can self-regulate by avoiding, turning or walking away from the trauma?

Wanting to do something to help is appreciable, but it needs to be in partnership and timed considerably with those impacted. Though resilient and adaptable, children and adults impacted by traumatic events will benefit from longer-term recovery support and/or may develop post-traumatic stress disorder (PTSD). Children may also mirror how their parents and caregivers handle stress. The impact of trauma doesn't just fade away. Therefore, reaching out in service with those impacted should be a consideration long past the crisis or event.

(Note: Chapter 9 goes deeper into trauma informed care)

Put It Into Practice: Support Circles or Groups

Consider putting in place groups or circles at your site to support students who are going through challenges such as death, divorce or changes in the family, friendships or other needs. Some schools have their licensed school social worker, therapist or other trained staff facilitate groups. Topics and responses are sensitive, so it is important to have a trained specialist leading these groups if possible.

If there is a traumatic event that impacts many people (e.g., natural disaster or mass shooting), bring in additional support, ideally from within the community. This may also be less formally trained folks who can set up circles to allow people space to process their grief, fear and begin healing. Circles provide a confidential space for people impacted by a similar trauma to speak openly, be received with compassion and begin to heal and recover (utilize the Peace Circle guidelines – see Lesson p. 259).

Seeking Peace Through Service

There are so many ways to make a positive difference, and by allowing students to discover, vision and enact their plans, educators are leaning into culturally relevant teaching. With voice and choice in how they *Reach Out In Service*, students are empowered and motivated.

When children and adults *Reach Out In Service*, it is a way to *Seek Peace With Others*, as it connects us and strengthens the community. It provides opportunities to engage with diverse people respectfully and to *Protect Our Environment*. Service is also a way to *Seek Peace Within Yourself*, as giving and helping others and nature can reduce stress, support a sense of purpose and increase health and happiness.

More Peaceful Practices: *Reach Out In Service*

Family & Community Connections

Families have powerful connections to the community and are a child's first role models. What are caregivers at your site passionate about? How do they *Reach Out In Service*?

◆ Involve families and community members in various stages of service projects.

- Have students interview family and community members to see how they *Reach Out In Service.*
- Ask parents and community members to come and speak to your class or a group of classrooms about how they give back to the community (hospitals, Peace Corps volunteers, veterans, animal shelters, volunteering, tutoring etc.).
- Reach out to local service-related organizations (food shelves, animal rescue organizations, community centers) and see if there are projects that your interested students could support.

Table 7.7 Content Area Connections: *Reach Out In Service*

Content Area Connections			
Literacy	**Math**	**Physical Education**	**Science**
Read inspiring books and view media about people and projects that serve their community and/or the world. Reflect with learners about the steps of service and how this story might inspire their service action.	Research mathematicians who have used their skills to make an impact on the world. This creates compelling reasons for math and service around the world. For example, Katherine Johnson used her phenomenal math skills to support NASA's trajectory analysis for the first U.S. crewed spaceflights.	Ensure that P.E. is inclusive of all bodies. Each unit, guide students in creating modifications and adaptations that allows for participation of all, regardless of ability, mobility or disability. For example, if you are doing a dance unit, start simple and co-create options for all body types, levels of participation etc.	Make links between your unit content and formal and informal scientists who made a difference by reaching out to their community. Here are a few formal examples: • Aristotle • Sir Isaac Newton • Marie Curie • George Washington Carver • Dr. Ayana Elizabeth Johnson • Chien-Shiung Wu • César Milstein

References

Dewey, J. (1897). My pedagogic creed. *School Journal, 54*(January), 77–80. http://dewey.pragmatism.org/creed.htm

Goodall, J. (2021). *What we do makes a difference.* Jane Goodall Institute Canada. https://janegoodall.ca/what-we-do/

Youth.gov. (n.d.). *Service-Learning.* Youth.gov. Retrieved January 9, 2024, from https://youth.gov/youth-topics/civic-engagement-and-volunteering/service-learning

101st United States Congress. (1990, November 16). *S.1430 – National and Community Service Act of 1990.* Congress.gov. https://www.congress.gov/bill/101st-congress/senate-bill/1430

8

Be A Responsible Citizen Of The World

Never doubt a small group of thoughtful, committed citizens can change the world; indeed, it's the only thing that ever has.
~ Margaret Mead

Be A Responsible Citizen Of The World is an important culminating peace action because it encompasses all of the peace actions. As world citizens, it's about giving back and considering the broader perspective. For educators, it's about supporting students in having empathy for others, looking beyond their own needs and caring for their peers, community and the world. This peace action also speaks to acting on your core values. As anthropologist Margaret Mead stated, it only takes a small group of caring, dedicated people to change the world (Keys, 1982). Never underestimate the ripples of action and change!

In This Chapter:

DOI: 10.4324/9781003449249-9

Stories & Storytelling

A great place to start your (and students') journey to *Be A Responsible Citizen Of The World* is through the sharing, studying and appreciation of stories and storytelling. Folktales, myths, fables, legends and creation stories offer rich narratives for learning about cultures around the world. Storytelling fosters global awareness by helping us learn about traditions, beliefs, values and customs. This cultural awareness also connects to the peace action, *Respect Diversity*, as it invites a deeper appreciation for the human experiences of the past and present. Additionally, as we read, view and discuss stories, it supports the development of empathy and creates opportunities to consider the world from varying perspectives.

Take for example universal myth stories such as 'The Great Flood' that crosses cultures and religions. Christians and Jews know this as the story of Noah and the Ark, but other versions predate the Genesis version. The Ancient Sumerian Epic of Gilgamesh includes the story of Utnapishtim, who built a ship and filled it with animals to escape a flood, eventually escaping to the top of a mountain. The Greeks point to Deucalion, who survived a flood caused by Zeus. The Turtle Island creation stories of the Lenape, Haudenosaunee and other Indigenous peoples tell of a watery Earth. More versions appear in Hindu and Mayan tales as well! By making cross-cultural connections and comparing and contrasting stories, students identify common themes, appreciate multiple perspectives and refer to historical aspects that impact society even today.

◎ Pause & Reflect:

- What folktale, fable, creation story or myth was impactful in your childhood or upbringing?
- Do a little digging and compare and contrast this story to one in existence in another culture/background. What common themes and motifs exist?

In addition to deepening cultural awareness, most stories of this nature have themes that connect across the peace actions – ultimately supporting the development of responsible global citizenship and an understanding of our interconnected human experience.

Table 8.1 Practice: Story Theme Analysis

Put It Into Practice: Story Theme Analysis		
Story Themes	**General Questions/Prompts**	**Peace Action**
Conflict and Resolution Communication Skills	• What challenges or conflicts do characters face? • How do characters resolve conflict? • Discuss the effective and ineffective communication styles and methods featured.	*Seek Peace Within Yourself And Others*
Environmental Awareness	• Describe the relationship between humans and our environment in this story. • What does this story teach us about our responsibility to nature? • What animal symbolism is present? Explore its meaning.	*Protect Our Environment*
Cultural and Historical Context; Critical Thinking	• Evaluate the context of these narratives – how has this impacted culture and history (and vice versa)? • What are common themes from this story that exist in other stories and civilizations? • How does this story connect to your life experience?	*Respect Diversity*
Identity Belonging Self-Awareness and Personal Growth	• How does the character's identity shift (or stay the same) as they have new and differing experiences? • How does the character grow and change? • How do the character's experiences intersect with others? What is the impact?	*Seek Peace Within Yourself And Others*
Helping and Advocating for Others	• Identify harm, injustices and crises present. • How are the characters acting to solve the problem and explore possible solutions? • How does this story inspire critical thinking and problem-solving of real global problems?	*Reach Out In Service*

Folktales, myths, fables, legends and creation stories literally and figuratively teach us about the experiences of life. They allow us to explore the meaning of life and rites of passage from birth to death that occur within and beyond this Earthly journey. Stories provide keys to understanding all aspects of the human experience.

'We': Connected Through Global Citizenship

Receiving and sharing stories helps us to understand ourselves and others. Being a responsible global citizen means that we recognize our link with our fellow humans, nature and our environment. This peace action invites us to share connection and empathy for all life. A world system that works for all inhabitants of this planet is possible when we utilize all the people and resources available to our imagination, creativity and problem-solving.

Throughout the world, aggression, violence, conflict and war negatively impact the well-being of countless people. Making a real change in curbing and ceasing violence requires all of us to take action – as individuals and collective communities. This can be accomplished by embracing a *'we'* mentality, instead of a *'me'* mentality.

There are different perspectives and opinions related to harm, aggression, violence and war. There will always be multiple sides to the story. If we only look in one direction, root ourselves in only one viewpoint or are silent, we are complicit in perpetuating the *'us vs. them'* mentality that feeds violent conflict and war.

◎ **Pause & Reflect:**

- ◆ How do you typically respond to complex situations related to conflict, violence and war?
- ◆ Do you tend to center *'me'* (yourself) or consider *'we'* initially? And ultimately?
- ◆ What are the contributing factors to your response and perspective?

Problems with *'Us vs. Them'*

The opposite of *'we'* and a common mentality, rooted in scarcity, competition, retribution and fear, is *'us vs. them.'* This viewpoint places people and even our environment as an 'other.' This mentality categorizes people and identities into specific groups. This *'us vs. them'* viewpoint divides folks and contributes to the harm, aggression and violence reported, observed and experienced across our planet.

- ◆ Polarization deepens (political, social, cultural) making it difficult to dialogue, compromise and peacefully resolve conflict.
- ◆ People's confirmation bias leads to seeking out and accepting information that aligns with or confirms existing beliefs. This reinforces biases, prejudice and misconceptions, which are big contributors to harm, aggression and violence.
- ◆ Dehumanization of *'them'* group members reduces empathy and is often used to justify violence.

◎ **Pause & Reflect:**

- ◆ How does an *'us vs. them'* mentality show up in your life or community?

Shifting to *'We'* & Your Individuality

Being a responsible citizen means that we live by and help create a mentality of *'we.'* A *'we'* viewpoint encourages people to understand the interconnected nature of all life. *'We'* calls for people to come together to share and have all voices be heard, valued and honored. This provides an opening for us to develop peaceful solutions to problems in our communities, countries and world. A *'we'* mentality creates a collective identity and sense of unity that promotes justice and peace.

- ◆ Extending empathy and understanding, to those who might once have been considered outsiders or *'them'* reduces divisions and hostility.
- ◆ Prioritizing peacebuilding, communication, negotiation, meditation and compromise to reduce and prevent violence. These skills are valued, practiced and embraced in this *'we'* mindset.
- ◆ Social bonds are strengthened when we *Respect Diversity*, creating welcoming inclusivity within all groups and communities. A repaired social fabric deters antisocial behavior and violence.

Holding and acting in alignment with a *'we'* viewpoint is not about giving up your individuality! This is not an *'either-or'* situation (which is characteristic of *'us vs. them'* thinking). Both your individual identity and collective unity can exist together and in balance! Remember our learning in Chapter 3 about *'both/and'* (p. 64)? We can hold true multiple ideas, experiences and beliefs at the same time. It is important to maintain a healthy sense of self, to celebrate your uniqueness and embrace your freedom of choice. *And* of equal importance, balance that individuality with a strong collective identity. You can *both*:

- ◆ Maintain your uniqueness *and* be part of various groups.
- ◆ Share your ideas *and* seek out and engage with diverse perspectives.
- ◆ Privately support your well-being and growth *and* embrace belonging and leverage resources of a supportive network.
- ◆ Share your skills, values and goals *and* honor the contributions of all.

Table 8.2 Pursuit: Needs, Choices & Actions

Peace Pursuits: *Be A Responsible Citizen Of The World*	
I consider my needs and the needs of others in my choices and actions.	• Distinguish between needs vs. wants, hopes and desires. • Consider the impact on the entire class, community and/or society with choices, decisions, behaviors and actions. • Guide learners in understanding the differences between the collective *'we'* and an individual *'me'* viewpoint. • Ask: How does this choice or action impact the greater good of our classroom? Community? Our world? • Continue to refer back to the *both/and* practice in Chapter 3, p. 64, especially when those teachable moments arise. How can we honor and balance *both* our needs *and* those of others? When we have to choose *either/or*, how does that impact us and others (empathy)?

Table 8.3 Practice: We Over Me

Put It Into Practice: We Over Me		
Discuss how everyone is part of the community. Co-create a Y chart in which the class could share ideas for all of the ways that the space needs to be *'we over me.'* Ideas: • Cleaning up the space (environment) • Sharing materials • Helping one another • Peer support (coaching, editing etc.) • Getting along at recess		
Emerging	*Intermediate*	*Advanced*
Why is it important to think about the needs of others as well as your own?	How do your choices and actions positively and negatively impact others?	View and discuss examples of *'us vs. them'* mentalities and/or actions and their short- and long-term impacts.
This could be part of coming up with a class charter at the beginning of the year (see Lesson p. 259), or it could be a 'reset' as needed to address an issue.		

Collectivism, Individualism & Pluralism

As discussed in Chapter 5, our cultural upbringing and epistemology play a part in how we view ourselves and our relationships. Generally, there are many worldviews. For example, in the United States, we have a much more individualist outlook, yet globally there is a much more collective view.

It may feel impossible to have a deep understanding of all of the cultures and worldviews represented within the classroom and beyond. Dr. Zaretta Hammond (2015) responded to this conundrum by breaking down cultures into archetypes. She stated,

> *There are two cultural archetypes that I think are important for the culturally responsive teacher to know, Collectivism and individualism. Dutch sociologist, Geert Hofstede, found that approximately 20% of the world has an individualistic culture, while 80% practice a collectivist culture. (p. 25)*

These statistics align with non-White, People of the Global Majority representing around 80% of the world's population. Hammond (2015) continued:

> *Most European cultures were rooted in an individualistic culture, while the collectivist worldview is common among Latin American, Asian, African, Middle Eastern, and many Slavic cultures. Collectivist societies emphasize relationships, interdependence within a community, and cooperative learning. Individualistic societies emphasize individual achievement and independence. (p. 25)*

Many early immigrants to the present-day United States came from Europe, which aligns with the tendencies of White American culture to be more individualistic. However, communities in the United States composed of People of the Global Majority and Native American cultures and ethnicities, typically are more collectivist.

It is important to note that there are continuums that operate within cultures and individual people; and people can change and evolve. For example, a person from a European country or a White U.S. citizen may embody a more collectivist perspective because of their cultural upbringing, family outlook or personality.

Conversely, someone raised in a collectivist culture may adopt an individualistic approach to feel successful in more individualistic systems. For example, a child raised with the core value and multidimensional African philosophy of **ubuntu** may feel the need to lean into individualism in a U.S. school system. Finding a balanced approach allows us to embrace cultural dynamics and views.

> The African concept of **ubuntu** highlights: *"respect for human beings, for human dignity, and human life, collective sharedness, obedience, humility, solidarity, caring, hospitality, interdependence and communalism"* (Hailey, 2008, p. 5). Ubuntu speaks to wholeness, belonging and compassion – our shared humanity.

A third consideration are pluralistic societies, which align to the idea of a social contract. Generally, pluralism is social and political tolerance, when people from diverse religions, races and social classes work collaboratively for the common good. As peace educators, we must acknowledge the differences between individualistic, collectivist and pluralistic cultures and prioritize balancing these in learning spaces.

◎ **Pause & Reflect:** As you review the different features of individualist, collectivist and pluralistic societies (Table 8.4), consider:

   ◆ How does this align (or not) with your upbringing and values?
   ◆ How does your viewpoint impact your teaching practices?
   ◆ How do individualism, collectivism and pluralism show up in your classroom/school/community?

Table 8.4 Features of Individualistic, Collectivist & Pluralist Cultures

Features of Individualist, Collectivist & Pluralist Cultures		
Individualism	**Collectivism**	**Pluralism**
Independence and individual achievement are valued.	Group success and positive interdependence are valued.	Tolerating others' beliefs even if it doesn't match their own is valued.
• Self-reliant • Take care of self • Competitive • Linear and analytical • Me over We	• Harmony • Group dynamics • Care for each other • Relational	• Common good • Democracy • Shared power
Learning through studying and reading individually.	Learning through collaboration.	Learning through compromise.

Adapted from: *Culturally Responsive Teaching and the Brain*, Zaretta Hammond (2015, p. 26)

Levels of Humanity

As we discussed in Chapter 1, each level of humanity holds concern for the forms of harm, aggression and violence that currently exist within it (see Figure 8.1). All levels of humanity can also pursue peace, inviting us all to *Be A Responsible Citizen Of The World*.

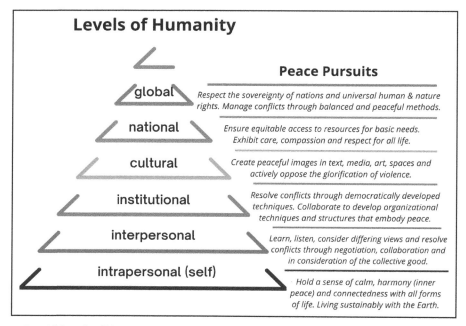

Figure 8.1 All Levels of Humanity Pursue Peace
Adapted from: *Peace Education, 3d ed. (p. 15)* (Harris & Morrison, 2013)

◎ **Pause & Reflect:**

- ◆ At the intrapersonal level, how do you hold a sense of calm and harmony within? What supports your inner peace, the foundations for global peace?
- ◆ As you consider the levels of humanity, how do or might you engage with pursuing peace at each level?

Author's Perspective

As a school administrator, I (Carey) have been in contact with several very young children who are navigating tumultuous home situations. For children in more unstable life situations (violence, abuse, trauma, unstable housing, unpredictable meals, ACE etc.), there may be additional impacts that trickle within all levels of humanity.

There are multiple ways people interact and intersect with each other, yet this is all built upon the intrapersonal or self-level of humanity. Many children are experiencing intrapersonal trauma and interpersonal challenges. These are areas in which it will take time to foster and deepen. There may be unlearning to do as they grow and develop. There is absolutely hope for all children, and yet it will take time and dedication to develop into peaceful and grounded human beings.

As you review these levels of humanity (Figure 8.1), you may be thinking about the violence that is pervasive around the world and wondering if peace and justice education can really help make a difference. We certainly hope and believe so! Remember that harm, aggression and violence, in their many forms, exist, in a very large part, due to the systems and structures holding it in place. Think about the many 'isms' that uphold and perpetuate inequities, injustices and the continuation of violence such as classism, sexism, ableism, racism, ageism, heterosexism, anti-semitism and colonialism.

When individuals choose the love of power over others, our social systems and structures become rigid and harmful, ultimately benefiting those few who wish to keep and gain power over others.

Peacelearning can help evolve all levels of humanity! When we take a global perspective, we can also see a great need for both local and international peace education. It's helpful to have a give-and-take between looking directly at your own community and holding a global perspective.

Peacemaker In Practice

Nurturing Peace and Unity:

How the American Montessori Society Educates for a Global Perspective

By Munir Shivji, Executive Director

An education capable of saving humanity is no small undertaking; it involves the spiritual development of [humans], the enhancement of their values as an individual, and the preparation of young people to understand the times in which they live.
(Montessori, 1972, p. 30)

True peace and justice education requires us to recognize our shared humanity while appreciating the richness of our differences. As we embrace global unity, we can work together for justice, rectify historical inequalities and bridge the gaps between diverse communities. In a world marred by conflict and discord, nurturing compassionate, responsible global citizens is of pivotal importance in the ongoing pursuit of peace.

Montessori education – and true peace education – encourage children to think critically, question the status quo and engage with real-world issues. Montessori students are exposed to various cultures, traditions and perspectives, which nurtures an inclusive mindset and a genuine curiosity about the world. Promoting diversity and respect from an early age helps build a compassionate, inclusive society, empowering individuals to positively influence the world in the future by advocating for universal human rights and working toward global peace and justice.

As peace educators, Montessori practitioners play a pivotal role in nurturing the next generation of peace advocates by creating transformative learning experiences that prepare children to be active agents of change:

➤ They explore the profound links between anti-bias, antiracist (ABAR) education and Montessori philosophy to understand personal beliefs, assumptions and observations. In so doing, they can address internal biases and identify bias in their environment, and embody the principles of peace from an equitable lens to ensure every student feels valued and respected, fostering a sense of belonging and unity. By demonstrating mindfulness, empathy and open-mindedness, teachers create a positive and respectful learning environment that serves as a model for students.

➤ They incorporate a global perspective into the curriculum to help students understand the interconnectedness of the world and humanity's shared responsibility for promoting peace and justice. This is achieved through multicultural studies, global current events discussions and collaborative projects with students worldwide.

➤ They advocate for universal human rights and social justice. Teaching children about human rights issues, both historical and contemporary, encourages critical thinking and empowers students to stand up against injustice.

A quote often attributed to Dr. Maria Montessori reads, *"The greatest gifts we can give our children are the roots of responsibility and the wings of independence."*

As educators and leaders, our commitment to nurturing peace must be unwavering, for it is through our collective actions that we can create a more harmonious and just world for generations to come. Since its founding in 1960, the American Montessori Society has supported peace and social justice efforts. Our longstanding Peace &Social Justice Committee sees the alignment between AMS's mission (empowering humanity to build a better world through Montessori) and the peace action, *Be A Responsible Citizen Of The World:*

Within the carefully and beautifully prepared Montessori environment, children are given responsibility from a very young age, and can exercise their freedom of choice. They learn to care for each other and resolve conflicts peacefully. They begin geography studies with maps of the world, and begin to learn about their wonderful, diverse Earth and the rich cultures of the people who inhabit it.

Themes of social justice, identity, and responsibility to society are investigated further, as students realize they have the power to make concrete, positive change in the world.
(By Chandra Fernando, Judi Bauerlein, Aimee Allen)

Learn more about American Montessori Society and Peace Seed Grants at: https://amshq.org/About-AMS/Donate/AMS-Peace-and-Social-Justice-Fund

◎ **Pause & Reflect:**

◆ What inspiration can you put into action from Montessori's ideas and approach to peace and social justice education?

Decolonization

A global perspective requires consideration of the current and historical impacts and effects of colonization. As peace and justice educators, we strive to be within a mindset of decolonization.

Moving toward a decolonized internal and external environment and ways of thinking takes courageous actions, learning and unlearning. Understand that decolonization has been hugely impactful in our socialization and throughout all levels of humanity with its legacies of White supremacy, capitalism and the patriarchy.

> *Decolonization is about cultural, psychological, and economic freedom for Indigenous people with the goal of achieving Indigenous sovereignty – the right and ability of Indigenous people to practice self-determination over their land, cultures, and political and economic systems. Colonialism is a historical and ongoing global project where settlers continue to occupy land, dictate social, political, and economic systems, and exploit Indigenous people and their resources. It is a global endeavor.*
> (Belfi & Sandiford, 2021)

◎ Pause & Reflect:

- Check your privileges: What are 'inherent' privileges you have (or don't have)?
- How are you/others exploited through capitalism? (For example, unpaid labor, consumption and scarcity mindset.)

In addition to questioning and reflecting on how colonization has impacted your mind, we must consider histories and relationships to the land we reside on. It isn't always an option for colonizers to just leave settled lands (for example, we don't believe this is realistic for much of North America) and yet honoring Indigenous sovereignty through shared power and repatriation is not only possible but is long past due. Though we can decolonize our minds through meaningful land acknowledgments, moving toward a mindset of reparations is essential and requires action.

The discussion of decolonization is more than we can attend to in this writing and is a continued place of (un)learning for us. We recommend these works to deepen and expand your mind, understanding and take action.

◆ Researchers Tuck and Yang (2012) provided a critical perspective that anchors why social justice and decolonization are not synonymous.

We ask you to take up the practice of awareness ... how the pursuit of critical consciousness, the pursuit of social justice through a critical enlightenment, can also be settler moves to innocence – diversions, distractions, which relieve the settler of feelings of guilt or responsibility, and conceal the need to give up land or power or privilege. (p. 21)

◆ Waziyatawin (Wahpetunwan Dakota) and Michael Yellow Bird's (Mandan, Hidatsa and Arikara Tribes) book *For Indigenous Minds Only: A Decolonization Handbook* (2012) shared how decolonizing actions must begin in the mind and empower positive change.

Put It Into Practice: Indigenous Land Acknowledgment

Explore where present-day and historical Indigenous peoples live(d) near your community. Foster conversations about colonialism, settler-Indigenous relations and Indigenous ways of knowing. Invite local tribal historians or family members to expand on your research and understanding. Co-create an Indigenous land acknowledgment for the school, as well as for other areas in the community or region.

Questions to consider:

➤ Who were the original inhabitants of this land?
➤ What was their relationship like with the land?
➤ How did colonialism impact/damage this land and the people?
➤ How can we learn from Indigenous peoples, nations and knowledge systems and be respectful stewards of the lands we live on? How can we honor this land?

United Nations & Human Rights

A global perspective or world order supports all human beings. By prioritizing opportunities for holistic learning and democratic leadership development, peacelearners can learn peaceful practices, handle conflict through nonviolence, celebrate diversity and advocate for themselves and others. Peace and justice education offers hope and empowerment for educators and learners across the world!

Understanding and respect for all peoples, their cultures, values, and ways of life; furthermore awareness of the interdependence between peoples' abilities to communicate across cultures and last, but not least to enable the individual to acquire a critical understanding of problems at the national and international level.

(Harris & Morrison, 2013, p. 75)

The United Nations (UN), with a mission to maintain international peace and security, has been a pillar of strength for peace and justice education since its founding in 1945.

The founding of the United Nations provided an impetus for an international effort to teach about the problems associated with war, violence, injustice, illiteracy, poverty and other sources of human conflict.

(Harris & Morrison, 2013, p. 80)

When schools focus on a global perspective, they offer opportunities for understanding and appreciation of other cultures and languages. As we explored in Chapter 5, culturally relevant teaching practices have an asset-based approach to diverse cultures, languages and perspectives.

◎ Pause & Reflect:

- ◆ What do you think needs to happen in your community to create a better sense of global citizenry?
- ◆ Within your own sphere of influence, what can you do to support change? (Not asking for outside assistance, just using what you have currently; but reimagining or reconfiguring resources.)

The United Nations Declaration of Human Rights (1948), viewed human rights through a global perspective. We highlight the first three of thirty articles that strongly demonstrate the essence of this peace action. When considering people's basic needs and universal human rights, it's important to acknowledge that different communities and cultures may vary in their interpretation and needs. Also, take into account the privilege that some have in comparison to others.

Article 1:

All human beings are born free and equal in dignity and rights. They are endowed with reason and conscience and should act towards one another in a spirit of brotherhood.

Article 2:

Everyone is entitled to all the rights and freedoms set forth in this Declaration, without distinction of any kind, such as race, colour, sex, language, religion, political or other opinions, national or social origin, property, birth, or another status. Furthermore, no distinction shall be made on the basis of the political, jurisdictional, or international status of the country or territory to which a person belongs, whether it be independent, trust, non-self-governing, or under any other limitation of sovereignty.

Article 3:

Everyone has the right to life, liberty and security of person.

⊚ **Pause & Reflect:**

- ◆ As you read through these articles, what resonates with you?
- ◆ Which Universal Human Right do you feel is being met in your community?
- ◆ Which is most pressing (needed) in your community?

Table 8.5 Pursuit: Universal Human Rights

Peace Pursuits for: *Be A Responsible Citizen Of The World*	
I identify people's basic needs and universal human rights.	• Understand the difference between needs and rights, and identify examples in your own life. • Consider how needs are communicated (verbally and non-verbally). • Look at the needs of all individuals (collective) and those needs that are (or may be) unique. • Practice asking or advocating for the needs and rights of yourself and others. • Support human rights across all systems and structures.

Table 8.6 Practice: Fairness & Human Rights

Put It Into Practice: Fairness & Human Rights		
Emerging	*Intermediate*	*Advanced*
Discuss scenarios of **fairness** and how it would feel to be left out or not allowed to do or receive something because of what you look like.	Extend from the *emerging* scenarios about fairness by breaking into smaller groups and discussing what they would do if something like this happened.	Have students read an article(s) about people not being allowed to be in school because of their gender or unless they could pay fees or buy a uniform.
• What if only students with curly hair received snacks for the day? • What if only students with brown eyes were allowed to use the drinking fountain? • What if only students with blue or green eyes got to have hot lunch and everyone else had to have a cold sandwich?	Come back together to debrief as a whole group about how fairness connects with universal human rights. • What rights do all humans have? • Does everyone really have those rights? Why/Why not? • How can we stand up or speak out for the rights of ourselves and others?	Work in partnerships or small groups to discuss how this intersects with basic human rights. • What is fair/unfair about this? • Is education a human right? • How would not being allowed to go to school impact someone's life? • What would you do to change this?

Sustainable Development Goals

The United Nations (2018) put forward 17 sustainable development goals (SDGs) that support world peace and sustainability in terms of quality of life (and survival). They are important for educators and leaders to understand regarding their connections and links to peace and justice education. They are also an excellent resource for class discussions, group or individual projects.

The 17 United Nations SDGs are not in any specific order of importance. Like the peace actions, they are interconnected. Explore them at https://www.un.org/sustainabledevelopment/

Note: The content of this publication has not been approved by the United Nations and does not reflect the views of the United Nations or its officials or Member States.

Figure 8.2 UN Sustainable Development Goals

In order to address our global problems, we have to face the challenges and injustices throughout the world. The intent is to achieve the SDGs by 2030.

◎ Pause & Reflect:

◆ Review the seventeen goals. Which do you feel most connected to? Concerned about?

Table 8.7 Pursuit: Cause & Effect of Hurts & Harms

Peace Pursuits for: *Be A Responsible Citizen Of The World*	
I reflect and wonder about (system) causes of the hurt and harm that I see in our world. I consider the effect of this on myself, others and the environment. (justice)	• Learn and share ideas about sustainable development goals. Propose creative and peaceful solutions for reaching the SDGs. • Explore different types of harm and hurt in this world through cause-and-effect relationships. • Reflect on how individuals and groups can harm and heal one another. • Utilize restorative practices to heal disagreements and harm inflicted intentionally and unintentionally.

The Earth Charter

The Earth Charter (EC) is a guiding international document that shares 16 principles that *"seek to turn conscience into action"* (2023). This is another tool that can be applied to schools, organizations and businesses that are interested in building a sustainable, just, peaceful, ethical and environmentally conscious environment. You can find more information on their website: https://www.earthcharter.org

The Earth Charter Four Pillars:

- ◆ *Respect & Care for the Community of Life*
- ◆ *Democracy, Nonviolence & Peace*
- ◆ *Ecological Integrity*
- ◆ *Social and Economic Justice*

Like the Five Peace Actions, the EC pillars and UN SDGs are interconnected. As you review Table 8.8, reflect on the connections and intersections with peace and justice education.

Table 8.8 Earth Charter, Sustainable Development Goals & Links to Peace Education

Earth Charter (EC) Pillars & UN Sustainable Development Goals (SDGs)	Links to Peace & Justice Education
	The Five Peace Actions are also interconnected! • *Seek Peace Within Yourself And Others* • *Respect Diversity* • *Protect Our Environment* • *Reach Out In Service* • *Be A Responsible Citizen Of The World*
EC: Democracy, Nonviolence & Peace **SDGs:** • Peace, Justice and Strong Institutions • Quality Education • Gender Equality • Reduced Inequalities	• Education is for life: social emotional learning, being a life-long learner, having a growth mindset, critical thinking and problem-solving and basic academics (literacy, math etc.). • Educators foster relationships, connection, belonging, empathy, caring and well-being for all. • An inclusive, accessible and equitable education for all human rights embraces diversity. • Everyone has the freedom to learn, explore and discover self, knowing that ideas and beliefs may shift and change throughout life. • Identifying harms, injustices and helping reduce inequalities is key to social justice and advocacy efforts. • Violent conflict can be prevented and transformed when justice and peace are prioritized. Processes such as Peace Circles (Lesson p. 259) are crucial.
EC: Social & Economic Justice **SDGs:** • No Poverty • Zero Hunger • Good Health and Well-Being	• Quality education leads to economic and personal empowerment. • Addressing the root causes of poverty fosters conditions that promote social justice and nurture the well-being of all life. • Taking care of self (inner peace) is foundational to well-being. Sufficient, healthy food is essential. • Respecting diversity leads to greater social cohesion and reduces marginalization, which in turn creates more access to economic opportunities and resources. • Countries and regions with historical and current conflict struggle to develop and/or maintain economic infrastructure. Conflict resolution and transformation are key skills for stability.
EC: Respect & Care for the Community of Life **SDGs:** • Industry, Innovation and Infrastructure • Decent Work and Economic Growth	• The foundations for understanding and identifying infrastructure issues begin locally with young learners. • Helping to create and refine solutions for advancing communication and information technologies, clean energy, transportation and irrigation embraces innovation that supports equitable opportunities for all people. • Empowerment to advocate, act and engage civically creates reform and change. • Families' work and economic opportunities impact learner education and well-being and are considerations for educators.

(continued)

Table 8.8 Earth Charter, Sustainable Development Goals & Links to Peace Education (continued)

Earth Charter (EC) Pillars & UN Sustainable Development Goals (SDGs)	Links to Peace & Justice Education

EC: Ecological Integrity
 	
SDGs:
 	
• Climate Action
• Clean Water and Sanitation
• Affordable and Clean Energy
• Sustainable Cities and Communities
• Responsible Consumption and Production
• Life Below Water
• Life On Land
	• All people worldwide are impacted by forms of climate change, and understanding this is crucial to *Protect Our Environment* and all life.
	• 'Green' efforts can be advocated for at school, district and city levels to emphasize affordable, sustainable and clean energy
	• Having a short- and long-term understanding of choices and decisions and how they impact others and our environment is crucial peacelearning.
	   ○ Do I waste food? Water?
	   ○ Can I reduce my energy usage?
	   ○ What happens with garbage and litter?
	   ○ How does plastic usage impact nature and us?
	   ○ How are animals and plants in my region impacted by humans?

EC: Respect & Care for the Community of Life **SDGs:** Partnerships for the Goals	• Creating partnerships with people and organizations that engage in learning and work aligned to UN SDGs and Earth Charter pillars is important. • Partnering on projects with other peacelearners locally and/or globally through the use of technologies deepens understanding.

◎ **Pause & Reflect:**

◆ As you consider Table 8.8, what resonates?

◆ What is your hope for global issues? Think about what you are passionate about in your own community.

◆ Choose one interconnected goal area and set an intention: How can you be an advocate for justice in your community and the world? How will you empower learners in taking peace action in this area as well?

Table 8.9 Practice: Sustainable Development Goals

Put It Into Practice: Sustainable Development Goals (SDGs)		
The SDGs set forth by the United Nations align with the Five Peace Actions and provide excellent topics for students to explore, research and make links to in their community. • What are connections and needs in your community? • If you could speak to the current United Nations leadership, what would you say?		
Emerging	*Intermediate*	*Advanced*
Review the SDGs and determine an area of interest for your class. Example: #15. Life on Land #14: Life Below Water Prompt learners to identify life on land and below the water. Why are they important? Read a mentor text about land or sea animals local to your community. Highlight threatened or endangered species. For example, in Minnesota (U.S.), moose are native and used to thrive in the state but are now listed as a species of special concern. Questions to consider: • Why are they in danger? • How have people put them at risk? • How can we help this species and *Protect Our Environment*?	Review the SDGs and determine an area of interest. Discuss what global issue(s) is important to the class and community. Read and discuss connected mentor texts. Assign pairs/small groups to each of the 17 SDGs and guide learners in generating questions and researching examples of people or organizations taking peace action in alignment with the SDG. Create a one-pager or visual poster of findings. (See Chapter 4, p. 95 for jigsaw collaborative structure.) Example: #4: Quality Education #5: Gender Equality • Read about Pakistani peace activist Malala Yousafzai, who continues to stand up for gender equality in education. **Questions to consider:** • Why is it important for all children to have equal access to education? • Does our school provide a quality education? • Are there still countries where girls/women have limited access to education? • Is there equality in access to sports, academic clubs and extracurricular activities for all genders? • How does this connect with the Five Peace Actions?	

UNESCO

Founded to prevent another World War and to create cultures of peace, the United Nations Educational, Scientific and Cultural Organization (UNESCO, 1945) continues to focus on *"peace and security by promoting international cooperation in education, sciences, culture, communication and information."* Throughout the world there are threats and challenges being made against freedom of expression, science and diversity, which makes UNESCO's vision and work of the utmost importance.

In 2023, UNESCO and its 194 member states updated their 1974 recommendations about peace education and education for international understanding, cooperation, human rights and fundamental freedoms. Areas of emphasis fully align with the Five Peace Actions and can be utilized by all education stakeholders and we suggest the document be reviewed in its entirety as part of implementation. Here are a few example recommendations:

◆ Ensure health and well-being (physical, mental, social, emotional).
◆ The SDGs in lessons and learning (glocalized).
◆ Empathy, critical thinking, fostering resilience, environmental stewardship and intercultural understandings are crucial focuses and competencies.
◆ Utilizing and creating technologies for good; media and information literacy.
◆ Promotion of cultures of peace and nonviolence; youth play important roles in peacekeeping and peacebuilding.
◆ Appreciating and embracing diversity; inclusivity.
◆ Place-based learning; natural, cultural and outside learning sites.
◆ Professional learning and collaboration to update, re-design and enhance curriculum and resources to align with human rights, peace and justice education.
◆ More at: https://unesdoc.unesco.org/ark:/48223/pf0000386924. locale=en

Peace and justice education empowers educators, families and children. *Be A Responsible Citizen Of The World* is a culminating peace action and draws on the rich multicultural foundation built through a well-rounded peace and justice education curriculum.

Honor & Celebrate All Life

Honoring and celebrating life is important to *Be A Responsible Citizen Of The World*. As we affirm and celebrate humankind, the environment and the world, opportunity and hope are fostered. Being able to find joy in life, promoting and honoring cultures and various forms of life on Earth are empowering. As discussed in Chapter 6, in Indigenous cultures, there is a beautiful way of celebrating *"we are all related,"* which means all life forms. This includes humans, animals, plants, mountains, soil, water and all of the interconnected beings on our planet.

Table 8.10 Pursuit: Celebrate Life

Peace Pursuits for: *Be A Responsible Citizen Of The World*	
I celebrate life (mine, others, environment).	• Explore all of the forms of life and celebrate how life is interconnected. • Find ways to foster a sense of care and belonging with socially isolated and socially stressed people locally. • Research and learn about people and life throughout the world. • Use technology to connect with the world, including other peacelearners; celebrate your similarities and differences. • Discuss: Who needs help? How will you advocate? What actions can you take?

For the most part, *'we'* all have the freedom to decide when, how and to what extent to engage with various groups and communities. This autonomy is flexible, and adaptable, inviting growth, not perfection. Peaceful communication and democratically co-created brave spaces (Chapter 4, p. 81) can help address concerns about balancing individuality and collective identity. As more and more shifts to *'we'* occur, it becomes possible for open wounds to heal, resulting in reductions in harm, aggression and violence. Our communities can be woven, repaired and, as a result, transformed. World citizenship calls for people to come together to be heard, valued and honored, which in return provides an opening for us to come together to develop solutions for our global problems.

We stand with and for humanity. We believe that all life has basic rights and deserves to live in dignity and peace. **If we want to end violence and live in a world with sustainable, just and positive peace, then we need peace education to be an integral part of all schools and communities**.

We believe deeply that peace education is for everyone, at every age and stage of life. Its success requires all of us to take action – as individuals and collective communities. This can be accomplished by embracing a *'we'* mentality and taking peace action to *Be A Responsible Citizen Of The World.*

More Peaceful Practices: *Be A Responsible Citizen Of The World*

Family & Community Connections

- ◆ Create a shared definition of characteristics of learners being a responsible world citizen.
- ◆ Provide opportunities for families to share their experiences, perspectives and ideas about global citizenship, individualism vs collectivism and the SDGs.
- ◆ Foster cultural exchanges, sharing, presentations and demonstrations.
- ◆ Host community organizing and cultural events that celebrate peace and global citizenship (e.g. march, parade, showcase)

Table 8.11 Content Area Connections: *Be A Responsible Citizen Of The World*

Content Area Connections			
Art	**Math**	**Music**	**P.E**
Share artists and works that highlight the intersection of art and social justice across the world. Connect to how art is a form of storytelling and helps deepen understanding of what is happening globally. Guide learners in creating an art piece that promotes positive change and/or demonstrates a key characteristic needed to *Be A Responsible Citizen Of The World.*	Model and practice reading and analyzing data and statistics from graphs and tables related to global issues. As learners answer basic questions about graphs, develop and discuss predictions and inferences.	Explore music from around the world. Identify and chart characteristics, similarities and differences. • Traditional songs • Instruments • Rhythms • Themes • Purposes	Share about international sporting events like the Olympics. Highlight how the Special Olympics invites more inclusivity of all people. Setup games inspired by the Olympics, perhaps in a station model. This could be a community field day, too!

References

American Montessori Society, & Allen, A. (n.d.). *AMS peace & social justice fund*. Amshq.org. Retrieved January 3, 2024, from https://amshq.org/About-AMS/Donate/AMS-Peace-and-Social-Justice-Fund

Belfi, E., & Sandiford, N. (2021). Decolonization series part 1: Exploring decolonization. In S. Brandauer & E. Hartman (Eds.), *Interdependence: Global solidarity and local actions*. The Community-based Global Learning Collaborative. Retrieved from: https://www.cbglcollab.org/what-is-decolonization-why-is-it-important

Earth Charter International. (2023). *Turning conscience into action*. Earthcharter.org. https://www.earthcharter.org

Hailey, J. (2008). *Ubuntu: A literature review*. Document. Tutu Foundation.

Hammond, Z. (2015). *Culturally responsive teaching and the brain: Promoting authentic engagement and rigor among culturally and linguistically diverse students*. Corwin/Sage.

Harris, I. M., & Morrison, M. L. (2013). *Peace education* (3rd ed.). McFarland & Company, Inc. Publishers.

Keys, D. (1982). *Earth at omega: Passage to planetization*: In *The politics of consciousness*. Branden Books.

Montessori, M. (1972). *Education and peace*. Henry Regnery Company.

Tuck, E., & Yang, K. W. (2012). *Decolonization is not a metaphor* (Vol. 1, No. 1). Decolonization. Indigeneity, Education & Society. https://jps.library.utoronto.ca/index.php/des/article/view/18630

UNESCO. (1945). *UNESCO in brief*. Unesco.org. Retrieved January 3, 2024, from https://www.unesco.org/en/brief

UNESCO. (2023). *Draft revised 1974 recommendation concerning education for international understanding, cooperation and peace and education relating to human rights and fundamental freedoms*. https://unesdoc.unesco.org/ark:/48223/pf0000386924.locale=en

United Nations. (1948). *Universal declaration of human rights*. https://www.un.org/en/about-us/universal-declaration-of-human-rights

United Nations. (2018, May 17). *Take action for the sustainable development goals*. United Nations Sustainable Development; United Nations: Sustainable Development Goals. https://www.un.org/sustainabledevelopment/sustainable-development-goals/

Waziyatawin, & Bird, M. Y. (Eds.). (2012). *For Indigenous minds only: A decolonization handbook*. SAR Press.

9

Becoming Trauma Informed
Best Practices for Peace Guides, Educators & Leaders

I consider it an important quality or virtue to understand the impossible separation of teaching and learning. Teachers should be conscious every day that they are coming to school to learn and not just to teach. This way we are not just teachers, but teacher learners. It is really impossible to teach without learning as well as learning without teaching.
~ Paulo Freire

A peace educator (guide, leader) understands their role as a teacher in children's lives. Yet, as educational leader Freire (1985) shared, we are not only teachers but *"teacher learners."* There is so much we can learn from and with children. Exemplify democratic principles by co-creating an environment that eliminates hierarchy and power dynamics between adults and children. Through connection and care, foster the many gifts within children and grow their sense of hope.

Encourage all children to explore, wonder, imagine, question and embrace life! Empathetic, caring and reciprocal relationships are crucial. As feminist educator, Nell Noddings (2005), emphasized, *"to care and be cared for are fundamental human needs"* (p. xi). Dedicate yourself to teaching and learning grounded in care. Resist judgments and give grace to mistakes and growth areas. Focus on cultivating appreciation for our interconnected world, enhancing harmony and deepening self-awareness and joy. In partnership with children, learn and teach about the Five Peace Actions. This process

DOI: 10.4324/9781003449249-10

deepens individual and collective sense of self, purpose, connection and compassion.

◎ **Pause & Reflect**: Reread the Paulo Freire quote that opened this chapter.

- ◆ What professional learning has most impacted your teaching?
- ◆ How have the children been your teachers?
- ◆ What peacelearning are you most interested in deepening?

In This Chapter:

First, you may benefit from reviewing the trauma terminology table in Chapter 2, p. 34–36 to refresh on the forms of trauma, meanings of being trauma aware, sensitive/responsive and informed and connections with peacelearning.

See Appendix E, p. 290 for a table summarizing culturally relevant and trauma aware/sensitive strategies and best practices to support your peace-learning implementation.

Becoming Trauma Informed

Becoming trauma informed begins with foundational awareness of the prevalence and manifestations of various forms of trauma. According to The Substance Abuse and Mental Health Services Administration (SAMHSA, 2023), *"more than two thirds of children reported at least one traumatic event by age 16."* And that is just what is reported! Trauma is stored in the non-verbal part of the brain, so it can be challenging to identify or talk about, especially for children. We are unlikely to know the exact events or prevalence of trauma experienced by children in our schools. By universally implementing this peace action framework and practices, built upon trauma aware, sensitive and informed approaches, we can provide the care all children deserve. Chicano/a scholars, Jaime-Diaz and Méndez-Negrete (2021), offered this guidance for teacher education:

> For a trauma informed care approach, educators must gauge the complicated ways that traumatic experiences may be affecting the lives of students. Trauma is not a noticeable or fixed entity, but vast and fluid in definition; it is attributed to being upset or in distress, such that experiences result in trauma related symptoms.

Experiences or events that are distressing, emotionally painful and overwhelm a person's capacity to cope leave us with trauma. Indeed, this is complicated, vast and fluid. A traumatized person may regularly be in an activated or alarmed state even without a specific trigger being present. When stress is prolonged, extreme and unpredictable our systems become sensitized. Chronic or toxic stress can create an overly reactive system, which looks and feels like trauma. Communities that have endured histories of racism, colonization, enslavement, discrimination and biases may manifest symptoms of historical trauma or historical trauma response (Brave Heart et al., 2007). Additionally, intergenerational or multigenerational trauma is passed down, which keeps many children in survival mode and in need of supportive, healing tools and spaces. How trauma impacts us is related to the 3Es: event, experience and effects.

> Individual trauma results from an **event**, series of events or set of circumstances that is **experienced** by an individual as physically or emotionally harmful or life threatening and that has lasting adverse **effects** on the individual's function and mental, physical, social, emotional and spiritual well-being.
>
> (SAMHSA, 2014, p. 7)

Trauma is not only what happened to us, but what happens within us because of such experiences.

Keep in mind that when adverse childhood experiences (ACEs), neglect, toxic stress or other forms of trauma occur as a baby and/or in early childhood there is an even more significant impact on our later physical, social and mental development (Centers for Disease Control and Prevention, 2022).

◎ **Pause & Reflect:**

- ◆ Without going into specific detail or reliving an experience, consider how trauma, in its varied forms, has impacted you and your family/friends.
- ◆ How have you seen trauma show up in your students? School community? (Often, we don't know much of the specific history, but being compassionate and empathetic is crucial.)

Regulate – Relate – Reason

Psychiatrist, teacher and researcher, Dr. Bruce Perry, has been instrumental in deepening understandings of the effects of ACEs and trauma in children, adolescents and adults. Dr. Perry's Neurosequential Model of Education (NME) examines the behavioral, emotional, social, physiological and cognitive effects of neglect and trauma on the brain and provides a neurobiologically and developmentally sensitive approach (Child Trauma Academy, Featuring Dr. Bruce D. Perry, 2004, 2008). Notably, the brain's sequence of engagement and processing is easily remembered as the *3Rs: Regulate, Relate, Reason* (Perry, 2008, 2020 and Perry & Winfrey, 2021). This is the flowing process of the brain that is necessary for a child (and any person) to engage deeply in teaching and learning.

Author's Perspective

Having been trained in this approach, I (Julie) find aspects of Dr. Perry's *Neurosequential Model of Education* and the 3Rs: *Regulate, Relate, Reason* provide foundational understandings necessary for pursuing peace within all levels of humanity.

Being a comprehensively trauma informed site is an ongoing process responsive to the needs of the community. It includes ongoing collaboration, training, coaching, support, self and collective care. It is far more than we can cover in the context of this book, though note that our professional learning offerings include creating trauma informed peacelearning communities.

This peacelearning framework and lessons are designed to support regulation through the implementation of calming and peaceful strategies and democratically co-created brave and supportive spaces. **When the body and mind are in a regulated and calm state, the person feels supported and safe through relationships and the environment, then they**

can reason. Reasoning means one can reflect, remember, articulate, analyze and synthesize – or simply being 'ready to learn' or 'ready to process.' Our goal is for educators to provide culturally relevant and trauma informed care based on learners' development, needs, strengths and their unique backgrounds.

Our Sequential Brain

There are many possible reactions to trauma. Energy from trauma becomes trapped in our bodies and if not discharged in a healthy manner, it will wreak havoc with our minds, bodies and spirits. Understanding the basic development of the brain is important because our brain state impacts:

- ◆ Automatic reactions
- ◆ Behavior
- ◆ Responses
- ◆ Comprehension
- ◆ Communication
- ◆ Connection
- ◆ Processing
- ◆ Learning

Our interconnected brain essentially develops from the bottom up. As you see in Figure 9.1, part of the hindbrain, our brainstem takes in sensorial input internally and from our external environment. This area also helps coordinate basic regulations like our breathing, heart rhythm, swallowing and sense of balance. The midbrain and interbrain include the diencephalon. This is our relay and processing center of sensory information (arousal, movement) and autonomic nervous system control (sleep, appetite, body temperature) parts of the brain. Connecting into our limbic system, this is where our emotions, sense of connection, memory, behavioral and motivation responses occur. For example, the amygdala is constantly evaluating what is safe and unsafe or dangerous, therefore highly connected with the emotion of fear. Also part of the limbic system, the hippocampus can shrink in response to trauma, impacting memory and learning storage. A key point is all our brain and body input goes through the emotional parts of our brain before reaching the rational forebrain. The cortex holds our capacity for creative thinking, language, reflection, reasoning and learning. This rational and reasoning part of our brain is essentially the last to know and/or be accessed.

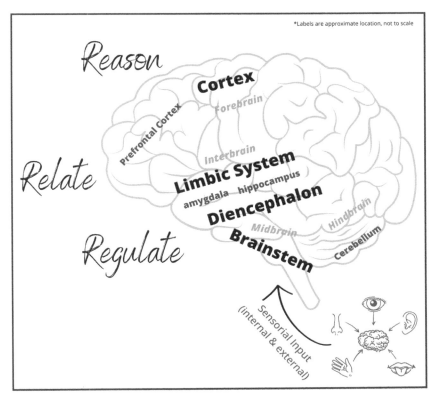

Figure 9.1 Brain Structures & Parts
Adapted from: What Happened to You? (p. 143) (Dr. Perry & Winfrey, 2021).

◎ **Pause & Reflect:**

◆ As you review the basic brain structure and parts (Figure 9.1), describe how this connects with the sequence of engagement (regulate, relate, reason)?

The Nervous System: Reactions & Responses

Our autonomic nervous system regulates many body processes and is divided into two major functions, the sympathetic and parasympathetic. The parasympathetic nervous system is our state of maintaining homeostasis, our 'rest and digest.' This is when we usually have a lower heart rate and our muscles are relaxed. Conversely, our sympathetic nervous system prepares the body for any potential damage, which is associated with an increased heartbeat, perspiration and tensed muscles. Toxic stress, trauma, post-traumatic stress disorder and feelings of powerlessness, fear and danger (perceived or actual) typically activate our sympathetic nervous system. The sympathetic nervous system can become sensitized so that even when the person is technically safe, their inner world does not feel at ease and is instead overactivated.

As our physiological state changes, so does our capacity for regulation, relating and reasoning. Dr. Perry and Szalavitz (2006) and Dr. Perry and Winfrey (2021), outlined a continuum of five internal states that we shift between depending on internal and external input and our trauma histories. These states are:

1. *Calm*
2. *Alert*
3. *Alarm*
4. *Fear*
5. *Terror*

These arousal states correlate with our sense of time, behavior, regulating brain regions and cognition. Basically, as a person moves across the continuum toward terror, their cognition and functional IQ lower because they have less access to the cortex of the brain (see Figure 9.2). For example, a child continually in an alarm state can appear to function pretty well or have 'street smarts,' but they are likely to be more challenged academically. In the higher arousal states, academic learning and reasoning are more difficult, sometimes even inaccessible.

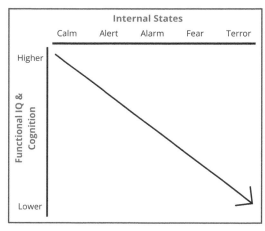

Figure 9.2 Correlation of Physiological States With Functional IQ & Cognition

Adapted from: What Happened to You? (p. 90–91) (Dr. Perry & Winfrey, 2021).

Dissociation, our capacity to disengage from our external world and bring ourselves inward, also corresponds with this continuum of internal states (see Figure 9.3). Many ways we self-regulate are actually adaptive dissociation. For example, most healthy humans 'zone out' from time to time. When we get bored, lost in a book, absorbed in a creative project or tuned into a video game or TV, we are at the initial stage of the dissociation continuum, which is adaptive. The very nature of learning is to tune in and out, so there will be many moments when kids will not be listening to you teach. Same goes with adults, even in an engaging conversation we shift from actively listening to reflecting internally.

◎ Pause & Reflect:

◆ Think about your academic instructional blocks and your lessons.
◆ Considering there is a lot of natural dissociation occurring, what changes or strategies might you implement for more engaged learning? (Hint: revisit cooperative learning Chapter 4, p. 93.)

If there is a threat (perceived or actual), we become more alert and move out of adaptive and into a moderate level of dissociation. If unable to avoid the threat, the internal state becomes more alarmed. If the threat continues, in the fear state we fully dissociate, meaning we are 'gone' or disconnected from the outer world and much of the inner world. At the most significant level of dissociation, we can be completely detached from the body and/or the body shuts down (see freeze, fawn, flop/ faint in Table 9.1).

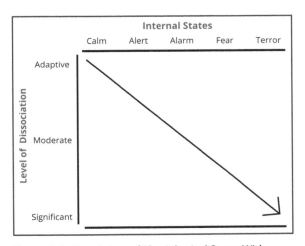

Figure 9.3 Correlation of Physiological States With Level of Disassociation

Adapted from: What Happened to You? (p. 90–91) (Dr. Perry & Winfrey, 2021).

Let's look closer at these automatic reactions in higher states of arousal (fear, terror) and some of the manifesting behaviors. Keep in mind that adaptive responses can take place simultaneously, especially with complex trauma. We can shift from different states, reactions and responses very quickly.

Table 9.1 Sympathetic Nervous System: Automatic Reactions & Adaptive Responses

Sympathetic Nervous System: Automatic Reactions & Adaptive Responses		
Type	**Description**	**Behaviors**
Fight	High energy readiness to confront or combat; anger, rage, assertiveness, defensive	• Talking back • Defiance • Blaming others • Aggression (self, others) • "It's _'s fault!"
Flight	Stamina energy to flee, escape or remove oneself; survival action	• Running away, missing class • Overwhelmed and anxious • "I need to get out of here!"
Freeze	Tension energy, decreased response and overwhelm; when the body feels fight or flight aren't an option; hide, stuck in place or remain unnoticed	• Spaced out, not seeming to listen • Panicked overwhelm • "I give up." • "I can't."
Flop/Faint	Similar to freezing, except muscles are loose, body goes floppy to reduce pain; may actually lose consciousness (faint) or to 'play dead'	• Appear disengaged, apathetic, hopeless or depressed • Collapsed • "__ (silence)"
Fawn	Covering up the distress or damage; a common reaction to child abuse	• Appease, be helpful, agreeable • Please the threatening person or situation • "Whatever you want."
Flock or Friend	Seeking comfort and support from others; often low confidence, helplessness or powerlessness; allows us to access co-regulators!	• Reliance on others • Placating, pleading or negotiating • "Please, help me!"

In general, we all experience these various states of arousal and automatic stress reactions and adaptive responses. Ideally our nervous system allows for a pretty quick recovery and resumed regulation after the stress or danger has passed. This usually happens when we are connected with our own resilience, have regulation strategies and/or support from others. However, for someone who has experienced trauma, this dysregulation can take a long time to settle or deactivate. When triggered and/or the system becomes sensitized a person can be stuck in overly active and reactive states of arousal. Access to the cortex is essentially shut down when the brain is (or thinks it is) under threat.

Developmental Considerations

Educators understand that brain development in infancy and early childhood provides the foundations for future development, regulation, relating and learning. When developmental trauma occurs during this time, the brain's neural pathways are prioritized to respond to the trauma and its attention is focused on survival. **This is why developmental considerations and approaches to relating and learning are so crucial – trauma and toxic stress literally change the brain and body.**

Put It Into Practice: Trauma 3Es & Developmental Stage

Uncover some details related to the 3Es to narrow in the developmental stage of the learner:

> ➤ **Event:** How old was the child when the traumatic event(s) occurred?
> ➤ **Experience:** What was the type and duration of the experience(s)?
> ➤ **Effect:** What are the known effects on the child's well-being (mental, physical, social, emotional spiritual)?

Awareness of a child's history helps bridge understanding to their current stage and level of functioning.

◎ **Pause & Reflect:**

- ◆ Think about a child whose development has been impacted by trauma. Considering the 3Es, what developmental stage is this child likely in?
- ◆ How does this compare to their chronological age and what is expected of them socially, emotionally and academically in their assigned grade level?

As a result of brain changes, an individual's worldview is impacted. For example, a child who has *not* experienced significant trauma or adverse experiences may view their world as predictable and safe. Alternatively, a child with developmental trauma may feel unsafe, afraid and that no one will help them. These children could be sitting right next to each other in your learning space and be having an entirely different experience. Their behaviors can be misinterpreted, as the underlying distress may be hidden.

The negative impact of ACEs and trauma on the brain can be changed, but that doesn't mean that the impacts aren't long-lasting, especially for the developing child. In their book *What Happened to You* (2021), Dr. Perry and

Oprah Winfrey emphasized that for the most part, it is impossible to go back to the self that existed prior to the traumatic event(s), including our biology and gene expression.

> *Trauma will change everyone, in some way. And these changes will be there, even if they don't result in any apparent real life problems for the person. Even if the person demonstrates resilience. A child may continue to do just as well in school, for example, but it may take much more energy and effort. Or we may find that a child is able to return to his previous level of emotional functioning, but changes in his neuro-endocrine system may make him more likely to develop diabetes. (p. 191)*

Although trauma does change a person, there is hope and healing is very possible. Becoming trauma informed means that we understand the impact trauma has on the brain and body, and are sensitive and responsive to the developmental stage learners are actually in as a result. Creating new neural pathways in the brain happens through repetition that is registered as safe and familiar. From one generation to the next and with compassion, empathy and love, we can heal and create more peace-filled people, environments and systems.

Regulate & Co-Regulate

Now that you have a foundational understanding of the neurosequential brain, states of arousal and nervous system reactions to various forms of stress and trauma, let's go deeper into the first in the sequence of engagement: regulate. When we are regulated, there is a sense of calm and a feeling of psychological safety. If dysregulated, we are in a heightened state of arousal and/or a stress response is activated. Dysregulation is the enemy of processing and learning (reasoning) because in this state, functioning is primarily in the hindbrain. To optimally pass information to the midbrain and then on to the cortex, we need to be regulated. Regulation is also the state in which healing can happen.

Our goal as peace guides is to support learners to be in calm and alert states as much as possible. However, for some learners with complex trauma, the goal may be supporting them to move from terror and fear to be more in alarm. Regardless, for us to support the regulation of another person, we must be regulated.

If you are dysregulated, you cannot co-regulate, instead you will co-dysregulate! Similarly, if you are dysregulated, you can then dysregulate a student who had previously been regulated! *Seek Peace Within Yourself* and prioritize your well-being and needs so that you can bring the best version of yourself to those in your care.

◎ Pause & Reflect:

- ◆ Reflect on people you've interacted with today, as well as your own internal states.
- ◆ As you identify the primary state, (calm, alert, alarm, fear and terror), consider what behaviors and signs were observable.

If someone is in a fear or terror state, and/or reacting with fight or flight, the first step in supporting regulation is to de-escalate. When someone is in crisis, exhibiting a stress response or there are warning signs (such as sudden and extreme changes in mood, agitation, refusals, trouble with usual tasks, isolating behaviors), there are many techniques that can be used to reduce the intensity and support regulation.

Put It Into Practice: De-Escalation Techniques

- ➤ Be patient, take time to mindfully decide your response unless there is an immediate risk of harm.
- ➤ Speak minimally, slowly, calmly and with respect (more on this in the next section).
- ➤ Give the child space and time to recover, make sure you both can move.
- ➤ Only use eye contact if welcomed.
- ➤ Share/show a possible distraction.
- ➤ Do not touch without permission. (Though for some light touch or even weighted blankets can be soothing.)
- ➤ Instead of trying to take control, offer two to three options or choices of what they can do.
- ➤ Model regulation strategies and invite them to join (e.g., breathing, movement, drumming).
- ➤ Don't try to reason – they aren't accessing that part of the brain right now!
- ➤ Only once regulated (recovered) ~20+ minutes after, engage in debriefing conversations. Listen, acknowledge their feelings and co-develop strategies for handling similar situations in the future.

Heightened states of arousal can vary in their observable presentation. For example, a child trying to connect with someone, talking or distracting oneself by joking or playing around may actually be a coping strategy!

Similarly, behaviors like stimming, rocking, doodling, fidgeting and tapping are likely attempts to regulate. Consider that these self-regulation attempts are often perceived as disruptive or maladaptive and are associated with diagnoses like Attention Deficit Hyperactivity Disorder (ADHD) and Oppositional Defiant Disorder (ODD). Remember, the more dysregulated, the less the cortex (learning brain) is available.

◎ **Pause & Reflect:** Wonder about how many kids with special and exceptional education labels and diagnoses are dysregulated and in heightened states of arousal due to trauma.

There is a great deal of evidence that points to significant disproportionality in special education representation for children of the global majority, particularly Black and Hispanic students from low-income backgrounds (National Center for Learning Disabilities, 2020). This same disparate trend exists for disciplinary measures like referrals, suspensions and expulsions, which correlate with an increased risk of future incarceration (the school-to-prison pipeline). ACEs and trauma, much extending from historical and current structural oppression and systemic racism have many consequences – trauma and resulting dysregulation being big factors!

Imagine a child who experienced stretches of neglect as a baby. Their primary caregiver, impacted by generational trauma, struggled to maintain safe and stable housing. As an incoming kindergartener, this child is at the developmental stage of a three-year-old due to several ACEs. The demands and expectations of kindergarten are overwhelming and unrealistic for this hypervigilant and dysregulated child. Attempting to self-regulate, they hum and tap on the tables, which usually results in negative interactions with the teacher or other classmates. On top of that, the shoes a classroom associate educator (AE) frequently wears remind the child of a traumatic memory from when they were in a shelter. Every time this AE approaches, the child reacts aggressively, once even throwing a pair of scissors at the AE. Three months into kindergarten, the child has been sent home and suspended several times and their primary caregiver is exhausted and 'not sure what to do.' The under-resourced school does what it can to arrange interventions and support with their single social worker for 600 students. Still at the developmental stage nearer that of a three-year-old and only intermittently regulated, this child isn't getting the benefit of the standard grade level social emotional learning or academic curriculum. Each year, socially promoted, they get further and further behind and receive frequent behavioral referrals. As the academic content increases, the social emotional and regulation supports decrease. The child has low self-esteem, feels like they are dumb, that something is wrong with them and shuts down easily. As they advance more grades, aggressive behaviors continue, resulting in more negative interactions, including with the school resource officer and more suspensions. Eventually, they give up, stop coming to school and move through the final stages of the school-to-prison pipeline.

Scenarios like this continue to play out across our schools. We must do things differently if we are going to get different results. How do we break the cycle?

Prioritize developmentally sensitive peacelearning (actions and pursuits), culturally relevant pedagogy and trauma informed care!

◎ **Pause & Reflect**: Think about your students. How many start their day regulated and 'ready to learn?'

◆ For those who are not 'ready to learn,' consider their stage of development and their state of arousal. How can you support their regulation before anything else?

◆ What are you (school) already doing or providing that generally supports learners' regulation? Is this effective for all students?

Put It Into Practice: Soothing Environment

When we calm the brain, we also calm the behavior, so creating a warm and predictable physical environment is important. Advocating for and implementing these recommendations is another way to *Protect Our Environment*!

➤ Clear routines and expectations (modeled, practiced, retaught)
➤ Predictable structures and previewing schedules (including visuals)
➤ Taking intentional breaks (beyond transitions)
➤ Relationally focused: support is in alignment with guidance for *Seek Peace With Others* and *Respect Diversity*
➤ Soft lighting, windows, natural light
➤ Flexible, comfortable and adaptable kid-size furniture
➤ Regular access to safe green/nature space, play areas and kitchen
➤ Spaces and time for quiet, decompression, breaks and processing (inside and outside)
➤ Limited sensory input (e.g., minimal wall hangings, posters)
➤ Natural highlights such as plants; perhaps animal(s)
➤ Space for comfortably circling together

In addition to a soothing environment, it is important to explicitly teach and guide learners in a variety of regulation strategies. Generally, practice regulation strategies even when learners are regulated, so that these tools can be more easily accessed during stress and heightened states! Be aware that when engaging in *Seek Peace Within* practices, blocked personal and/or collective trauma can be dislodged and released. This may appear as increased dysregulation or moving into heightened states of arousal. Go slowly and regulate first, which then allows for (re)connection. **That which regulates, also heals.**

Put It Into Practice: Regulation

➤ Patterned (structured) rhythmic movement, music or activity. Examples are rocking, dancing, yoga, walking, kicking a ball back and forth, preparing food, cooking, baking, art, hand-clapping games, breathwork and drumming.
➤ Go back to practices from Chapter 3: *Seek Peace Within Yourself!*
➤ Coach learners to be aware of what is happening in their body and notice when their nervous system is aroused.
➤ Predictable interactions are important. Be in tune with non-verbal cues (facial expression, tone of voice, body movements).

Relate: Embodying Equanimity

Fire can warm or consume, water can quench or drown, wind can caress or cut. And so it is with human relationship, we both create and destroy, nurture and terrorize, traumatize and heal each other.
~ Dr. Bruce Perry and Maia Szalavitz (2006)

Another example of the *'both/and,'* in the duality of human nature, we can *both* benefit *and* harm one another. Building healthy, supportive, consistent and safe relationships challenges the trauma template existing within a student and assists in healing. Co-creating spaces to reduce and manage the power differential between adults and students is one key nurturing aspect. As is neutral and supportive non-verbal and verbal communication.

For decades, the clear, calm and kind communication and actions of educators have been cited by researchers, theorists and students as keys in positive relationships and a general sense of belonging and well-being in schools (Hulburt et al., 2020 and Jennings & Greenberg, 2009).

It is also foundational for trauma informed care. Hulbert and colleagues (2020), highlighted the immense value in *"teachers who are calm in body in challenging situations, clear in mind when making decisions in complex classroom environments, and kind in approach to interactions with others."* This peaceful and patient way of being is (further) developed by embodying the peace actions and living mindfully with empathy and compassion.

Cultivating a greater sense of equanimity is a skill that is developed with consistent practices such as mindfulness, breath, meditation, self-reflection and self-care. Embodying this calm and balanced mental-emotional state of being equanimous is a process! There will be ups and downs, ebbs and flows.

Put It Into Practice: Embody Equanimity

These best practices will support you (and learners) in the process of embodying equanimity:

- Engage in meditation, breathwork, mindful movement and/or other stress-management practices every day.
- Deepen your self-awareness through processes such as those lessons outlined in Chapter 3: *Seek Peace Within Yourself.*
- Be patient and extend yourself compassion and grace, just as you would do when supporting a loved one.
- When stressed or challenged, take a break or pause and breathe to shift from reacting to responding mindfully (see Lesson: PBNA Strategy, p. 250).
- Embrace the power of now – being in the moment with your senses. Be present.
- Put your energy toward what you can influence or control.
- Set healthy boundaries.
- Connect and learn with others on this path (*Seek Peace With Others*); have a strong support network.
- Celebrate progress and reflect on growth.
- Practice gratitude.

◎ Pause & Reflect:

- ◆ Choose one to two practices for embodying equanimity and set intentions for how to deepen this practice in your life and with learners.
- ◆ Have you ever felt like you were doing all the 'right things' with learner interactions and the environment, but a child was behaving in an undesirable or confusing way? Why might that be?

It's important to understand that even if you embody equanimity, you could still trigger someone unintentionally. This is what Dr. Perry (2021), called an evocative cue, "…*basically any sensory input, like a sight, sound, smell, taste or touch can activate a traumatic memory*" (p. 28). For example, imagine you were embodying neutral communication as you model and guide learners in math. As you approach a child new to the class you notice that they recoil away in discomfort. You give a little space and calmly say, "*I'll check back in a minute to see how I can support you*." When you return, you move to their level, approaching side-by-side and gently smile and say, "*I'm here to help*," yet the child responds similarly, this time even more fearfully and moves to the corner of the room and begins pacing. The next few days, similar flight responses occur every time you are near the child. You feel you're doing all the right 'moves' and so wonder, "*what's wrong with them?*"

Even though you're embodying equanimity and compassionate care, there is a signal within the child that they are unsafe. The evocative cue could be as simple as the smell of your shampoo, the timbre of your voice or the sight of the ring you always wear. If this child (knowingly or unknowingly) associates some sensory input from you with a traumatic memory, it filters through the brainstem, the first step of the sequence of engagement, dysregulates them and initiates a stress response. In this dysregulated, survival state, they are not able to process the communication (words) or be 'ready to learn.'

Generally, stress responses are activated when we don't feel safe. Triggers can also happen in power dynamics, which is another reason we emphasize co-creating brave, democratic spaces. For example, if learners of the global majority have a White teacher, there may be some association or categorization (overt or implicit) based on historical trauma that leads to the White teacher prompting a stress response, dysregulation or a feeling of being threatened. The teacher may be feeling that the child was reactive, disrespectful or defiant for "*no reason at all*"! However, when learners experience predictable, positive and nurturing relationships and a sense of belonging, this can reduce or change the association and create new patterns.

These scenarios remind us of the importance of not taking the behavior of others so personally (it may not have anything to do with you directly). This can be difficult sometimes, but rarely do we know a person's history and experiences. As we navigate interactions, relationships and learning, be mindful of your language, which informs perception and action. Trauma informed expert and psychiatrist Dr. Sandra L. Bloom (1995), offered this wisdom in creating a sanctuary in school:

> *The goal of this educational change is to deliberately shift attitudes, to move the fundamental question that we pose when we confront a troubled or troubling person from "What's wrong with you?" to "What's happened to you?", and "How can we help?" (p. 9)*

Through this discovery process ("*What happened, how can we help?*"), perhaps the evocative cue can be reduced or eliminated, and the child guided on a path to healing in alignment with their stage of development. It is always important to communicate and interact with learners through an empathetic stance. Even and especially when the behavior is challenging and difficult, the outcomes for the child and our experience are always better when we center compassion. It's easier to have patience and respond with grace when we focus on preventing retraumatization, supporting regulation and connecting with care.

Put It Into Practice: Relate

➣ Be regulated and model emotional and self-awareness. Regulate, then relate!
➣ Build relationships and create a sense of belonging (see Chapter 4).
➣ Hold high expectations that are firm, but also flexible.
➣ Try to have predictable interactions.
➣ Respond to student needs, concerns and behaviors privately. Address them with low-key, calm and lower-level volume.
➣ Validate feelings, and respond with curiosity and not judgment.
➣ Offer gentle observations and ask directly how you can help.
➣ Co-establish auditory, visual or sensory cues to meet the child's needs.
➣ Create ample opportunity for each child to develop connected and meaningful relationships with classmates, other children and adults. Allow them to have as much control as possible in relational opportunities.
➣ Model, explicitly teach and reinforce methods for resolving conflicts (see Peace Circles Lesson, p. 259)
➣ Honor that children already have the internal instructions for peace and help them to understand, deepen and embody this through engaging in the peace actions and pursuits.

Reasoning & Neurodiversity

When we are regulated and feel connected, we can fully access reasoning. Our cortex is the logical and rational thinking brain, where our ability to draw conclusions from evidence and to make decisions happens. Our intellect (which we are referring to generally as reasoning), includes our cognitive abilities to think creatively, abstractly and critically, to problem solve, reflect, analyze, evaluate, ask questions, clarify understandings, synthesize and engage in new learning. These are the cornerstones of academic learning and problem-solving! Once regulated and relationally connected, the aftereffects of the trauma can be processed, released and healed.

We challenge the assertion that there is a 'normal' or 'right' mind or brain. If a person is considered neurotypical, this indicates functioning (sociability, learning, mood, attention) that the dominant society and standards label as 'normal.' However, in reality everyone is within the spectrum of neurodiversity. One of the many beautiful biological truths in our human experience is that we all have a unique way of processing information. When we *Respect Diversity* this includes neurocognitive functioning, as we are a neurodiverse species! It is crucial that we offer multiple strategies, modalities and paths to learning and demonstrating understanding that honors the neurodiversity of all of our students.

Just as we all have a unique way of processing information, so do we have varied responses to our experiences. What impacts, stresses or traumatizes a person, as well as how they react and respond varies greatly. We all have different sensitivities and vulnerabilities. Adverse childhood experiences, historical and current trauma further impact our capacities to self-regulate, demonstrate resilience and connect. Being trauma sensitive and informed includes understanding that individuals respond differently to stress, stimuli and events such as sensory experiences, communication and social interactions.

◎ **Pause & Reflect**: As you review Table 9.2, consider how you view, think and talk about the neurodiversity and needs of learners. What in your mindset and language can be shifted?

Table 9.2 Practice: Language & Mindset

Put It Into Practice: Language & Mindset	
Instead of this...	**Shift to this...**
Deficit-based language	Asset-based language:
Troubled, disadvantaged, at-risk, vulnerable, dangerous, acting out, out of control, manipulative, defiant, disobedient	*Strengths, efforts, motivation, resourced, skilled, determination, hard-working; exhibiting dysregulation or characteristics of a flight/fight/ freeze response; seeking safety or connection*
Reactive, adversarial or aggressive	Embody equanimity & care
Hollering: *You shouldn't be in the hallway, get into class right now or I'll call the principal to deal with you."*	Approach calmly and offer gentle observations and support: *Are you okay? I'm here to help.*
Labeling learners:	Person-first language with rich descriptions: *Roy does well with his regulation needs when he has structured peer interactions and choices.*
Roy is Tier 3 and EBD (Emotional and Behavioral Disability), so he will have issues on the playground.	
Praising generally on performance and outcome	Positively reinforcing process and progress; encouraging effort
Nice work, that is correct.	*I like how you went back to that problem and tried a different strategy!*
No, this is wrong.	*It was wonderful watching how you worked as a team and supported each other.*
You are a good student.	
This _ is so well done!	*Would you share with me how you created this...*
Making assumptions	Seeking to understand and building on strengths
Student: I don't get it.	*Student: I don't get it.*
Teacher: Just try your best.	*Teacher: Tell me what you do understand... Let's work together to figure it out...*

Our students are sometimes puzzles, but they are not problems. Same goes for families and caregivers. Do not judge situations or reactions of others, but instead respond to the physical, social and emotional challenges they face and offer developmentally sensitive support and guidance to remove barriers to learning. With needs addressed, regulation supported and a calm, strength-based relational approach our students are able to be 'ready to learn,' reason and heal.

Resilience & Healing

We all face challenges, setbacks and adversity. Resilience is our dynamic ability to counter this, recover, to still achieve a successful or positive outcome and heal. Predictable, mild and moderate challenges or stressors foster our ability to demonstrate resilience. Challenges should be within the child's zone of proximal development and/or scaffolded from already mastered skills. Though all humans need to leave their comfort zones to learn, find the line between having just enough challenge and avoiding a sense of overwhelm. Failure and making mistakes are an important part of learning and building resilience, but if it is too far beyond development and skills, it does not promote healthy growth. Moderate and predictable stress is an important part of learning and resilience.

As discussed earlier, the brain and nervous system's reactions to stressors are varied and complex. When stress is repetitive, intense or long-lasting (i.e., toxic stress, trauma), there can be profound and lasting impacts on brain development. **However, all brains and especially that of children, can adapt, change and recover.** This neuroplasticity involves the reorganization of neural connections, the formation of new neuron connections (synapses) and can even change the structure of the brain over time. Repetition is key to growing, creating and changing neural pathways. Educators should provide moderate, predictable doses of developmentally sensitive challenges – this develops resilience.

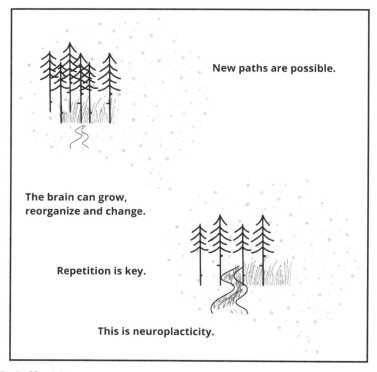

Figure 9.4 Brain Plasticity

◎ **Pause & Reflect:**

- ◆ There are many analogies for understanding neuroplasticity, the creation of new neural pathways and neuron connections. Come up with your own or use one of these examples to solidify your understanding of how the brain forms new habits and learnings.
- ◆ Examples:
    - – A new path through the forest
    - – Wheel(s) grooves on a dirt road
    - – A tree with thinner and thicker branches
    - – Fresh snow on a sledding hill
    - – A fresh notebook and newly sharpened pencil.

Like the creation of new neural pathways, with repetition and support, recovery and healing of a sensitized stress response is possible. In a therapeutic model, this happens in moderate, controlled and small doses. Yet, throughout human history, people have navigated the impacts of traumatic events and experiences. So how did people heal without weekly therapy appointments? The answer … through community healing!
Dr. Perry and Oprah (2021) described pillars of traditional healing; three of which are applicable to our school environments:

1. *Connection to clan and the natural world.*
2. *Regulating rhythm through dance, drumming and song.*
3. *A set of beliefs, values and stories that brought meaning to even senseless, random trauma. (p. 200)*

These pillars of traditional healing have been found in communities around the world since time immemorial. Most healing happens within a person's network: friends, family, teachers and others in their community. A healthy community is a healing community and vice versa. One person should not be expected to support all of the needs of a developing child or a person healing from trauma. The clan (network, community) must do this together.

Table 9.3 Practice: Trauma Resilient Spaces

Put It Into Practice: Trauma Resilient Spaces	
1. Connection to clan and the natural world.	• Regulate and relate! • Reduce screen time and prioritize usage that allows for creativity and connection. • Advocate for and reduce child-to-adult ratios and have the opportunity for varied, diverse relationships: ○ On-site counselor, therapist, social worker, nurse, librarian, community and volunteer coordinator, associate educators ○ Community & volunteer partnerships and mentoring: non-profits, businesses, healthcare, agencies, sports and recreation, parks, religious organizations, college/university, elders ○ Older/younger student mentoring; multi-age classrooms • Opportunities for mutual support with and for caregivers/parents: family stabilization, housing, classes, interventions and recovery. • Ample options for playing, being and learning in nature and connecting with all life – go back to Chapter 6! ○ Outdoor classrooms; Garden ○ Green space as part of the building design ○ Walking field trips, nearby parks ○ Space for meditation, breathwork, observation, sensory exploration
2. Regulating rhythm through dance, drumming and song.	• Singing, spoken word, rap; creating rhythms, rhymes or chants about concepts being learned, as well as for fun; nursery rhymes and sing-alongs. • Listening to diverse music and dance breaks (dance party!); mindful movements. • Construct drums, regular drum circles, drum lines. • Invite in local drumming, dance and singer groups and individuals (also a great way to celebrate and *Respect Diversity*). • Music, arts and sports are indispensable for regulation, can be therapeutic and provide an opportunity for social connection. • Learn while we move – not while sitting fixed all day in a desk!
3. A set of beliefs, values and stories that brought meaning to even senseless random trauma.	• Deepen awareness of how our beliefs, values, knowledges and experiences shape our worldview, interactions and reactions/responses (including implicit bias). • Literacy, language, stories and storytelling help us learn, explore, heal and make sense of our world. These are foundations for connection and healing! • All of the peace actions and peace pursuits can be lifted up and explored through diverse sets of beliefs, values and stories. So many of our practices align, a few highlights: ○ Chapter 1: Belief Intersections (p. 6); ○ Chapter 3: The whole Chapter! ○ Chapter 4: Co-creating brave spaces allows for developmentally and trauma sensitive sharing, reflection, dialogue and healing (p. 81). ○ Chapter 5: Windows, Mirrors, Sliding Glass Doors (p. 113) ○ Chapter 6: Inquiry Process & Stories (p. 138) ○ Chapter 8: Stories & Storytelling – folktales, myths, fables, legends, creation stories (p. 161) ○ Chapter 12: Language and literacy-based Belonging & Harmony Unit of Lessons (p. 245) ○ Highlight peacemakers; List on our website: www.thepeacepad.org

In a trauma informed peace site, our classrooms, schools, adults and peers provide small, controlled doses of sharing, listening, dialogue, compassion, love, predictability and safety – the needed medicine for transformative healing.

◎ **Pause & Reflect:**

- ◆ Review the three pillars of traditional healing (Table 9.3). For each pillar, outline what next step(s) you will take to co-create trauma resilient spaces in your classroom or school.

The prevalence of mental health disorders, trauma, adverse experiences, PTSD, direct and secondary exposure to traumatic events, violence and harm have underscored the necessity for all schools and spaces to deeply support the social, emotional and mental health needs of children, parents/ caregivers, educators and our communities. Connectedness with others who are present, regulated, nurturing, supportive and caring are keys for fostering resilience. Resilience can be built and deepened. Coping capacities can be strengthened.

Peace and justice education plays such a crucial role in navigating adversity, fostering resilience and supporting healing – individually and ultimately at all levels of humanity. Here are key aspects of resilience and healing that are also core to this peace action framework:

- ◆ Emotional and creative intelligence; deepening self-awareness
- ◆ Mindfulness and regulation strategies for coping with trauma and managing stress
- ◆ Practices centering gratitude and promoting overall well-being
- ◆ Conflict resolution and transformation
- ◆ Empathy, compassion and understanding
- ◆ Positive relationships, social supports, a sense of belonging, social cohesion and connectedness
- ◆ Communication, listening and cooperation
- ◆ Supportive and inclusive environments, usually co-created democratically
- ◆ Critical thinking and questioning; creative problem-solving
- ◆ Empowerment, a heightened sense of agency and reaching out in service
- ◆ Advocacy and action to address systemic issues such as the root causes of harm, aggression, violence and injustice

Our ability to bounce back, to be resilient when there is trouble and tragedy, is anchored in our protective factors, namely relationships. We need to support students (and families) in understanding the impacts of trauma and chronic stress on learning and behavior, as well as that resilience is a protective factor! Our learners also need to be trauma aware to aid in healing and deepening resilience.

Table 9.4 Practice: Neuroplasticity & Resilience

Put It Into Practice: Neuroplasticity & Resilience		
Use developmentally appropriate techniques to access schema and create a basic understanding of brain development and nervous system reactions/functioning. • View and create images, videos, models, interactive visuals, games. • Highlight the neuroplasticity of the brain – that it grows and changes throughout life and especially as a child. • Extend this to sensitively teach students about the impact of ACEs and various forms of stress and trauma. • Emphasize learners' understanding of their own resilience, protective factors and learning preferences.		
Emerging	*Intermediate*	*Advanced*
Basic explanation of main parts of the brain and nervous system and functions. Brain is built from the bottom up! (building analogy) • Basement or Downstairs = body functions, survival • Middle = emotions • Upstairs = thinker, problem solver Introduce connections to regulate, relate, reason – *"what happens when/if…"* Like a muscle, the brain gets stronger the more you use it. The brain changes; try new things. Making mistakes helps us learn and strengthens the brain. No one brain is exactly the same. What helps us have a healthy brain? (food, exercise, learning, connection etc.) What can make the brain less healthy? (introduce ACEs/trauma)	Extend brain and nervous system learning to sensory input, neurons, pathways (analogy: a bridge), memory and automatic stress responses. Explore how the brain is also unique (special talents, for example) and the impact of life experiences, ACEs/trauma. (Empathy!) Regulate, relate, reason – the why and connecting to practices, environment setup, relationships. Brain seeks and likes patterns. Creating new patterns requires repetition. Challenges and mistakes create and strengthen neural pathways. Research amazing brain facts. Identify what supports healthy brains and set a goal for strengthening.	Extend learning to more detailed brain evolution, neuroscience, parasympathetic & sympathetic: systems, parts, functions and roles. (Chemicals, cortisol, neurotransmitter, hormones) What does your brain have to do with your attitude or motivation? Synthesize the connections to regulate, relate, reason. Explore the impacts of brain injuries, trauma, toxic stress, ACEs and evocative cues. Discover neuroplasticity, dendrites – new experiences, learning, repetition, mistakes, healing. Identify what/who supports your resilience. Reflect on personal experiences; foster hope and empowerment

Individual and collective healing is possible, and it happens within supportive environments and relationships like those we advocate and guide throughout this book. With healing there is a great transformative power, change, growth and (un)learning that occurs. What was once a painful open wound can become a healed scar that holds great insights, compassion and an awakened perspective. Dr. Perry and Oprah (2021) referred to this as **post-traumatic wisdom**. Oprah stated so beautifully,

> *Social connection builds resilience and resilience helps create post-traumatic wisdom and that wisdom leads to hope. Hope for you and hope for others witnessing and participating in your healing. Hope for your community. (p. 203)*

Though many in our modern and technological world are navigating injustice, instability, trauma and disconnection, there is hope for and within our communities. The children who may be the most sensitized and/or challenged right now, also hold such deep potential for developing post-traumatic wisdom that becomes the catalyst for healing at all levels of humanity. We must disrupt, advocate and take action to create learning communities that align with the needs, research, best practices and visions of what it will take to create just and peaceful futures for all.

Hope begins within all our children, rippling outward and enlightening our world.

References

Bloom, S. L. (1995). Creating sanctuary in the classroom. *Journal for a Just and Caring Education*, 1(4), 403–433.

Brave Heart, M., Bussey, M., & Wise, J. B. (2007). *Trauma transformed: An empowerment response*. Columbia University Press.

Centers for Disease Control and Prevention. (2022, March 17). *About the CDC-kaiser ACE study*. Cdc.gov. https://www.cdc.gov/violenceprevention/aces/about.html

Child Trauma Academy, Featuring Dr. Bruce D. Perry. (2004). *Understanding traumatized and maltreated children: The core concepts*. Linkletter Media & Child Trauma Academy.

Child Trauma Academy, Featuring Dr. Bruce D. Perry. (2008). *Neurosequential model of therapeutics*. Child Trauma Academy.

Freire, P. (1985). *Reading the world and reading the word: An interview with Paulo Freire*. Language Arts, Vol. 62, No. 1, Making Meaning, Learning Language. pp. 15–21. National Council of Teacher of English

Hulburt, K. J., Colaianne, B. A., & Roeser, R. W. (2020). *The calm, clear, and kind educator: A contemplative educational approach to teacher professional identity development*. In O. Ergas & J. K. Ritter (Eds.), *Exploring self toward expanding teaching, teacher education and practitioner research* (Advances in research on teaching, Vol. 34, pp. 17–36). Emerald Publishing Limited. https://doi.org/10.1108/S1479-368720200000034001

Jaime-Diaz, J., & Méndez-Negrete, J. (2021). *A guide for deconstructing social reproduction: Pedagogical conocimientos within the context of teacher education*. IntechOpen. https://doi.org/10.5772/intechopen.96213

Jennings, P. A., & Greenberg, M. T. (2009). *The prosocial classroom: Teacher social and emotional competence in relation to student and classroom outcomes*. *Review of Educational Research*, 79(1), 491–525. https://doi.org/10.3102/0034654308325693

National Center for Learning Disabilities. (2020). *Significant disproportionality in special education: Current trends and actions for impact*. Ncld.org. https://ncld.org/wp-content/uploads/2023/07/2020-NCLD-Disproportionality_Trends-and-Actions-for-Impact_FINAL-1.pdf

Noddings, N. (2005). *The challenge to care in schools* (2nd ed.). Teachers College Press.

Perry, B. D. (2008). *Child maltreatment: The role of abuse and neglect in developmental psychopathology*. In T. P. Beauchaine & S. P. Hinshaw (Eds.), *Textbook of child and adolescent psychopathology*. Wiley.

Perry, B. D. (2020, April 2). *Regulate, relate, reason (sequence of engagement): Neurosequential network stress & trauma series*. Info NME. https://www.youtube.com/watch?v=LNuxy7FxEVk

Perry, B. D., & Szalavitz, M. (2006). *The boy who was raised as a dog*. Basic Books.

Perry, B. D., & Winfrey, O. (2021). *What happened to you?: Conversations on trauma, resilience, and healing*. Flatiron Books.

Substance Abuse and Mental Health Services Administration (SAMHSA). (2014). *Concept of trauma and guidance for a trauma informed approach*. HHS Publication No. (SMA) 14-4884. Rockville, MD. https://store.samhsa.gov/sites/default/files/sma14-4884.pdf

Substance Abuse and Mental Health Services Administration (SAMHSA). (2023, March 17). *Understanding child trauma*. Samhsa.gov. https://www.samhsa.gov/child-trauma/understanding-child-trauma

10

Staying the Course

Peace Education in the Face of Obstacles & Challenges

Peace is a daily, a weekly, a monthly process, a gradually changing opinions, slowly eroding old barriers, quietly building new structures.
~ President John F. Kennedy

Peace guides, educators and leaders need to be prepared to address challenges made to peace and justice education efforts. As President Kennedy said when addressing the United Nations (1963), peace is a slow process of *"eroding old barriers, quietly building new structures."* That is our goal in writing this book. We want to help dismantle oppressive structures and create brave spaces for students to be critical thinkers, have an opportunity to engage with the peace actions and feel empowered in shaping their future. As peace and justice education becomes part of the identity and values of a space (a home, classroom, school, district, organization and/or community), there may be some who express opposition, anger, fear or propaganda.

DOI: 10.4324/9781003449249-11

◎ **Pause & Reflect:**

♦ What do you anticipate being a challenge for (to) you with implementing peace education at your school/site?
♦ Which stakeholders do you think will be the most receptive?
♦ Are there any stakeholders you are concerned about collaborating with regarding peace education?

Author's Perspective

As a public school leader, I (Carey) have seen many examples of school district's support of equity-focused initiatives. However, I have also experienced examples of leadership not fully committed to making real change. It's one thing to have a framework for equity and culturally relevant teaching practices, and it's another thing to act in alignment with anti-racist and anti-bias education. Power and privilege are challenging things for districts to navigate and overcome.

In alignment with my core values, I've made hard choices about where to work, put my energy, and efforts. School districts are complex and can be bureaucratic, but if you don't feel supported in working for social and racial justice, it can be a difficult hill to climb.

One piece of advice to fellow educators and leaders is to reflect often on your core values in relation to what you see really happening in practice at your school and district. How does this relate to stated school core values?

If a school district espouses being culturally relevant and/or trauma informed, what does this look like? What does this sound like? How is your district supporting anti-racist and anti-bias education? Do you feel supported as a leader/educator?

Leadership Recommendations

These recommendations will support educators and leaders in staying the course and navigating challenges to peace and justice education efforts. In Chapter 11 we provide further guidance for leading for peace.

Find a group of leaders and/or mentors for mutual support.

♦ Do you have a group of equity-focused peers to learn, unlearn and grow with?
♦ Do you have mentors who can listen and support you with your peace, equity and social justice goals?

Consider coaching.

- ◆ Find a leadership coach dedicated to this work. This could be a coach outside of your system. Julie and I (Carey) decided to write this book after I engaged her for this type of support!
- ◆ Determine clear goals and check in regularly. Evaluate your progress and setbacks and be sure to celebrate even small successes.

Check in with your leadership.

- ◆ Consistently check in with your supervisor to make sure there is alignment and understanding of the social justice, equity and peace work. Do you have support?
- ◆ If not, can you coach up? (Coach upward to your supervisor?)
- ◆ If not, is it time to make a change?

Listen and learn with your teams.

- ◆ Check in with teams you support and supervise. Are you holding space for equity of voice?
- ◆ Are you remaining open to different perspectives and checking your own biases during meetings?
- ◆ Are you supporting teacher leadership and peer coaching when possible?
- ◆ How are you building and empowering teacher leadership?

Listen and learn from your stakeholders.

- ◆ How are you seeking out and inviting in family/caregiver, community, parents and other stakeholders? Is there equity of voice?
- ◆ Are you remaining open to different perspectives and checking your own biases during meetings and parent/community interactions?
- ◆ How are you fostering parent/community leadership? Are you delegating and inviting folks in when possible?

The goals of peace education, trauma informed care and culturally relevant teaching are possible and require dedication personally and with all stakeholders.

(Challenging) Questions & Guidance

As you are becoming a peace site and/or are adding an emphasis of peace education into your classroom or school, questions and potentially some challenges or concerns may arise. We have tried to anticipate many of these and have designed this section as a question-and-answer format: a question or concern (in bold, italics) with our guidance and suggestions that follow.

Peace Education: Philosophy & Process

How do you summarize the basic elements of peace education?
We emphasize the Five Peace Actions as a framework for creating cultures of peace.

- *Seek Peace Within Yourself And Others*
- *Respect Diversity*
- *Protect Our Environment*
- *Reach Out In Service*
- *Be A Responsible Citizen Of The World*

Peace education has short-term goals related to the immediate needs and situations in our homes, classrooms and schools. Additionally, longer-term goals transform people, systems and structures of human society to live with nonviolence, compassion, and respect for all life. The tenets of our peacelearning approach include:

- Dedication to holistic, whole-person learning and nurturing inner peace.
- Exploring identity, beliefs and how these intersect with ideas and goals of peace and justice.
- Practicing nonviolence and harm-reduction; conflict transformation.
- Prioritizing co-creating brave spaces that honor all voices and allow for developmentally sensitive learning about harm, injustices, structural violence, systematic oppression and the exploration of peaceful alternatives and solutions.
- Being inspired and empowered by other peacemakers and their actions; cultivating literacy in peace.
- Wondering about the states of life and having a flexible mindset and understanding that change is always happening.
- Grounding in a social justice approach; thinking about all stakeholders and how actions taken by one or a small group may impact others (now and future).
- Taking a decolonized viewpoint on peacebuilding and honoring Indigenous worldviews and knowledge.
- Working toward positive peace, which is ultimately more systematic, proactive and preventative.

◆ Realizing a vision of a more just future for all life (human, nature).
◆ Creating a sense of hope. Hope for one's future, that others have all the possibilities they will need for a fulfilling life and for the protection and restoration of our planet.

Isn't violence inevitable in society? Is violence a natural part of being human?

We emphasize that inner peace is the foundation for building and sustaining positive peace in our families, communities, nations and world. If our mental-emotional well-being and energy are compromised, it will be challenging to skillfully navigate the stress and challenges in life and the cycles of violence will continue.

Violence has been a part of society and our history for thousands of years, but it has not proven to be an effective path for humanity. Nonviolence and living in harmony has also been part of societies for thousands of years and we can clearly see the difference in the short- and long-term well-being of communities and societies. As we outlined in Chapter 1, violence, in its many forms, exists, in a very large part, due to the systems and structures holding it in place. It is a public health issue and is something peace education can help change.

Take for example the impact of violence and war on military veterans. According to the U.S. Department of Veterans Affairs (2023), veterans are more likely to develop post-traumatic stress disorder (PTSD) than civilians and those deployed (in conflict, war) have even more likelihood of PTSD. According to the National Veteran Suicide Prevention Report in 2020, suicide rates for veterans was 57.3% greater than for non-veteran U.S. adults (2022, p. 5). If the myth of people being inherently violent was true, then why would violence, conflict and war be so harmful at the moment and also have a lasting impact on peoples' minds, their physical and social emotional well-being and ultimately our communities and societies?

In his book, *Will War Ever End?* (2009), peacemaker and former U.S. Army captain, Paul K. Chappell, outlined that humans are not naturally violent, but when it is believed we are, it makes war seem unpreventable.

> *… hatred and violence, like an illness, are not necessary expressions of our humanity but occur when something has gone terribly wrong. By improving our understanding of human nature we can begin not only to understand what has gone wrong when it occurs, but how we can prevent the causes of violence and conflict. (p. 62)*

When we understand the human condition and the impacts of trauma and prioritize our foundational inner peace, we can take paths to justly and peacefully solving conflicts and ultimately living in positive peace. Why not do better for our collective good by choosing and teaching nonviolence?

Even if violence isn't inherently natural to humans, many children learn violence from their homes, schools and society, so the cycle continues. How do we break the cycles of oppression and violence?
The social reproduction theory argues that the social, economic and political stratification that exists in society are largely replicated in schools (Bourdieu & Passeron, 1990). Similarly, violence is reinforced through glorification in history, culture, curriculum, textbooks, media and gaming. Many children are direct observers and experiencers of violence within their families, schools and communities. If not healed, this hurt, harm, aggression, violence and trauma can go on to be reproduced.

So, how do we break the cycles of oppression and violence? Well, this is precisely what trauma informed, culturally relevant peace education seeks to do! The reality of the complexities of this question provides a compelling why for creating just cultures of peace in schools. We assert that implementing this peace action framework, practices and the guidance throughout this book will help address the root causes of violence and over time break these cycles and allow for the creation of truly peaceful societies.

Author's Perspective

We both have experienced scenarios similar to this …. A student becomes angry and hits another child. In contacting the caregiver about the incident, they say there will be consequences and go on to let the child know, *"I'm gonna whoop you when you get home."* In addition to the legal considerations for child abuse, there is a compassionate understanding for the generational reproduction of the aggressive or violent behavior. The lines of parental discipline versus abuse may vary given cultural or ethnic context, but the question lingers of whether you now unintentionally did more harm for this child by contacting the caregiver about the incident. Comprehensive peace education interrupts the cycles of violence.

Implementation Considerations

What are challenges to peace education that leaders and educators may be able to address upfront with stakeholders?
Challenges to peace education will vary across settings. Transparency, listening and dialogue are important. Here are a few considerations and the

rest of this chapter offers more guidance!

- ◆ Peace and justice concepts may clash with parent/caregiver attitudes, values, beliefs or opinions.
- ◆ Concern about developmentally sensitive peacelearning related to 'isms' or 'phobias;' for example, racism, sexism, ableism, classism, heterosexism, anti-semitism; transphobia, xenophobia, islamophobia and homophobia.
- ◆ Finding curriculum and materials that are balanced (historically, diverse people and perspectives); textbooks being unbalanced or centering war and conflict and not inclusive of peacemakers and peacebuilding throughout history.
- ◆ Positions related to the role of schooling should be only about academics.

What should I do if I am an educator who is interested in teaching peace education, but feel there is not enough time in the day to teach everything that is required by the school/district?
As we outline in Chapter 2, p. 40, begin by making explicit connections between the peace actions and your existing curriculum, programs and requirements. Then, you might choose one peace action to go deeper with – this could be for the whole school year or a smaller amount of time. Perhaps this is decided as a teamed approach so that as you collaborate, ideas, materials and resources are shared! Identify a specific space in your schedule for integrating peace education more intentionally such as a morning meeting or literacy block. The teachers in our pilot group felt that the more they engaged with the Five Peace Actions, it became easier to naturally embed the framework and lessons into their regular planning and school schedules. Keep yourself an ongoing learner and reflector of peace and justice education as well!

What should we do if our school does not have enough mental health support?
As we outlined in Chapter 2, p. 32, mental health needs are high. Some districts receive additional funding for mental health support, but it is still not enough. The needs highlight the importance of fully implemented peace education and whole-person learning for all. In a multi-tiered system of support (MTSS) framework, this is called Tier 1, meaning proactive and preventative instruction that is universally delivered or provided. The practices and conferring outlined in Chapter 3 are extremely valuable for supporting the mental and emotional well-being of learners. Additionally, trauma awareness and becoming trauma informed (Chapter 9) is key.

You will likely be implementing interventions with many students, which in MTSS is Tiers 2 and 3. As you evaluate and plan interventions, be sure to start with the student's strengths and continually return to these gifts, which are likely keys to healthy relationships, self-acceptance, confidence and growth. Implementing integrated interventions that are trauma sensitive, culturally and linguistically responsive and evidence-based, as well as conducting data-driven progress monitoring, is part of an MTSS model.

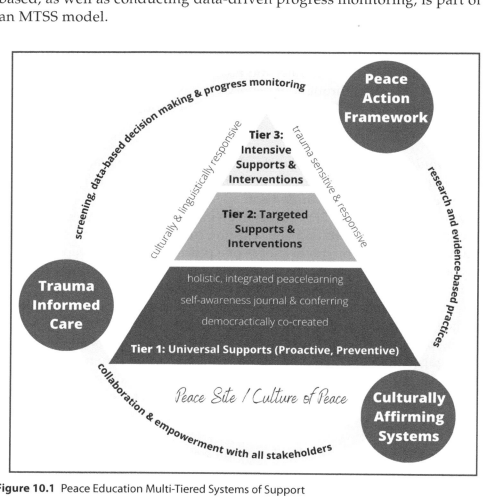

Figure 10.1 Peace Education Multi-Tiered Systems of Support

Needs should also be addressed in your school leadership team and if applicable brought to district leadership. Bringing data to the table is essential. If your school has an 'MTSS,' or 'child study' team, they should have access to data about all students who need tier 2 and 3 mental health support. Connect with site staff: social worker, therapist, psychologist etc.

◎ Pause & Reflect:

◆ Review Figure 10.1. Describe the relationships and connections between MTSS and creating cultures of peace (peace sites).

Though we must advocate at the national and state level for additional funding, in collaboration with the community, peace sites (schools) can become centers of connection and healing.

As a leader, what should I do if there are staff and/or parents and caregivers who are adamant that they "don't believe in (or are opposed to) peace education"?

First, evaluate roughly how many stakeholders hold this view or concern. It is crucial to create ongoing and meaningful feedback loops between leadership, staff, parents/caregivers and students. A Peace Leadership Team (more in Chapter 11) should be composed of all stakeholders and their feedback, recommendations and guidance are important for any school. Providing anonymous feedback channels like surveys or forms can help get a pulse on how the community understands peace education and the actions, as well as related questions, concerns and suggestions. If overall the school stakeholders are 'on-board' to create cultures of peace in school, then proceed!

In the beginning, you might keep your initial focus on creating calm classrooms and fostering relationships, connection and a sense of belonging (community). Most people respond well to classroom and school environments that are calm, respectful and focused on preventive solutions and peaceful problem-solving.

Put It Into Practice: Feedback Loops

As your advisory committee(s) and leadership team(s) go deeper into peace education and the peace action framework, keep those feedback loops going! Create continuous opportunity to deepen stakeholder engagement with peace education and the Five Peace Actions, such as:

➤ Curriculum night, open house, carnival
➤ Volunteer options; joining for special events, field trips
➤ Parent-teacher associations (PTA/PTO)
➤ Child-led conferences, home-visits
➤ Parent and caregiver workshops or info sessions (virtual and in person)
➤ Staff meetings, professional development, professional learning
➤ Online portals, communication platforms, emails, newsletters, social media

What should I do if my administration or district leadership is not supportive of peace education?
Set up rituals and routines that focus on fostering a classroom community with a sense of care and belonging. Model, invite and practice calm, kind and clear communication. Engage learners in processes that require critical thinking skills, meaningful discussion, as well as peaceful and constructive dialogue and conflict resolution. Incorporate diverse peoples and perspectives into content and curriculum. Basically, focus on trauma informed and culturally relevant best practices (see Appendix E, p. 290). The language and literacy-based lessons (Chapter 12, p. 245) also align to standards. Most people/leaders are supportive of classrooms that embody calmness, and mutual respect and engage in meaningful and responsive teaching and learning.

With fellow interested educators, explore your understanding of the peace actions, the tenants of peace education and how they intersect with your existing standards, curriculum and administrative/district priorities. Through dialogue and collaboration, go deeper into what the concerns or objections are, seeking to compromise and find common ground that ultimately best serves your primary stakeholders – the children.

Depending on your circumstances, you could also evaluate your core values and determine if it is time to make a change in your work environment.

What are the pros, cons and considerations of advancing technologies?
Advances in technology, artificial intelligence (AI), large language models (LLMs) and virtual and augmented realities offer additional evidence and opportunity to shift out of the industrial-era educational structures, priorities and norms and into holistic peace and justice education. There are concerns and challenges related to advancing technologies such as bias, stereotyping, cultural insensitivity, equitable access, training, ethical use and data privacy. Social media and other smartphone apps and platforms, advancing technologies, can be addictive, harmful, used to bully, sow mistrust and be weaponized. However, generative AI (chatbots) can be anthropomorphized in children's interactions, which can provide a place to practice inquiry and social emotional skills, but ultimately this doesn't replace real human interaction and connection. It is important that we understand how to responsibly utilize technologies.

There are many positive opportunities new technologies offer, some which don't even exist yet! Current technologies can help with language translations, reduce educator administrative tasks and assist in the initial development of curriculum, materials and individualized resources. For students, learning platforms are becoming more adaptive, providing real-time feedback and increased engagement, accessibility, and enhanced personalized learning. The near future technologies can be used for good in society, which is why it is critical to equip and foster learners with critical consciousness, peace-centered problem-solving, empathy and care for all life; something technologies may not yet be equipped to do. Advancing technologies must be constructed for the benefit of children and to create cultures of peace.

Pause & Reflect:

◆ Reflect on your understanding and integration of advancing technologies. What would you like to know more about or have more experience with?
◆ What attitudes and values will help humanity use future technologies for good?

Socio-Political & Socio-Cultural Challenges

How do you handle accusations that call peace and justice education 'woke indoctrination or ideology?' What if there is pushback against diversity, equity, inclusion (DEI) and/or anti-bias and anti-racism efforts? And/or LGBTQI+ inclusivity?
If you encounter this type of accusation, it is usually in connection to a relatively small but vocal minority and/or well-funded, organized groups who are strategically stoking fear and misinformation within the socio-political climate. These 'advocacy' groups are attempting to and/or are spreading propaganda, censoring and banning curriculum, books, content and learning, as well as undermining the fabric of (public) education. It's an attempt to create or reinforce an *'us versus them'* mentality and increase polarization.

Focus on building and maintaining trust with the families of the children you serve – they are your most vital partners to ensuring all children have access to a well-rounded education. Support families and invested community members in understanding and connecting with the *Five Peace Actions*. Provide ongoing and meaningful opportunities for parents and caregivers to learn about the goals of peace education and how children are engaging with peace actions in developmentally sensitive ways. Co-create brave spaces for conversations, questions and concerns (see Chapter 4, p. 81).

Peace and justice education values that all children have the **freedom to learn**, be themselves and pursue their dreams – no matter how they look, where they are from or how they identify. This is the foundation of inclusivity and a basis of human rights. Check out We Make The Future (2021) for more messaging guidance.

Indoctrination points to only one specific point of view being taught/ learned, whereas this framework is quite the opposite, emphasizing exploring and listening to many points of view from a variety of sources! Learners construct their understanding, honoring that as new information or experiences arise, their ideas might change. **Freedom to disagree** (peacefully) or come to one's own opinion or decision is part of peace education. Practices of non-judgment and leaning in with curiosity, wonder and inquiry are attributes of peacelearners. As are characteristics such as critical, conscious, creative thinking and problem-solving.

It is our goal that peace educators, guides and leaders are informed and conscious of prejudice, bias, discrimination, injustices and inequalities. Being more awakened helps create positive change and supports our collective evolution. We must defend the freedom to learn and resist that which seeks to censor and/or oppress universal human rights.

How can I respond to community member or parent/caregiver concerns about 'values education?'
This concern may have similarities with pushback against diversity, equity and inclusion (DEI) efforts (discussed above). We suggest guiding the conversation toward the peace actions, particularly *Be A Responsible Citizen Of The World* and emphasize forming supported, caring and connected communities.

Additionally, remain open-minded! Peace guides should model constructive dialogue and the benefit of exploring different ideas, beliefs, perspectives and concepts, as well as acknowledging, accepting and/or respecting differences. Respect the right of individual learners to independently hold, explore or reject values. Show respect for diversity in your students and their families. Avoid being on a 'soap box' or potentially positioning yourself as preaching or proselytizing.

Creating calm and harmonious learning environments and people should not be controversial, but if it is viewed as such, you could go deeper into showing the positive outcomes of the strategies and practices within peace education. "Show, don't tell" with these – we learn from experience. Go back to the family and community connections at the end of Chapters 3–8.

> **Put It Into Practice: Values & Language Expressions**
> A conversation(s) with stakeholders could connect to the use of language
> that perpetuates and normalizes harm, aggression and violence. After
> all, our values, mindset and language are often deeply connected. Hate
> speech, toxic masculinity, objectification, threats, name-calling, war
> metaphors, dehumanization, victim blaming, stereotyping, belittling and
> discriminatory language negatively impact people and contribute to a
> culture of harm, aggression and violence. Co-create a brave space (see
> CARE agreements Chapter 4, p. 83), and for exploratory unlearning and
> learning, examine "normal" expressions and patterns of language. Here
> are some specific examples to get this conversation started:
>
> ➢ Stick to your guns
> ➢ An eye for an eye
> ➢ I will kill you if …
> ➢ Kill two birds with one stone
> ➢ You're … a wimp; crazy; drama queen; dumb
> ➢ Sticks and stones may break my bones, but words will never hurt me
> ➢ Be a man
> ➢ They're the good guys

Our inner work, as well as models for positive social change and
connectedness, require compassion for ourselves, others and our
environment. If you encounter concerns from stakeholders related to
valuing universal human rights, start by creating a brave space for
listening, asking questions, sharing and as much as possible holding
a stance of empathy. In this listening and dialogue, anchor back to the
peace actions. You aren't tasked to change someone's mind or convince
them, but your job is to create a space where all children have the
freedom to learn and be.

What do you recommend regarding the banning of diverse books?
Book censorship, banning and other actions meant to restrict access to
diverse, developmentally sensitive literature are major concerns. As
discussed in Chapter 5: *Respect Diversity*, p. 113, it is crucial that the books,
media and curriculum shared and accessed by learners reflect themselves
(mirrors) as well as represent other peoples and cultures (windows, sliding
glass doors).

Studying the impact of banned books, First Book (2023) found,

> *…that the conversation and actions to ban and/or censor books in schools, libraries and programs are having a negative impact on educators' ability to teach and students' ability to learn – and these negative impacts reach far beyond just the districts that are facing bans.*

Fostering a love of reading, an appreciation for diversity and addressing the short- and long-term harm of book bans and censorship are key points to address, including with our older learners. We encourage you to focus messaging and your actions on the freedom to learn, which also includes the freedom to read and access diverse, developmentally sensitive books.

What do you advise if your school/district/state has taken a stance against social emotional learning (SEL) and/or culturally relevant teaching, which are elements of this peace education framework?
This scenario is indeed challenging and creates additional stress in navigating how to best serve the needs of all children. Fundamentals of SEL have and always will be integral parts of human development. These skills, behaviors and attitudes are infused through every part of our daily lives and can't just be 'turned off' or ignored! Additionally, long-standing best practices of teaching are connecting to students' cultures, languages and life experiences, which is being culturally responsive. Holding clear and high expectations is part of culturally relevant pedagogy.

We recommend keeping your emphasis on your immediate classroom/school community while you advocate. Classrooms thrive if they have strong rituals, routines and a sense of belonging. Democratically co-create the environment. Hold daily morning and/or afternoon meetings (circles) that support reflection and community building. As conflict and issues arise in your class, model, practice and empower techniques that contribute to a culture of peace.

A few basic strategies:

- ◆ Restorative practices: How do we make things 'right' when someone has been hurt (either physically or mentally)?
- ◆ Peace circles to support conflict resolution and transformation (see Lesson, p. 259)
- ◆ Listening strategies to support students' cultivation of empathy and collaboration vs. reactive conflict
- ◆ Providing students ongoing opportunities for leadership, choice and voice in their learning

Some people don't think racism, sexism or other 'isms' should be addressed in school, let alone with elementary-aged learners. How can I respond to this?
The reality is that even young children experience racism, sexism and other 'isms' through discrimination, microaggressions, stereotyping, bias and existing inequities within our systems and structures. We believe that since children are not 'too young' to experience 'isms,' then it is also imperative they have the freedom to learn about it, explore and seek out solutions for positive change through developmentally sensitive methods. The lessons and practices throughout this book provide a foundation for this anti-bias and anti-racism learning. Respect for diversity and inclusiveness, which is an ultimate goal of peace education, does not discriminate based on gender, race, sexual orientation, age or other factors. To create a just and harmonious society, our children can, should and will be the leaders of this transformation.

How is critical race theory (CRT) connected with culturally relevant teaching and peacelearning?
In PreK-12 education, there has been some conflation of CRT. Originating in higher education and legal fields, CRT focuses on interrogating the historical and sociological role and impacts of race and racism. CRT is characterized by the acceptance that racism is pervasive in our systems and looks at how White supremacy and privilege operate (Lawrence & Hylton, 2022). The philosophy of peacelearning has some connection with CRT in the sense that in developmentally sensitive ways learners engage in inquiry about root causes of conflict and injustice. Peacelearning also inspires activism for equity, justice, inclusivity and social change. Culturally relevant teaching is focused on empowerment, helping students understand themselves and others, as well as honoring diverse cultures and perspectives.

Peace education could be viewed as politically contentious, especially when topics related to war, militarism, security, defense and foreign policy are involved. How can we respond to these concerns and what can be addressed with elementary learners?
Inviting many diverse perspectives and critical thinking about the military industrial complex and violent conflict is an important topic in peace education. Though certainly there are developmental considerations for how we engage with elementary learners in these topics, this topic is of great significance for ultimately creating societies that are just and peaceful.

If there are concerns raised about engaging learners with these topics, first get grounded in the reality that children are most certainly aware of these topics from adult discussions, news, media, textbooks, video games and through play. War and violence is often glamorized and normalized in society and culture through books, movies, television and games. So many children, unfortunately, also have direct experiences with violence and war. Remind anyone raising concerns that the goal of peace education and this framework are to empower learners in their freedom to learn – for their whole lives.

Table 10.1 Practice: Violence & War Inquiry

Put It Into Practice: Violence & War Inquiry		
Utilize an inquiry process, where learners can pose their questions about violence and war. Then, find appropriate resources and information to investigate these questions, ensuring that this is inclusive of varied and diverse perspectives. As learners make connections and engage in recording, analyzing, interpreting and evaluating the information, additional questions will likely be generated. Encourage learners that this is in a cyclical process and that as they learn, grow and encounter new information and perspectives, their opinions and beliefs related to these topics may also shift.		
• Look at examples of violence and war in what kids are already exposed to: the actions of others, books, games, media and play. How does this impact how we view or interact with fellow humans and our environment? • Look for examples of justice and peace in the actions of others, our books, games, media and play. How does this impact how we view or interact with fellow humans and our environment?		
Emerging	*Intermediate*	*Advanced*

• What are the basic needs and rights of humans?
• Why is there violence? War?
• What is war? Why does it happen?
• Are there options besides violence and war?
• What role(s) does the military have in our safety? In peace?
• What jobs help create peace?
	• Is violence normalized and/or glamorized in your community and/or society?
	• How much money is spent on military defense and war?
	   ○ What feels/seems necessary?
	   ○ What else might this money be spent on?
	• In _____ (a violent conflict or war), what were (are) the different perspectives and positions? Were (are) there more peaceful alternatives?
		• What is the role of peacekeeping and peacebuilding by the world's military? What could it be?
		• What are nuclear weapons? Are they needed in the world?
		• What are the root causes of structural violence? How can these be addressed so all humans can live in peace?
		• What is the difference between cultures of peace and cultures of war?
		• What is the difference between positive and negative peace?
		• How does the military have a presence in schools? Should they?

We encourage you to reach out to us for support as you stay the course in your implementation of peace and justice education. Working toward a culture of peace and/or being a peace site does not mean that you work in utopia, rather, it's a framework in which social justice, equity and care for self, others and our environment are at the center of your mission, vision and every day actions.

References

Bourdieu, P., & Passeron, J. C. (1990). *Reproduction in education, society and culture* (2nd ed.). SAGE Publications.

Chappell, P. K. (2009). *Will war ever end?: A soldier's vision of peace for the 21st century*. Easton Studio Press.

First Book. (2023). *Educator insights on the conversation around banned books*. First Book. https://firstbook.org/solutions/banned-books-study/?utm_source=firstbook&utm_medium=homeslider&utm_campaign=bannedbooksstudy

Kennedy, J. F. (1963, September 20). *Address by President John F. Kennedy to the UN general assembly*. U.S. Department of State. https://2009-2017.state.gov/p/io/potusunga/207201.htm

Lawrence, S., & Hylton, K. (2022). Critical race theory, methodology, and semiotics: The analytical utility of a "Race" conscious approach for visual qualitative research. *Cultural Studies*, 22(3), 255–265. https://doi.org/10.1177/15327086221081829

U.S. Department of Veterans Affairs, Office of Mental Health and Suicide Prevention. (2022). *2022 National veteran suicide prevention annual report*. Retrieved December 29, 2023 from https://www.mentalhealth.va.gov/suicide_prevention/data.asp

U.S. Department of Veterans Affairs. (2023, February 3). *PTSD: National center for PTSD*. Ptsd.va.gov. https://www.ptsd.va.gov/understand/common/common_veterans.asp

We Make The Future. (2021). *Resources*. We Make The Future. https://www.wemakethefuture.us/resources

11

Leadership & Peace Site Guidance

*Systems don't change just because we identify them,
they change because we disrupt them.*
~ Cornelius Minor

We hope you feel empowered to shift toward a culture of peace in your school or organization. This involves taking a fresh stance or new approach to the world of education. The time is now to transform and evolve! Just because something has been done one way, doesn't mean that this pattern or system should continue. When we think of our students of the global majority, there is an even greater need for systems change. As educational leader Minor (2019) stated, systems only *"change because we disrupt them"* (p. 31). Evaluate your mission, vision and values to create an environment where all students and educators thrive.

Counselor and social emotional learning (SEL) leader, Dr. Jennifer Rogers (2019), outlined that despite an agreement for the need to transform schools to value SEL and be inclusive and celebratory of diversity, *"It requires a tremendous effort from all stakeholders to make systems change work"* (p. 3). She goes on to highlight that, *"Changing and sustaining school culture can require an examination and transformation of the infrastructure, norms and policies within school environments as well"* (p. 4).

Making these disruptions and transformations requires collaboration, diligence, grit and determination. We urge you to take steps toward needed change. Our students are waiting for us! Creating Peace Sites

DOI: 10.4324/9781003449249-12

and places where students truly feel welcome and celebrated is an invitation; join us!

Disrupting for Culturally Affirming Systems

If you are in a leadership position (positional or otherwise) and bringing peace education to a school or organization for the first time, be thoughtful in how you set out to enact this vision. Set up a team of people to grapple with what peace education looks, sounds and feels like in your community. It's always important to gather diverse perspectives and to build a group of people to ask questions, lead through change and support one another. Consider adult learning theory and where people are coming from regarding their views on justice and peace. Though this is a collective journey, everyone is on their own journey as well. This peace action framework offers a different way of learning and being. **We encourage you to think about how you can disrupt systems that are not serving all students.** Perhaps at your site this is not a complete disruption, but we really do want you to think about ways of being and practices that are not serving all children.

As discussed throughout the book, we urge you to prioritize culturally relevant pedagogy and trauma informed care; this must be at a systems level. Teachers who do great work in one classroom will impact those students, but to impact a whole school or district, we need to work within the big picture. That's why we make a case for culturally affirming systems.

Pause & Reflect: Review Figure 11.1: Culturally Affirming Systems and the corresponding Put It Into Practice (Table 11.1). In relation to this:

◆ Evaluate aspects of your system that are working for all students. What is your evidence?
◆ Evaluate what is not working for students (regardless of the number of children). What is your evidence?
◆ Aspects that are not working should be disrupted. What ideas can you generate for disrupting and transforming this? Get creative, don't create limitations as you brainstorm.
   – Note that student voice & choice are the foundations for culturally relevant pedagogy (Ladson-Billings, 1995, p. 160), culturally sustaining pedagogy (Paris, 2012, p. 1) and culturally affirming systems (Seeley Dzierzak, 2021, p. 163).

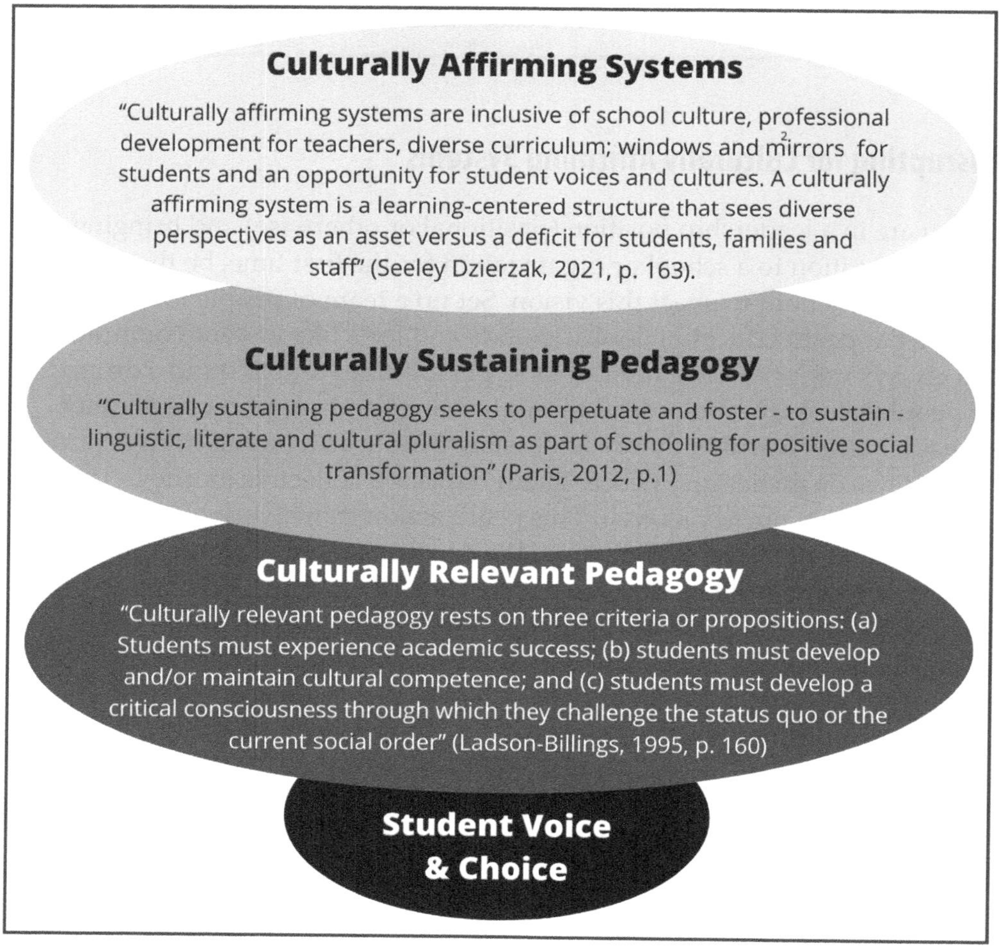

Culturally Affirming Systems

"Culturally affirming systems are inclusive of school culture, professional development for teachers, diverse curriculum; windows and mirrors [2] for students and an opportunity for student voices and cultures. A culturally affirming system is a learning-centered structure that sees diverse perspectives as an asset versus a deficit for students, families and staff" (Seeley Dzierzak, 2021, p. 163).

Culturally Sustaining Pedagogy

"Culturally sustaining pedagogy seeks to perpetuate and foster - to sustain - linguistic, literate and cultural pluralism as part of schooling for positive social transformation" (Paris, 2012, p.1)

Culturally Relevant Pedagogy

"Culturally relevant pedagogy rests on three criteria or propositions: (a) Students must experience academic success; (b) students must develop and/or maintain cultural competence; and (c) students must develop a critical consciousness through which they challenge the status quo or the current social order" (Ladson-Billings, 1995, p. 160)

Student Voice & Choice

Figure 11.1 Culturally Affirming Systems (Seeley Dzierzak 2021, Paris 2012 and Ladson-Billings 1995)

Table 11.1 Culturally Affirming Systems

Put It Into Practice: Culturally Affirming Systems	
Instead of this...	**Shift to this...**
Giving into power & privilege.	Define privilege and highlight how it shows up.
	Identify and address bias, discrimination and prejudice. (Self-awareness included!)
	Prioritize the well-being and success of every student and family through peace actions.
Students and families are expected to conform to the school culture and/or code-switch.	Recognize when/how the school is upholding characteristics of White (supremacy) culture as the norm.
	Co-create shared leadership, agreements and expectations. Partner with the whole community.
Upholding the 'status quo.'	Speak up and advocate for students, families and staff. This may include advocating for policy and legislative changes.
	For example, many Muslim students are fasting and celebrating during Ramadan and Eid, yet the school calendar doesn't reflect this consideration. Some state testing is even scheduled during this time!
Outcomes of standardized assessments are the primary measure for success.	Positive relationships, social emotional well-being, peace and justice education (actions, pursuits) are prioritized.
	Assessments are designed to be developmentally, linguistically and culturally relevant.
Structures, curriculum, materials and communication that uphold Whiteness as the 'norm.'	Lift up diversity! Include multiple perspectives.
	Communicate in a variety of formats and ways to increase accessibility, engagement and access (not just written).
	Evaluate the 'hidden curriculum' (see next section).
Implicit and explicit messaging related to 'don't question authority.'	Children are co-creators of their environment. Invite and allow children to be our teachers.
	Identify injustices and collaborate on peaceful solutions.

Hidden Curriculum

Being an effective change agent requires advocacy, leadership and cooperation in order to align curriculum, management, systems and structures with the peace actions. **Be on the lookout for the 'hidden curriculum,' or that which continues patterns of injustice, social oppression and racial stereotyping.** Keep in mind that for some, schools are historical sources of collective trauma. Take into consideration the history of education and educational access in your community. For example, this may exist in the form of White-centering, overt and covert White supremacy, colonization and patriarchal systems and curricula. The underlying school climate, messages being sent (unconsciously and consciously), as well as the ways teaching and interactions happen, can stay hidden when the emphasis is only on 'what' is being taught. Leading urban scholar, Pedro Noguera (2008) explained, *"The stereotypical images we hold toward groups are powerful in influencing what people see and expect of students. Unless educators consciously try to undermine and work against these kinds of stereotypes, they often act on them unconsciously"* (p. 11).

Paralleling the systems and structures that continue to uphold racism and oppression across the world, the hidden curriculum has persisted in so many schools despite reform efforts. Peace guides and leaders reflect on, engage in discourse and act in ways that move to dismantle systems of injustice, racism and oppression.

Put It Into Practice: Analysis of Hidden Curriculum

➤ What hierarchical structures exist? What power dynamics are in place?
➤ What obedience is expected? How is respect defined?
➤ What happens if authority is questioned? How is defiance defined?
➤ What implicit and explicit bias may be occurring through discipline policies and practices?
➤ What stereotypes exist and how are they being reinforced (consciously and unconsciously)? Are counternarratives provided?
➤ Is the atmosphere competitive or cooperative? How does competitiveness contribute to divisions between individuals and the overall climate?
➤ Is the structural violence that exists in communities and societies being reinforced?
➤ How is nonviolence communicated and practiced? Are there feelings and demonstrations of compassion for all forms of life?
➤ What voices are centered in stories, curriculum, materials and interactions? Whose voices are not included or are silenced?
➤ How is history presented? Is it centering Whiteness and patriarchal views? Are war and militarism glorified? Is there balance with how peace is presented?
➤ Are diverse peacemakers, peacebuilders, nonviolent strategies and practices for seeking peace amplified?
➤ How are students assigned to classes, groups and interventions? How do children sit in the cafeteria and play outside? Is segregation occurring that in turn reinforces stereotypes?
➤ Are conversations about race and racism occurring? What is deemed acceptable and unacceptable in regard to these conversations? Whose voices are centered and/or silenced?

As you examine your systems, structures, management, curriculum and resources, remember that great teaching and learning do not show up in a box. Continue to advocate for culturally relevant (Chapter 5) and trauma informed (Chapter 9) practices. Work as a team to evaluate needs and weave peace actions and pursuits into the school culture.

Once you've identified what needs disrupting, consider how peacelearning plays a role in creating culturally affirming systems. We must advocate for the inclusivity, well-being and success of <u>all</u> students and this occurs within all levels of humanity.

Cultures of Peace and/or Peace Site?

Disrupting systems, creating culturally affirming systems and acting for justice leads to the establishment of cultures of peace. This peacelearning framework and practices guide this effort. This does not mean that there will never be conflict, challenges or issues, but there will be an infrastructure of peace and justice in which these issues can be resolved with humility and care.

While these may feel to be lofty goals, we believe in them deeply and encourage you to access your creative intelligence and reimagine schools as we know them. In his book, *Peace Is Every Step*, Thich Nhat Hanh (1991), offered a beautiful reminder to slow down and really take the time to imagine a different world. He shared, *"There is nothing to chase after. We can go back to ourselves, enjoy our breathing, our smiling, ourselves, and our beautiful environments"* (p. 132). When you become frustrated, feel despair or hopelessness, pause, rest and return to your center. After all, inner peace is the foundation for peace in our external world.

As we introduced in Chapter 2, your commitment to creating cultures of peace can be deepened and expanded by becoming a Peace Site. Let's differentiate a bit between having a culture of peace and becoming a formally declared Peace Site. As an example, perhaps your school focused on creating shared understandings and practices for how to solve conflict. You might decide to use restorative peace circles, which emphasizes learning from mistakes and making amends. This is helping to create a culture of peace.

If your school/site wants to become a Peace Site, there are collaborative steps to take with all stakeholders. Becoming a Peace Site involves aligning your mission, vision and values with the Five Peace Actions and prioritizing peacelearning implementation.

World Citizen Peace (2014), defined an International Peace Site as "*an organization, school, home or community that makes the decision to live out the Five Peace Actions.*" They offer an option to register as a Peace Site and to purchase a Peace Action Pole. This visible reminder of the Five Peace Actions can be installed at a prominent and trafficked area of the site such as a main entrance.

A functional Peace Site has a strong identity and culture of care, hope, peace and is inclusive of all life. The process of creating cultures of peace and/ or becoming a Peace Site will likely occur over three to five years. In the remainder of this Chapter, we consider key aspects of the four stages of implementation (see Figure 11.2).

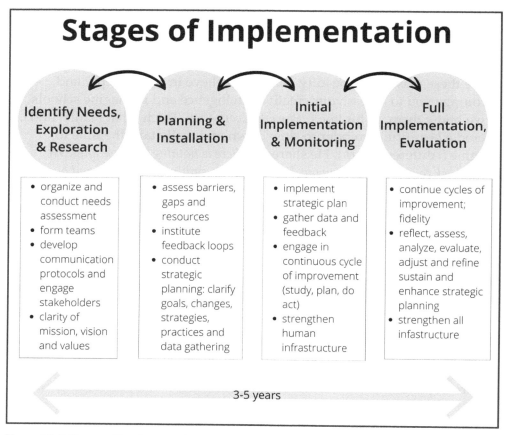

Stages of Implementation

Identify Needs, Exploration & Research	Planning & Installation	Initial Implementation & Monitoring	Full Implementation, Evaluation
• organize and conduct needs assessment • form teams • develop communication protocols and engage stakeholders • clarity of mission, vision and values	• assess barriers, gaps and resources • institute feedback loops • conduct strategic planning: clarify goals, changes, strategies, practices and data gathering	• implement strategic plan • gather data and feedback • engage in continuous cycle of improvement (study, plan, do act) • strengthen human infrastructure	• continue cycles of improvement; fidelity • reflect, assess, analyze, evaluate, adjust and refine sustain and enhance strategic planning • strengthen all infastructure

3-5 years

Figure 11.2 Stages of Implementation

Stage: Identify Needs, Exploration & Research

Whatever led you to this book shows that the first stage of implementation has begun! You've been exploring peace and justice education-related research and practices. Through this you've been envisioning how to transform your site.

◎ **Pause & Reflect:**

◆ Have you conducted an **assessment of needs** (children, educators, staff, families, community)?
  – If you have, what needs have you identified?
  – If not, this is where your work begins! Though you can likely identify many known needs right now, gathering feedback and data is important.

The structure of a Peace Site is based on shared leadership and democratic modeling. At the structural, leadership, classroom and student levels, strive to exemplify peace, justice and student voice and choice. This means understanding dynamics and collaborating to co-create power with, not hold power over others.

Put It Into Practice: Peace Site Process & Considerations

➤ Have you set up a team of dedicated educators and stakeholders to help lead the site? (We refer to this as your 'Peace Leadership Team')?
  ○ Do you have diverse representation on the team (race, gender, culture, positionally etc.)
➤ Do all stakeholders (staff, educators, administrators, families/ caregivers, students, community) have time and space to grapple with what peace and justice education means to them, to ask questions and give input?
  ○ How will you include stakeholders throughout the process?
  ○ What communication protocols are being put into place?
  ○ Do you have support from district leadership?
➤ Are spaces co-created, brave and democratic?
➤ Are there different ways for adults to enter into the pedagogy of peace education?
➤ What resources (lessons, books, people etc.) are being offered to support peace education implementation?
➤ How have you included student leadership and student voice?
➤ What will you do if people are not open to or challenge peace education?
➤ How are you connecting with other schools that have similar missions, visions & values?

Always return your focus to fostering the gifts of all children. All are capable of fostering peace within themselves and others, acting for justice, exploring, wondering, thinking critically and problem-solving. Emphasize methods & techniques across the site that model peace: child participation and shared decision-making, respecting similarities and differences; discovering children and educator's needs and building programming to be trauma informed and culturally affirming.

Build a Network

Whether you are a positional leader or otherwise, finding a group of like-minded peace and justice educators is critical in this work. This work can be a lonely venture if you do not have the support from your colleagues, leadership and community. It will also be challenging to bring peace education into focus without a strong infrastructure. Take the time to gather folks and get momentum behind the mission, vision and values surrounding peace and justice education.

There is a worldwide collective of peacemakers and Peace Sites to join with others dedicated to advancing peace and justice education. There is hope in education and our students deserve our very best. Let's step up and support them to be peace leaders, activists and to discover and be the best versions of themselves.

Stage: Planning & Installation

As you begin strategic planning, this is an opportunity to clarify goals and assess barriers, gaps and resources in collaboration with the Peace Leadership Team, stakeholders and your network. A key component are **feedback loops**, cyclical processes that allow for:

- ◆ The identification of needs and goals
- ◆ Gathering of input and data
- ◆ Clarification and affirmation of shared understandings, concerns and needs
- ◆ Reflection that supports the next steps in implementation
- ◆ Determination of strategies and practices
- ◆ See Chapter 10, p. 219, for Put It Into Practice

Also consider the intersections of peacelearning goals with existing programs and initiatives. Folks who have been in education for several years have likely had training or experiences with a variety of programs such as:

◆ Responsive Classroom
◆ Envoy
◆ Positive Behavioral Interventions and Supports (PBIS)

Many of these programs are beneficial and have influenced our teaching practices as well. Consider how the implementation of our flexible peace action framework may incorporate aspects of these programs or work in tandem. Strategic planning brings the focus and goals to the Five Peace Actions and lifts up a powerful mission, vision and values.

Table 11.2 Planning & Installation Stage

Planning & Installation Stage		
Focus Area	**Action**	**Considerations**
Engage district leadership	Institute feedback loops with all stakeholders. Discuss that your school is considering becoming a Peace Site. • Share the identified needs and emerging vision.	Are there other schools in your area that are interested in becoming (or are) Peace Sites? Share ideas, successes and problem-solve together.
Engage students, staff, parents, caregivers and community stakeholders	• How can you foster and leverage their support? • What questions, barriers or challenges arise? • Compromise and collaborate!	Are there organizations and people in the community that might assist in this process?
Visioning hopes and dreams Mission, vision & values	Led by the Peace Leadership Team, engage stakeholders in visioning their hopes and dreams. Use this to create the mission, vision and values (shared identity) of the Peace Site.	This is the core strategic plan development, which is part of School Improvement Plans/Goals and initial steps for continuous cycles of improvement.
Goals, strategies and data	Clarify the specific and actionable goals. What strategies and practices will be implemented? What data will be gathered to monitor implementation? How does this inform Multi-Tiered Systems of Support (MTSS)?	This process involves returning to stakeholders for input, insight, perspectives and feedback.
Adult learning and leadership plan	In collaboration with the Peace Leadership Team, create a professional learning and adult implementation support plan. • Professional development • Coaching • All staff engagement • Team planning • Family learning • Leadership support or coaching	This plan should be outlined in the site calendar. How will feedback be gathered to inform the next steps, refinements and needs? (More on this later in the Chapter!)

Stage: Initial Implementation & Monitoring

Keep in mind that becoming a Peace Site is not an endeavor that happens quickly. It's a three-to-five-year plan and there will be cycles of implementation reviewed and repeated (especially when there are new staff, students and families).

That being said, consider your initial implementation monitoring process. What checkpoints are you planning for? How are you mindfully reviewing these aspects with the Peace Leadership Team?

Table 11.3 Initial Implementation & Monitoring

What	Who	How
Implement strategic plan	Peace Leadership Team, teachers and staff	Be sure to have a clearly articulated plan that addresses all stakeholders.
Gather data & feedback	Peace Leadership Team	There are lots of ways to collect data and feedback from stakeholders: • Survey (staff, students & families) • Focus groups • Poster session (key questions with time to share feedback/ideas) • Team interviews
Engage in continuous improvement cycles	Peace Leadership Team and teachers	Meet weekly or bi-weekly to engage in a Plan, Do, Study, Act cycle. Collect data, reflect and respond to information.
Strengthen human infrastructure	Peace Leadership Team and all stakeholders	Engage in ongoing professional learning, gather feedback and consider needed adjustments to staff and student support. (i.e., If restorative circles are not going well, train additional staff and/or students).

◎ **Pause & Reflect:**

   ◆ What is your stakeholder feedback and data showing? What can be celebrated?
   ◆ How is your Peace Leadership Team responding when data is not favorable?
   ◆ How can you engage more student leadership?

Stage: Full Implementation & Evaluation

Full implementation requires fidelity. It is a process of continued data and input gathering, evaluation, reflection and analysis. Be mindful that it will take time and energy to disrupt, change, transform and evolve education; and we can make it happen, now! As strategic planning and implementation are refined and enhanced, return to the mission, vision and values of being a Peace Site. Continue to monitor progress and make changes as needed.

There are many considerations as you continue your journey of creating cultures of peace and sustaining as a Peace Site:

- ◆ How will you support peacelearning of new staff and educators and acclimate them to the goals, mission, vision and values? What about new students?
- ◆ How will the Peace Leadership Team handle challenges that do not promote a culture of peace?
- ◆ How does connected community programming align with or enhance the Peace Site's goals?
- ◆ Are there other partnerships that can strengthen infrastructure and implementation?
- ◆ What needs to be advocated for with district, city, state and country leaders (i.e., funding)? How can students and families be empowered in this process?

Table 11.4 Full Implementation & Evaluation

What	Who	How
Strengthen human infrastructure	Peace Leadership Team	Reduce adult-to-child ratios! Schools need to be fully funded, staffed and have an on-site counselor and/or social worker, nurse and librarian.
	District, city, state and country leaders and government	A site that can host and cultivate relationships with community resources such as mental and physical healthcare professionals, government agencies, non-profit organizations, artists and park systems will be able to create spaces of healing and peace. These partnerships will support students and families, strengthen civic connections and positively contribute to greatly improved overall health and education outcomes. Schools can become trauma resilient and healing spaces.

(continued)

Table 11.4 Full Implementation & Evaluation (continued)

What	Who	How
Strengthen environmental infrastructure	Community partners All stakeholders	Update and/or re-design the environment to support the development and well-being of peacelearners. • Outdoor areas for learning and play • Windows and natural light • Reusable food trays and utensils • Composting food waste; garden • Library and media center with adequate and up-to-date technology • Spacious classrooms, comfortable and varied seating and standing options • Flexible gathering and common areas • Spaces to regulate with support: 'Peace Pads' • Powered on clean, green energy

As we work to transform and evolve education and systems, continually return to these seven areas of focus that we presented in Chapter 2, p. 30:

1. Address structural oppression and systemic racism.
2. Increase per pupil funding and access to quality education.
3. Value the profession.
4. Reconstruct teacher preparation programs and professional learning.
5. Extend educator planning and collaboration time and update curriculum.
6. Honor student voice and development.
7. Support mental health and social emotional needs.

Fully funded, implemented and sustained peace and justice education can transform and ultimately evolve education, our systems and all levels of humanity. Advocate! Disrupt!

Sustaining Peace & Justice Education

Regardless of whether you become a formal Peace Site, sustaining peacelearning implementation takes time and persistence. We encourage you to stay the course and work toward a culture of peace, despite challenges that will arise. Continually evaluate your needs, priorities and implementation. Consider the following questions:

◆ What are our needs?
◆ What are our priorities?
◆ What needs to be removed/disrupted to focus on peace and justice education?
◆ How do we balance expectations, hopes and needs?

- ◆ How do we connect peace education with culturally affirming systems?
- ◆ How are we deepening our peacelearning implementation?
- ◆ Have we become trauma informed across the site? (see Chapter 9).

Many schools have challenges, including inadequate funding, trauma and other systemic barriers. These can and must be faced. Dedication to creating a culture of peace is a start. The mission, vision, values and actions that come with being a Peace Site can be the impetus to deeper solutions and real change. As students encounter barriers and challenges, having a school that is committed to being a Peace Site, may be the answer they are seeking. Everyone needs a place where they can feel safe and be brave. A Peace Site provides an answer; for fostering hope, resilience and providing a refuge and the support needed for individual and collective healing.

Professional Development, Learning & Curriculum

Striving toward and sustaining a culture of peace requires an ongoing professional development plan focused on peacelearning, self-care and mental, emotional and social well-being. This includes peer coaching and team support to maintain this work. As teams are getting set up, this can also be a focus of professional learning communities (PLCs). We encourage you to co-create brave spaces (see Chapter 4, p. 81) and to support teams with collaboration.

Preparation for educators is essential. Think about how you will plan and co-create professional learning and training for teachers and staff that focuses on peace and justice education. Many school districts have time limitations, so how can your site think outside the box and offer professional development, coaching and other team support? And advocate for change that extends educator planning time for collaboration and updating curriculum!

Teacher preparation and ongoing professional development need to be programmed around the realities of the needs of those ultimately served. Regardless of geographic location, teacher training in culturally relevant pedagogy and trauma informed care will ensure all students have the knowledge, skills and practices to help evolve our society and put an end to structural oppression. In addition to developing critical thinking skills to recognize and solve real-world problems, culturally relevant models honor the identities of all people. Growing students' intellect (academics), reasoning, creativity, decision-making and social emotional skills, invites student ownership of their education, as well as meaningful engagement with the larger world. These are the skills that transfer to all contents, relationships and areas of life.

Developing and implementing curriculum that aligns with the developmental needs and unique interests of students and is delivered with ample modeling, practice and real-world application empowers learners. Our flexible and adaptable peace action framework, along with scheduling that prioritizes problem-solving, critical thinking, creativity, connection, communication and mindful awareness fosters meaningful learning that will extend through a lifetime.

Engaging & Empowering Learners

To create a sustained approach to peace and justice education, it's important to put students at the center of this work. School leaders are there to serve and ensure an environment of voice and choice for students. Reflect on these questions at different checkpoints throughout the school year to guide your work.

- ◆ How do you elicit student voice and input in creating cultures of peace and/or being a Peace Site?
- ◆ Have you established a system for peer mediation (peace circles, restorative practices etc.)?
- ◆ Do you have school-wide student leadership input opportunities (student council, leadership team etc.)?
- ◆ Are there opportunities for all children to be classroom leaders?
- ◆ What is in place for ongoing student feedback loops? Are all children engaged?

Caregivers & Community Engagement

We believe that by involving all stakeholders in the planning and implementation of curriculum and learning methods that honor diverse voices, identities and strengths and take in account systemic inequities, an evolved education system can (and will) be created!

Parents and caregivers are the first education system for children and their voices should be honored and uplifted. In the spirit of sustainability and shared leadership, consider how you will share and implement feedback loops about building a culture of peace and/or Peace Site. Look for ways to engage families and community members throughout the school year by including them in this process. Refer back to the guidance at the end of Chapters 3–8 for each peace action.

Events to Celebrate & Sustain Peace Education

◆ Invite families and community members for monthly/bi-monthly peace rallies that are focused on the peace actions and/or related to being a Peace Site. This is more powerful if planned with/by students!

◆ On September 21st, International Day of Peace, invite families to do a peace walk around your school that is led by students. Include peace posters and music to enhance this experience.

◆ Embed monthly SEL themes that connect with the Five Peace Actions. Have strengths-based student of the month celebrations that lift up learners for their peace and justice strengths (caring, curiosity, persistence etc.). This is a great way to include families and to celebrate students! See a sample calendar, Appendix C, p. 286.

◆ Hold a *Reach Out In Service* family event (see Chapter 7 for ideas).

◆ Link academic nights, goals and conferencing to the peace actions and pursuits.

◆ On April 22nd, celebrate Earth Day and how we *Protect Our Environment.*

◆ Plan a Spring Field Day. Highlight *Be A Responsible Citizen Of The World* with an Olympics theme; promote physical well-being and cooperation.

◆ Host an end-of-the-year rally where the Five Peace Actions are celebrated. Have each grade/class highlight their peacelearning throughout the year.

There are so many possibilities, what does your site/school want to celebrate?

Hope & Empowerment For Peace Education

Evolving our education systems, structures and methods to those that center peace and nonviolence can help us to finally eliminate disparities in discipline measures and gaps in academic achievement. As Minor (2019) stated, *"Creating a space where kids feel safe means that we must create a space where we share power. One can let go of power without letting go of control"* (p. 75). Feel empowered, you can make change - in community!

Creating spaces where power is shared is an act of care and love. By involving all stakeholders (including children), in the planning and implementation of this framework, practices and learning methods, we transform learning spaces and ultimately evolve into an education system grounded in justice and peace. Together we leverage the power of co-created democratic, brave spaces that honor and explore identities and foster belonging, harmony and hope.

References

Hanh, T. N. (1991). *Peace is every step*: The path of mindfulness in every day, edited by Kotler, A. Bantam Doubleday Dell Publishing Group.

Ladson-Billings, G. (1995). Toward a theory of culturally relevant pedagogy. *American Educational Research Journal*, 32(3), 465–491. Retrieved from https://doi.org/10.2307/1163320

Minor, C. (2019). *We got this: Equity, access, and the quest to be who our students need us to be*. Heinemann Educational Books.

Noguera, P. A. (2008). *The trouble with Black boys and other reflections on race, equity, and the future of public education*. Jossey Bass.

Paris, D. (2012). Culturally sustaining pedagogy: A needed change in stance, terminology, and practice. *Educational Researcher*, 41(3), 93–97. Retrieved from https://doi.org/10.3102/0013189x12441244

Rogers, J. E. (2019). *Leading for change through whole-school social emotional learning: Strategies to build a positive school culture*. A SAGE Publishing Company.

Seeley Dzierzak, C. (2021). *The case for culturally affirming systems of education: Exploring how professional development impacts culturally relevant and critical literacy teaching practices*. [Hamline University]. School of Education and Leadership Student Capstone Theses and Dissertations. 4516. https://digitalcommons.hamline.edu/hse_all/4516

World Citizen Peace. (2014). *World Citizen Peace*. https://worldcitizenpeace.org/

12

Belonging & Harmony Unit of Lessons

We are all connected; To each other biologically. To the Earth chemically. To the rest of the universe atomically.
~ Neil deGrasse Tyson

This unit launches your peace and justice education implementation and contains essential foundations for a positive, democratic classroom climate that fosters belonging, harmony and an understanding of the interconnection of all life. As astrophysicist Neil deGrasse Tyson (Symphony of Science, 2009) highlighted, all life shares common ancestry, molecules and atoms with each other, our natural world and the greater universe. Getting in touch with this sense of oneness is foundational peacelearning.

The belonging and harmony unit supports you in setting up the rituals and routines for the school year and, though can be started at any time, is especially recommended for the first six to eight weeks of school. The lessons have been carefully constructed to align with Common Core English Language Arts Standards (2024). Most will occur over multiple sessions, but the pacing and length will depend on your implementation decisions. The lessons are recommended in the specific order presented, but as always, use your judgment.

As you read through the lessons, think about how you will launch with care, vigor and diligence. Understand that as you get to know your students, you will make changes and adjustments. Take time with these foundations, get to know your students and enjoy the process! With a strong, caring community and well-established rituals and routines, you and learners will be able to navigate challenges that arise with more ease and collaboration.

DOI: 10.4324/9781003449249-13

In This Chapter:

Leadership Note: This unit is important for the whole school community! It is crucial to allow time for collaboration, planning, processing and reflection in teams and the whole staff. We recommend you plan a launch assembly and/or visit classrooms to highlight the Five Peace Actions and share a belonging and harmony-connected book. Reflect on your peacelearning vision, hopes and dreams and how this is being setup, modeled and practiced with all staff and students.

Note on Recommended Resources: Looking for the book/video indicated in the Lesson? Go to the Reference List (p. 279) for specifics and keep in mind that many picture books are available via YouTube (video). Please also check our website www.thepeacepad.org for select lesson plans that include digital links, printable anchor charts and presentation slides.

Table 12.1 We Are Interconnected

Launch: Storytelling & Key Vocabulary
We Are Interconnected

Peace Actions & Pursuits	Setup	Hook & Identity

All Five Peace Actions!
 	
• I have awareness of what makes me, me.
• I practice active listening, empathy and compassion.
• I view and am inspired by stories of peaceful people from around the world.
• I describe similarities between myself and people with different experiences, histories or cultures from my own.
• I learn about the interconnectedness between myself, others and the environment.
• I respect all forms of life.
• I celebrate life (mine, others, environment).
	1. Preview the lesson and materials.
	2. Reflect, plan and take action:
	  o How will you create excitement for the launch and highlight a special story? (e.g., gathering in a circle at a special outdoor space or dim indoor lighting and music)
	  o What collaboration can occur with others/all in your school community to share this story and teaching while creating a sense of belonging? (assembly)
	  o How will you make the Five Peace Actions visible and model them?
	  o What method and materials will you and learners use for the unit vocabulary? It will be added to routinely. (e.g., word wall, vocab notebook and/or digital slides)
		What does peace mean to you? (elicit background knowledge)
		
		In our classroom (school) we care about and seek peace. We do this by learning about and practicing the Five Peace Actions.
		
		• Share each peace action and invite children to give examples from their lives for each.
		
		(turn and talk)
		• *Who are your relatives?*
		• *How are you connected with all life?*
		
		(non-verbally respond)
		• *Are people who aren't in your family relatives?*
		• *Are plants, animals, rocks, dirt, water and nature our relatives?*

(continued)

Table 12.1 We Are Interconnected (continued)

Vocab & Mini Lessons

Belonging: It is important for us to feel acceptance and connection with others and our environments. In this classroom/school environment, we respect each other and our similarities and differences. Through that connection, we feel welcomed and that we belong. **Harmony:** When we feel a sense of belonging, care and respect of others and our environment(s), we are experiencing harmony (interconnection, peace and calm). It's important for us to try to live in peace and harmony with ourselves, others and our environment. **Vulnerable/Vulnerability:** In order for us to work together and support each other, we need to be open to learning and to be accepting of one another's strengths, gifts and areas for growth. Sometimes this can feel risky, uncomfortable or emotional. Being vulnerable means we show up just as we are; it takes courage.
 	
1. Introduce the vocabulary terms.
2. Share videos, stories and/or poems that align to the themes of interconnection, harmony and belonging. Honor Indigenous worldviews of how we are all related (see Chapter 6, Peacemaker In Practice, p. 134). A few suggestions:
  ○ *How Do You Say All of My Relatives in Ojibwe?* (Kaagegaabaw, 2022)
  ○ *Remember* (Harjo, 1983)
  ○ *Haudenosaunee Thanksgiving Address* (Six Nations Indian Museum, 1993)
  ○ *Walking Together* (Marshall & Zimanyi, 2023)
  ○ Note: Not Indigenous: *We Are All Connected* (Symphony of Science, 2009)
3. Discuss questions & prompts in whole, small groups or partnerships.
4. Utilize a Frayer model (Frayer et al., 1969) and co-create definitions of belonging, harmony and vulnerability.
  ○ Add this to your unit word wall, interactive notebook and/or digital slides.

(continued)

Table 12.1 We Are Interconnected (continued)

Questions & Prompts		
Emerging	*Intermediate*	*Advanced*
What does it mean to be connected? Describe your community. Where and with whom do you belong? How might it feel if someone didn't want you around or didn't allow you to join in a group? What can you do to help others feel they belong? Let's be vulnerable and support each other in our community. What is something that has been really hard for you?	Who do you have a relationship of harmony or a sense of belonging with? (nature, others) What does it mean to be interconnected with others? Share examples of how we are interconnected with each other and with nature. Do you refer to our planet as *Mother Earth*? Is Earth our mother? Explain. Why does it sometimes feel hard to show up, speak up and be just as we are?	Describe the relationship between yourself and other people. How are you all related or interconnected? How does that compare/contrast to your relationships with the four-legged, the winged and crawling ones and plants, rivers, trees, lakes and rocks? When is a time you felt vulnerable (as a learner)? How might some vulnerability help us grow, learn and work in harmony?
Check for Understanding	**Closing**	**Extension**
Turn & talk or pick one question to write about: • Who are your relatives? Are people who aren't in our family our relatives? • Are plants, animals, rocks, dirt and nature our relatives? • How are you connected with all life?	Create a peace action tree or other symbol and as children experience or notice one in action, they can draw/write to add it to the tree. Close the day with this reflection & sharing and encourage children to add to the peace tree/symbol routinely, keeping it growing. Highlight the connections and how we are all relatives!	Consider the many intersections in your environments and contents to make explicit connections to the peace actions in an ongoing and meaningful way. Model and encourage children to notice when a peace action happens in text, curriculum and the environment. Consider assigning one as a journal prompt. This might also occur as another lesson.

Gratitude to: Indigenous ways of knowing and being.

Table 12.2 I Am Peace: PBNA Strategy

Emotion Identification & Regulation
I Am Peace (Calm): PBNA Strategy

Peace Actions & Pursuits	Setup	Hook & Identity
Seek Peace Within Yourself • I identify my emotions and explore their messages. • I use strategies to calm and ground myself. • I explore and share ideas about happiness, love and safety.	1. Preview the lessons and materials. *I Am Peace: A Book of Mindfulness* by Susan Verde and illustrated by Peter H. Reynolds (2017) 2. Reflect, plan and take action: How will you incorporate the language of emotions in an ongoing and meaningful way? (e.g., word wall, feelings/emotion check-ins and responses, partner shares, journaling) Where/how will you set up a peace corner or area in your classroom? This could be called a peace pad!	*Everyone has a range of different emotions (feelings). We experience and share (express) those feelings in different ways throughout the day. Sometimes we feel more than one emotion at the same time! There are no 'bad' emotions, but some feel more intense or uncomfortable than others. Or it can feel bad when others express their emotions in harmful ways, but the emotion itself is not bad. Emotions are important messengers, telling us to stop, change, take action or keep going.* • What emotions can you identify (name)? What do those feel like in your body? • What does calm feel/look like?

Vocab & Mini Lesson

Calm: quiet or still in body and mind; neutral, soothed, tranquil, serene, chill; peaceful
Peaceful(ness): free from disturbances, untroubled; calm
Mindful(ness): a non-judgmental state of awareness of one's emotions, thoughts and experiences; being fully present with the senses

1. *Everyone experiences strong feelings, emotions, stress or uncertainty. When you do, it is important to Pause – Breathe – Notice – Act (model strategy). Noticing what is happening inside of us is called mindfulness. This mindful strategy helps us return to calm and peacefulness. As I share the story, listen to how the character finds peace.*
2. Share the text and discuss (see questions).
3. Utilize a Frayer model (Frayer et al., 1969) to explicitly teach and add 'Calm/Peaceful' to your word wall, journals and/or digitals.
4. *Like the character in the story, there are many ways we can find or return to peace and calm. Let's name a few ways:*
   ○ tell yourself: I am okay (alright, safe)
   ○ breathing practices
   ○ notice the here and now (present, mindful)
   ○ observe thoughts, feelings and let them go
   ○ draw, write (journal)
   ○ connect with a friend or animal

Table 12.2 I Am Peace: PBNA Strategy (continued)

Questions & Prompts		
Emerging	Intermediate	Advanced
There are times the character worries about what happens next and before… When have you worried? • I felt worried because… • I worried when… What did (or could) you do to find peace/calm? • I found peace/calm by… • I could have found peace/calm by…	The character tells themselves, I'm alright and notice the here and now… How can one be present or mindful to notice the here and now? (breath, tune into senses & self) • Being present looks/feels like… • When I'm in the here and now, I… What are the different ways the character seeks peace? How is this similar/different from when you seek peace? • The character seeks peace by… • This is similar/different from me because…	In the book, the seeds dropped and suddenly something started to grow… What are the seeds, seedling and tree representing (symbolizing) in the story? • The seeds/seedling/tree represent… • They symbolized… How does this relate to your life and learning? • It relates to my life… • This connects to my learning… How might you share your peace with others? When might a peer need space and time to find their own peace? • I can share my peace with others by… • My peer might need space and time to find their own peace when…
Check for Understanding	**Closing**	**Extension**
Have students practice the Pause – Breathe – Notice – Act (PBNA) strategy with a partner. Share noticings and when this strategy may be used. • Are there other ways to stop and pause that help to seek peace?	Share the peace corner (spot) in the classroom, model and share expectations for how this space should be used for finding peace within yourself. Include the PBNA anchor chart there. The PBNA strategy can take anywhere from 20 seconds to 20+ minutes!	Draw a picture of what (can) bring you peace when at school – these can be added to the peace corner (spot)! Refer to Chapter 3, p. 61 emotion vocabulary for ongoing instruction.

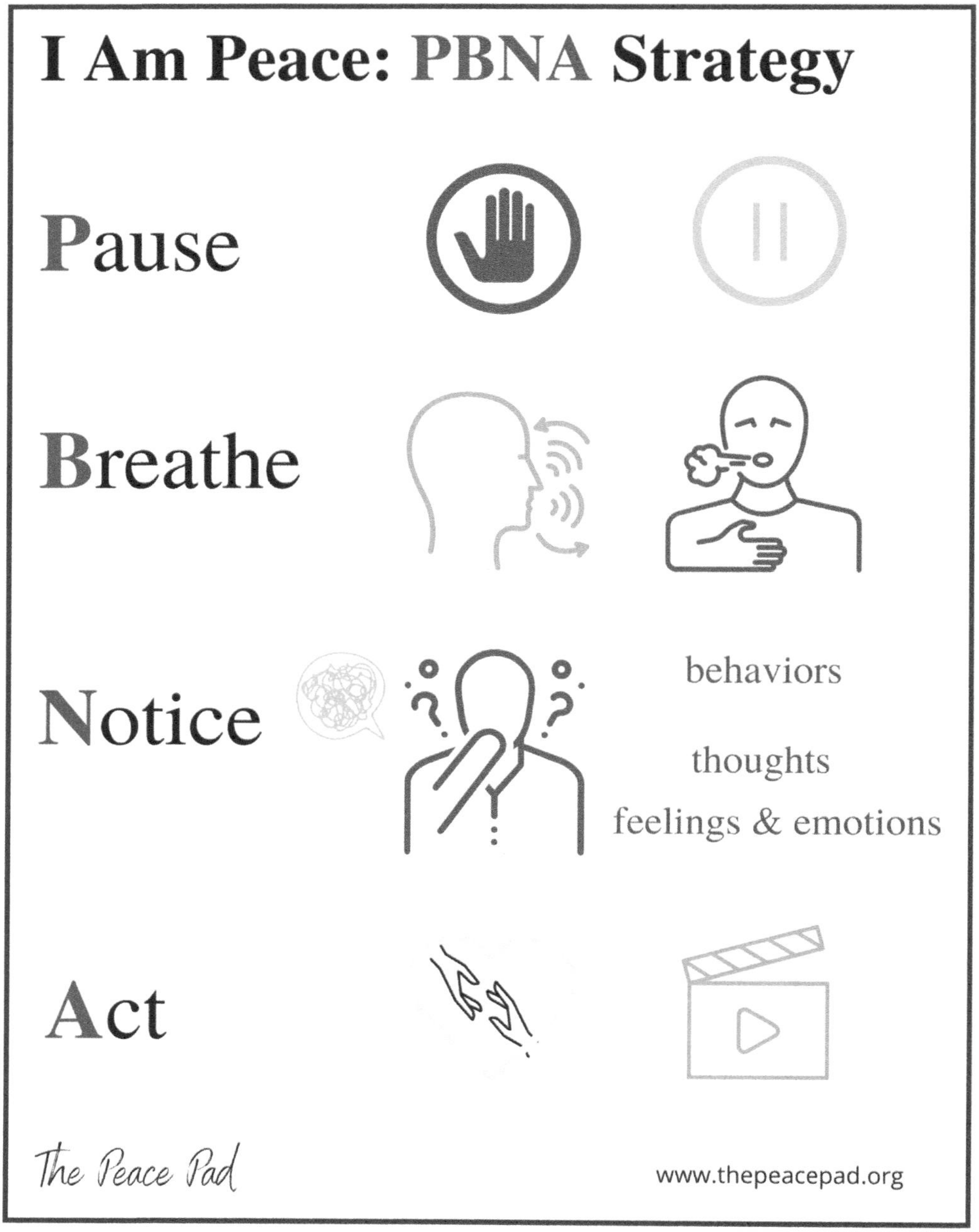

I Am Peace: PBNA Strategy

Pause

Breathe

Notice

behaviors

thoughts

feelings & emotions

Act

The Peace Pad

www.thepeacepad.org

Figure 12.1 I Am Peace: PBNA Strategy

Table 12.3 Heart Map: Who Am I?

Journaling & Joy Writing
Heart Map: Who Am I?

Peace Actions & Pursuits	Setup	Hook & Identity
Seek Peace Within Yourself • I have awareness of what makes me, me. *Respect Diversity* • I understand that every person experiences the world in their own unique way. • I describe similarities between myself and people with different experiences, histories or cultures from my own.	1. Preview the lesson and materials. 2. Reflect, plan and take action: Launch and practice your writer's workshop routine. What will it look, sound and feel like (expectations)? • journals/notebooks/ booklets • writing/drawing supplies • decorate the cover • sample entry (may include date, title) • option: make an entry private by folding the page in/over Consider what you will put on your heart map (for modeling)!	Everyone has special and unique identities. We have our areas of passion and interest and our life stories. We can learn about others by sharing our interests and experiences. Partner Share: • What are a few things that you are interested in? • What do you like to do?

Vocab & Mini Lesson

Identity: Who am I?: values, beliefs, passions, experiences, personality, ethnicity, gender, race, culture, interests
Unique: Special, your own person; be who you are!
Experiences: Life stories: Things you've done, places you've gone, people you've been with, how you've felt

1. Introduce vocabulary and add to your word wall, journals and/or digitals.
2. Model aloud brainstorming and drafting your heart map with sketches and key words, share and connect to identity. (*I am interested in… tennis and painting. I have a strong memory of… painting a mural (experience), oh and playing tennis at the park with my brother. I am adding people, places and things that are important to me as I keep that close to my heart.*)
3. Students share (new partner) about all that could go on their heart map. (*As you share with your partner about _____ (interests, beliefs, important people, memories etc.), be sure to carefully listen to their ideas, it might remind you of something you have in common and can add to your heart map!*)
4. Before releasing to independence (to create their heart map), have the student's name one interest they will put on their heart map. This also provides another opportunity to reinforce how we are unique and have commonalities (e.g., liking the same sport, having an injury before).

(continued)

Table 12.3 Heart Map: Who Am I? (continued)

Questions & Prompts		
Emerging	*Intermediate*	*Advanced*
Draw your heart map. Label with sounds and inventive spelling. Then, dictate, trace and write. What are you interested in? • I like… • I love…. Who are important people in your life? • I care about… What makes you special? • I'm special because… *I love going to the beach with my family.*	After drafting the heart map, make a journal entry or write about one part of your heart map. What makes you unique? • I like… • I am… • In my family/culture we… What experiences do you remember well (e.g., event, place, with family, memory, being hurt)? • I remember… • An important… *I love going to the beach. The beach is on the Outer Banks of North Carolina. This is a special place for my family because we have all been going there for many years!*	Extend *Intermediate* guidance: What is important to you? What makes up your identity? (interest, beliefs, values, culture, people, memories etc.) Narrow it into a special or important smaller moment that happened. Show, don't tell by adding details from the senses. (See intermediate example and add): *One time, my brother and I decided to make a sandcastle and we had it almost as tall as us. All of a sudden, the waves came crashing and it fell over. We felt sad at first, but then laughed so hard we snorted!*
Check for Understanding	**Closing**	**Extension**
Share with a partner or small group what is on their heart maps and why this is important to who they are.	Remind students that their heart maps will be used throughout the year and they can add to this and even make more heart maps and images to help them capture their stories of self.	Routinely refer children back to their heart maps to add more and to find inspiration for ongoing journal entries.

Gratitude to:
Heart Maps: Helping Students Create and Craft Authentic Writing (Heard, 2016)
Joy Write: Cultivating High-impact, Low Stakes Writing (Fletcher, 2017)

Table 12.4 The Great Peacemakers

Seminar Circle
The Great Peacemakers

Peace Actions & Pursuits	Setup	Hook & Identity
Be A Responsible Citizen Of The World • I peacefully share my ideas or opinions. *Seek Peace With Others* • I practice active listening, empathy and compassion. *Respect Diversity* • I listen to and consider others' ideas or opinions. • I honor the ideas, views or perspectives ('truth') of others, even if it is different from mine. • I view and am inspired by stories of peaceful people from around the world.	1. Preview the lesson and materials. Video: *Haudenosaunee's Legendary Founding* (PBS, 2018) 2. Prepare the pre-seminar work you will assign (access background knowledge and generate questions). Or this can be done orally with children. 3. Reflect, plan and take action: How is (will) your classroom be co-created as a democracy? • See Chapter 4, p. 81 • See next Lesson: Class Charter • Will learners gather in a full class circle or small groups for discussions?	*We are going to learn the story of the first democracy in North America. Our classroom is also set up as a democracy! Each of you belongs and has rights and responsibilities as an individual and as a member of our community.* • How does it affect you when someone hurts you, someone in your family or community? • What does it mean to *Be A Responsible Citizen Of The World?*

Vocab & Mini Lesson		

Democracy: government run by the people
Wampum: traditional shell beads of Eastern Woodlands tribes of Native Americans. Usually made from hard-shelled clams. Used in ceremonies today.
Haudenosaunee (hoe-dee-no-SHOW-nee): means 'people who build a house' and refers to the confederation or alliance between six Native American nations of the northeast of North America ('Turtle Island'). Also known as the Iroquois League or Confederacy.

• Introduce vocabulary and add to your word wall, journals and/or digitals.
• Share an image of the Hiawatha wampum belt. How might the symbols on the belt represent peace?
• Orient children to the location of the Haudenosaunee.
• View text and assign/conduct pre-seminar work.
  ○ What do I think… I know? And 'your truth' may change!
  ○ What do I wonder? (see Figure 12.3)
• View text again and conduct the seminar!

(continued)

Table 12.4 The Great Peacemakers (continued)

Seminar Basics

1. Gather in a circle
2. Center on a 'text' and refer back to evidence
  a. Written word (e.g., book, article, story, poem)
  b. Media (e.g., video, podcast)
  c. Art (e.g., image, music, sculpture)
3. Collaboration: all voices honored (harmony)
  a. Active listening
  b. Questioning (see Figures 12.2 & 12.3)
  c. Critical and creative thinking
4. Leader helps, keeps discussion focused, asks follow-up questions (not always the teacher)
 	
Guidelines:
• One person speaking at a time
• Don't interrupt
• Show it (body language)
• Can take notes
• Build on what others share
  ○ No need to raise your hand (conversational)
  ○ Come prepared with questions
  ○ See Builders (see Figure 12.2)
• Refer to the 'text'
  ○ Use evidence
  ○ Be specific (e.g., "on page 3…")

(continued)

Table 12.4 The Great Peacemakers (continued)

Questions & Prompts		
Emerging	*Intermediate*	*Advanced*
Who was Hiawatha? How did he help the Peacemaker? What was special about the Peacemaker? Who was Tadodaho? Why was he so important for bringing peace to the Haudenosaunee people?	How did the wampum shells help Hiawatha and the Haudenosaunee to heal? What was its power? How did Jigonsaseh, the first Clan Mother, help bring peace? Why do you think the Onondaga leader, Tadodaho, was described as evil?	What may have been some root causes (reasons) for why Onondaga leader, Tadodaho, was at first unwilling to be peaceful? How is the Law of Peace similar to the United States Constitution (and democracy)? How does the wampum Hiawatha belt represent the Law of Peace? And the tree?
Check for Understanding	**Closing**	**Extension**
Summarize the discussion (big ideas). How does this connect to self, others, environment and hopes for the future? What did Hiawatha and Tadodaho teach us about forgiveness and living in peace?	Reflect on participation and set a goal for the next seminar. • What was my participation like? Rate it. • How did this affect the group? Set a goal. Repeat as a group: reflect, rate, set a goal.	Read/view related stories and compare and contrast. Create or design a wampum belt to represent the harmony in your classroom. Gather two similar items from nature (not alive) and create a peaceful ritual like how Hiawatha was guided to use the power of the wampum shells to clear the eyes, ears and open the heart. Go deeper in exploring the relationship(s) between anger, love and forgiveness.

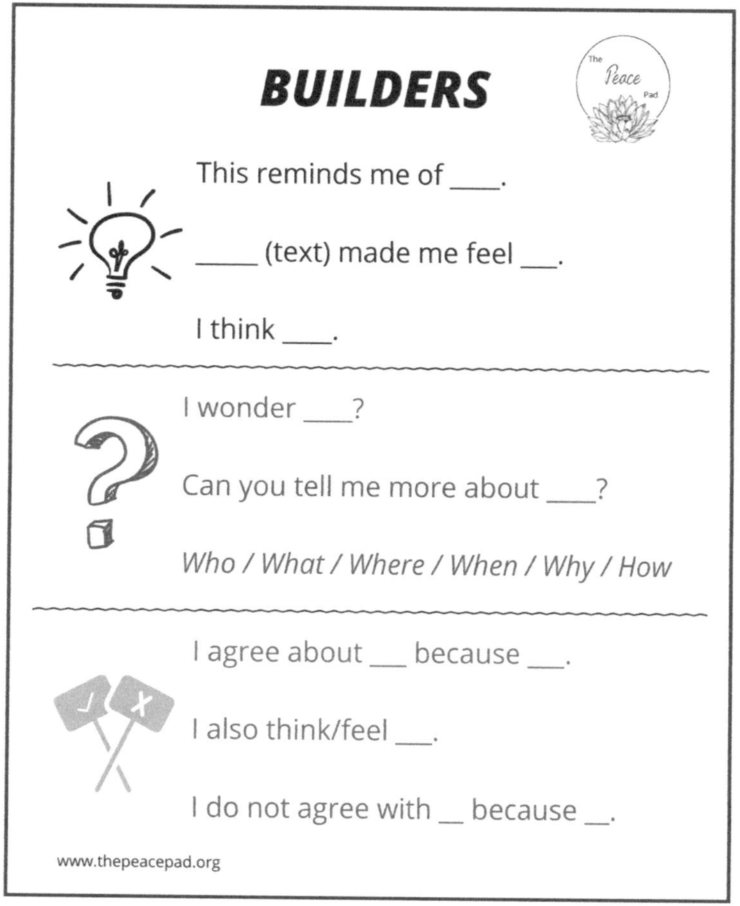

WONDERS

Who is /was _____?

When did _____?

What is _____?

How would _____?

Why do you think _____?

How are _____ and _____ alike?

How are _____ and _____ different?

What evidence supports _____?

Could a root (main) cause be _____?

What would you predict _____?

How does this impact _____?

How might this impact _____?

Could a missing voice be _____?

www.thepeacepad.org

Figure 12.3 Wonders

BUILDERS

This reminds me of _____.

_____ (text) made me feel _____.

I think _____.

I wonder _____?

Can you tell me more about _____?

Who / What / Where / When / Why / How

I agree about _____ because _____.

I also think/feel _____.

I do not agree with _____ because _____.

www.thepeacepad.org

Figure 12.2 Builders

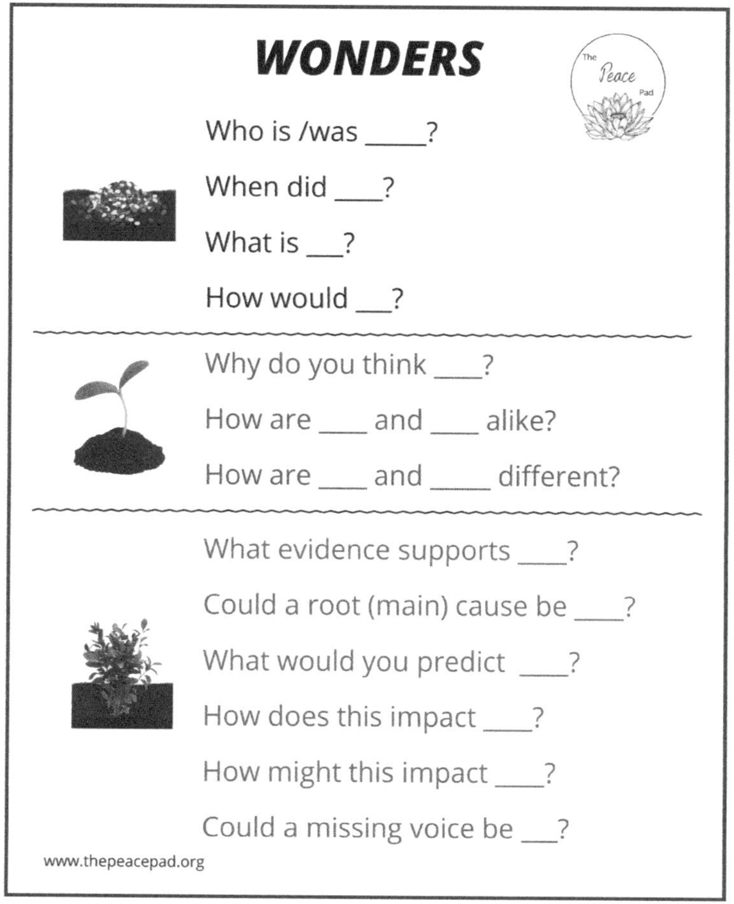

Table 12.5 Peace Circles & Class Charter

Communication & Conflict Resolution

Peace Circles & Class Charter

Peace Actions & Pursuits	Setup	Hook & Identity

Seek Peace Within Yourself
 	
• I recognize how my values, needs and wants impact my behavior and decisions.
 	
Seek Peace With Others
 	
• I practice cooperation and collaboration with others (problem-solving)
 	
• I practice peaceful (nonviolent) communication and actions when:
  ○ I disagree with someone
  ○ I feel hurt or wronged
  ○ My needs or wants are not being met
 	
• I practice active listening, empathy and compassion.
	1. Preview the lesson(s) and materials.
	
	YouTube @UNICEF (2021): *We All Have Rights*
	
	2. Reflect, plan and take action:
	
	How is (or will) the space be co-created and support principles of a democratic classroom?
	
	How will you visually communicate peace circle guidelines & expectations?
	
	Where will the class charter be posted for routine referencing?
	
	Where, when and how can student-initiated circles take place **throughout the school year?** (3+ children). Follow guidelines and/or co-create expectations. Consider partnerships with other classrooms.
		We all have conflicts or disagreements that happen with friends, family, classmates and people in our lives. How we handle conflict is at the center of peace education. Seeking peace within yourself and others means…
		
		(review the lesson peace pursuits)
		
		• Without saying any names, think about a conflict, problem or disagreement with someone. What was it about?
		
		Connect responses to the word harm as well as to feelings, values, needs and wants.
		
		• How did (or could) you solve the problem and come to a peaceful agreement?
		
		• How did (or could) you address the harm peacefully or nonviolently?

(continued)

Table 12.5 Peace Circles & Class Charter (continued)

Vocab & Mini Lesson
Peace Circle: First Nation and Indigenous peoples of North America have long used peacemaking circles as a process for peer mediation, conflict resolution, support, making decisions, sharing and healing. In a peace circle, all voices are valued. Using a talking piece, participants take turns respectfully sharing, problem-solving and coming to a consensus (agreement). Peace circles invite connection, community and individual & collective accountability and change and may vary a little based on the purpose. **Talking Piece:** An object that is passed around the circle and only the person holding the piece may speak (e.g., smooth stone or shell).
Circle Keepers: One to two people who help keep the circle a brave space and support others in following the guidelines; recommend all children have opportunities to serve in this role.
Class Charter: Co-created rights and responsibilities that all agree they will strive to follow, in order to foster a peaceful learning community. All members of the community contribute to the creation of the charter and visual.
1. Introduce peace circles, vocabulary (add to word wall, journal, digitals), review the guidelines (see Figures 12.4 and 12.5) and show the talking piece.
2. Gather in a whole group circle with the peace circle guidelines visual & a talking piece. Explain that you will serve in the role of circle keeper today. Open the circle positively and invite an open sharing (about anything, keep it open). Focus on practicing the guidelines for the first time in this brave space. Name active listening, empathy and compassion. Close by asking for feedback on the guidelines (revise as agreed upon) and set a group goal for the next peace circle.
3. Come back together for another whole group peace circle and explain the purpose is co-creating a class charter. Consider what materials will be needed to create the charter visual (see questions & prompts) and how each child will participate. *For this circle, everyone in the community needs to contribute in some way. What do you need to be able to learn? What rights, responsibilities and agreements will create a peaceful community?* Close in a positive way such as hanging up the co-signed charter visual.
4. For the next peace circle, come prepared with a harm or problem impacting the community. Open by visually sharing & modeling aloud the three parts of a peace circle for solving conflicts: 1. harm/problem identification, 2. healing & problem-solving and 3. reflection & goal setting (see prompts). Engage in the process, naming active listening, empathy and compassion. Close in a positive way such as a group fist bump, high-fives, a game or movement.
5. Practice a few more peace circle processes with children serving as the circle keeper; provide scenarios as needed. Consider setups (see circle seminar) such as a fishbowl where a small group goes through the process and the rest observe or hold simultaneous small group peace circles. Close in a positive way.

(continued)

Table 12.5 Peace Circles & Class Charter (continued)

Questions & Prompts: Class Charter		
Emerging	Intermediate	Advanced
Show the UNICEF video *We All Have Rights* (from start to 1:39).	Show the UNICEF video *We All Have Rights* (from 2:18 to 4:17).	Show the UNICEF video *We All Have Rights* (from 2:18 to 6:53 or end).
Use shared writing to record the charter rights & ideas as you hear from each child in the peace circle. Invite children to agree/disagree with the ideas non-verbally. Create a 'quilt' with the synthesized and succinct written charter in the middle.	Use interactive writing for all to record the ideas shared for the charter. Guide the grouping in combining alike responses of rights, needs, responsibilities and agreements. Orally co-create the synthesized charter and then write it on a large circle of paper for the center of a wall or bulletin display.	Interactively guide students in taking two column notes as they share and group: rights, needs, responsibilities and agreements. Co-create the synthesized charter, having each student record it in their planner or in the cover of a journal or a key notebook. Guide children in writing a personal goal, naming that the charter is a collective goal.
• What do you need to be able to learn? • What will you do to help create a peaceful learning environment?	• What are your rights and needs in life and in this learning community? • What is your responsibility in creating a peaceful environment? • Why is it important for each of us to write our name on the charter?	• *See intermediate* • How do we keep our space feeling safe for everyone? • What challenges might you or the community have in keeping the commitments and agreements of the charter?
Have each child design a colorful square to go around the outside that shows their name and an agreement.	Have each child design a strip with their name and a drawing of an agreement or commitment. Hang these around the charter to create a design (e.g., peace sign, sun or planet).	Post the charter and have everyone in the community sign it and/or create an artistic visual display.
Or create a poster/visual with the charter (e.g., Keeping the Peace in Room) and then have children make/color a hand with their name on it.		

(continued)

Table 12.5 Peace Circles & Class Charter (continued)

Questions & Prompts: Conflict Transformation, Problem-Solving & Healing		
Open: circle keeper shares the purpose of the circle. **Part 1:** What happened? What did you and others say, think and/or feel? **Part 2:** What might make it right (for you, others)? **Part 3:** How will there be peace in the future? What is each person's role for peace (connect to class charter)? **Close:** in a positive way.	**Open:** circle keeper shares the purpose of the circle. **Part 1:** What harm was experienced? Who was affected? **Part 2:** What might make it right (for you, others) and help heal the harm(s)? **Part 3:** How might this harm be prevented in the future? What is each person's role for peace (connect to class charter)? **Close:** in a positive way.	**Open:** circle keeper shares the purpose of the circle. **Part 1:** What led to the harm happening? Why was this experienced as harm? What was the impact on you and others? **Part 2:** What might make it right (for you, others) and help heal the harm(s)? **Part 3:** How might this harm be prevented in the future? What is each person's commitment for peace (connect to class charter)? What steps need to be taken and when? **Close:** in a positive way.
Check for Understanding	**Closing**	**Extension**
Reflect on the process, set intentions individually and as a whole group. How does this connect with the Pause-Breathe-Notice-Act (PBNA) strategy? Co-create: How can we respond to conflicts & class charter needs as they occur (in our classroom, recess, specialists, lunchroom)?	Remind children that all humans have challenging situations, possibilities of harm or conflict. The key to being peaceful is not to avoid conflict; it's taking a pause before deciding how to handle the situation peacefully. Set up a system for learners to be empowered to facilitate their own peace circles in the classroom. Share expectations for where, when and how student-initiated circles can take place.	How will peace circles occur in community spaces such as at lunch, recess? Collaborate on logistics, visuals/tools, modeling and reteaching across the site. Finish the UNICEF video *We All Have Rights* and keep connected discussions ongoing.

Gratitude to: First Nation and Indigenous peoples of North America.

Intermediate & Advanced

Peace Circle Guidelines

- Keep what is talked about in the circle confidential, meaning don't share it with others who weren't in the circle unless you have permission.

- Circle Keeper(s) will begin the circle and will help guide others to keep it a brave space. Circle keepers allow others to do the majority of the talking.

- One speaker at a time (use a talking piece).
- Speak loud enough so all in the circle can hear. Speak for yourself.

- Listen to each other. Listen to understand not to respond.

- If you do not want to share, that is okay. You can pass the talking piece and listen (staying part of the circle).

- If you need a break from the circle, that is okay. Just move outside the circle and listen/watch. Do not interrupt the circle.

The Peace Pad   www.thepeacepad.org

Figure 12.5 Peace Circle Guidelines (Intermediate & Advanced)

Emerging

Peace Circle Guidelines

- Keep what is shared private (shh!)

- Circle Keeper(s) - help to keep it a brave space.

- One speaker at a time (use a talking piece).
- Speak loud enough so all in the circle can hear. Speak for yourself.

- Listen (active listener)

- It's okay to pass (not share).

- Do not interrupt the circle. If you need a break move outside the circle and listen/watch.

The Peace Pad   www.thepeacepad.org

Figure 12.4 Peace Circle Guidelines (Emerging)

Table 12.6 The Hoop Dancer's Teachings

Seminar Circle
The Hoop Dancer's Teachings

Peace Actions & Pursuits	Setup	Hook & Identity
Seek Peace Within Yourself • I feel empowered that as I learn and grow, my opinions, ideas and understanding of myself and the world may change. *Respect Diversity* • I view and am inspired by stories of peaceful people from around the world. • I listen to and consider others' ideas or opinions. I honor the ideas, views or perspectives ('truth') of others, even if it is different from mine. *Be A Responsible Citizen Of The World* • I peacefully share my ideas or opinions.	1. Preview the lesson and materials. *The Hoop Dancer's Teachings* Written by Teddy Anderson and Illustrated by Jessika Von Innerebner (2019) Refer to the Great Peacemakers seminar circle (p. 255) for more guidance and materials. 2. Prepare the pre-seminar work you will assign (access background knowledge and generate questions). Or, this can be done orally with children. 3. Reflect, plan and take action: How can these Indigenous teachings (Medicine Wheel and Hoop Dance) be honored in your space?	*A young Lakota boy named Black Elk had a vision that showed him how all of Earth is connected with each other. He shared that all of life is a circle, not a square or a straight line.* • Where do you see circles in nature? (e.g., birds nest, sun, moon, rocks, spider webs) • Where do you see cycles in nature? (e.g., plants, animals, seasons)

(continued)

Table 12.6 The Hoop Dancer's Teachings (continued)

Vocab & Mini Lesson
Medicine Wheel: One of the oldest teachings of many Indigenous peoples in Turtle Island (North America) is that the circle shows the connection of all things, that there is no beginning or ending and that the equally divided quadrants show balance (harmony).
Elders: Native American elders are often referred to as "wisdom-keepers" and are considered leaders in many tribal nations who are treated with great honor and respect.
Hoop Dance: A dance practiced by some Native American peoples that uses hoops as a representation of the circle of life and that we are all connected (all relatives).
1. *Native American tribes across North America (Turtle Island) have a sacred dance that uses hoops to share the story of the power and importance of the great circle and of growth in the journey of life.* Show pictures of Medicine Wheels (sacred circles) and highlight the colors and attributes (Four: directions, seasons, life cycle, medicines etc.).
2. Introduce vocabulary and add to your word wall, journals and/or digitals.
3. Watch a video of Teddy Anderson hoop dancing (YouTube @Hoopdanceproductions).
○ Note: Teddy Anderson is of European and Turkmen descent. His hoop dance training was guided by traditional Metis Salteaux and he also received special permission to share the hoop dance publicly from a Lakota Elder. (Medicine WheelPublishing, 2023).
4. Assign/conduct pre-seminar work.
○ What do you think the hoop (and dance) might be teaching us (symbolize)?
5. *We are going to hear teachings from a Hoop Dancer, Teddy Anderson, about how to live in peace and harmony with others.* Share the text and conduct the seminar.

(continued)

Table 12.6 The Hoop Dancer's Teachings (continued)

Questions & Prompts		
Emerging	*Intermediate*	*Advanced*
What does the Medicine Wheel teach us about life?	Why do you think the Hoop Dance was created? What are its lessons?	When was a time in your life that you experienced growth or change? How does this connect to the circle?
What lessons did the Hoop Dancer learn?	How are the Medicine Wheel and the Hoop Dance connected?	Why do you think the lessons and symbolism of the Hoop Dance are important?
	Are there symbols that are special or sacred to you? Explain.	How do your ideas about human harmony compare to the Hoop Dancers (big family, elders, goodness in all)?
Check for Understanding	**Closing**	**Extension**
Summarize the discussion (big ideas).	Share that Hoop Dancers all have their unique way of sharing stories of the growth and cycles of life. Similarly, we are all unique individuals and interconnected with each other and nature.	Learn more about the Medicine Wheel through readings, stories and videos. *"Thousands of Medicine wheels have been built on Native lands in North America"* (Native Voices, n.d.).
Individuals self-reflect on their participation and set a goal.		
As a group, reflect on the quality of the seminar and set a goal.		Share: *Black Elk's Vision: A Lakota Story* by S.D. Nelson (2015)

Table 12.7 We Are Protectors

Constructing a Claim & Taking Action
We Are Protectors

Peace Actions & Pursuits	Setup	Hook & Identity
Protect Our Environment • I describe the habitat(s) near my community and explain why it is important. • I learn about the interconnectedness between myself, others and our environment. • I respect all forms of life. *Reach Out In Service* • I ask questions and stand up for the needs and rights of myself, others and the planet (empowerment, justice). *Be A Responsible Citizen Of The World* • I peacefully share my ideas or opinions.	1. Preview the lesson and materials. Gather article(s) or mentor texts that align with *Protect Our Environment* Suggested mentor text: *We are Water Protectors* by Carole Lindstrom, illustrated by Michaela Goade (2020) 2. Reflect, plan and take action: How will learners record their writing? (Consider a graphic organizer.) What areas of need do you recognize in your environment, local habitats or community? How can you highlight this in your model and brainstorming?	*If you are going to make a stand, you need to have a* **claim**. *A claim is your main point. When you state a claim, you also give evidence and reasons to support it.* *Being a protector of the environment and reaching out in service are important roles we have as humans.* • What in nature needs our help or protection? • How can you help make a change in your community? • What questions do you have about this need or change? • What are your ideas to take peace action?

(continued)

Table 12.7 We Are Protectors (continued)

Vocab & Mini Lesson

Advocate: a person who publicly supports or recommends a particular cause or policy. May also be a person working in support of another.

Community: a group of people living in the same place or having particular characteristics, ideas or beliefs in common.

Water Protector: activists, organizers and workers focused on protecting water worldwide; many leaders are Indigenous peoples.

Claim: a statement that answers a question.

Evidence: clues, data, facts

Reason: explains or supports the why or how

1. Introduce vocabulary and add to your word wall, journals and/or digitals.
2. Generate questions and ideas. Discuss and identify potential claims, evidence and reasons.
   - What do you care about in our natural world?
   - What changes do you think need to happen at our school to *Protect Our Environment?* In our community, country, world?
   - We are all protectors of our environment…. Who/what will you protect?
3. If you read, *We are Water Protectors*, discuss and co-create a claim, evidence, reasoning example:
   - How does the author show us the importance of water?
   - Why is water essential to our Earth?
   - Why is it so important to protect the water?
   - What does the snake symbolize in this text?
   - What questions can we generate from this book?
   - What is the **claim?**
   - What **evidence** backs up your idea/suggestion?
   - How will your idea/suggestion work? This **reasoning** should be tied to your evidence.
4. Guide learner in drafting a claim, evidence (research) and reasoning from an identified area of need to *Protect Our Environment.*

(continued)

Table 12.7 We Are Protectors (continued)

	Questions & Prompts	
Emerging	Intermediate	Advanced
Shared writing • Keep the playground clean • Pick up after yourself • Be respectful and caring with nature, plants, animals • Water waste Example: We believe Birch tree is hurt. **(claim)** We found out that when attached bark is torn off Birch, the tree is less protected. **(evidence)** We should protect the trees on the playground so they stay healthy. They give us beauty, shade and a home for animals like birds. **(reason)**	Through interactive writing, small groups, partners or independently My claim is… An idea I have is… Evidence shows… Research says… My reasoning says… because… That helps by… We know we need… Example: **My claim is** that we should use real silverware vs. plastic silverware in the lunchroom. **Evidence** shows that plastic silverware causes a lot of waste and pollutes our water and environment. **My reasoning** says that we should use real silverware for school lunch because this will reduce waste in the environment and in the rivers and oceans.	Extend the *intermediate* guidance by having learners prepare for a counterclaim they may encounter. **Potential counterclaim:** • If you encounter someone who says that silverware is more expensive and the water and soap needed cause more water waste… what will you say? • Plastic silverware may be cheaper initially, but over time it costs less to use real silverware and the impact on the environment is much less harmful.
Check for Understanding	**Closing**	**Extension**
Have students share with a partner. Emphasize that by bringing your ideas to the surface you have the power to make important changes in our community.	This is an opportunity to *Reach Out In Service!* As a class, make a plan and put it into action: What will we do to help *Protect Our Environment?*	Adapt this lesson template to a current event important to students.

Table 12.8 Noticing Nature: Looking For Harmony

Observation & Notetaking

Noticing Nature: Looking for Harmony

Peace Actions & Pursuits	Setup	Hook & Identity
Seek Peace Within Yourself • I have a sense of hope for my future and for what the world will be like for those who come after me. *Protect Our Environment* • I learn about the interconnectedness between myself, others and the environment. *Seek Peace With Others* • I practice cooperation and collaboration with others.	1. Preview the lesson and materials. Recommend one to three column notetaking in a science journal. Option: could take a close-up digital photo of observations. 2. Reflect, plan and take action: Students will routinely use observation throughout their writing experiences. This is an opportunity to be present and observe the world around them in small and big ways. • Where can outdoor observations occur? • What natural areas (even if very small) are within walking distance? • How can technology/media be utilized to share worldwide examples?	Taking time to observe the world around us will help ground us and deepen gratitude for nature. *As we look around our world, we can find lots of examples of harmony and collaboration in nature.* • Birds flying together and taking turns being the leader. • Ants working together to make an ant hill and carrying food. • Bees pollinating flowers and getting food for themselves. • Human food waste becomes compost that helps grow more food. • A pride of lions or pack of wolves hunting together.

(continued)

Table 12.8 Noticing Nature: Looking For Harmony (continued)

Vocab & Mini Lesson

Harmony: When people are peaceful and get along with one another, when we feel a sense of connection, belonging, care and respect for others and our environment(s), we are experiencing harmony.

Collaboration: When people (or nature) work together to get something done; teamwork.

1. Introduce vocabulary and add to your word wall, journals and/or digitals.

The world around us is amazing! There is so much to see and observe. We are going to go outside, notice, observe and take notes (draw/write) about the world around us. For this lesson, we are going to be looking for harmony in nature. All around us there are examples of collaboration, teamwork and animals and nature working together in harmony.

2. Model: notetaking of an observation (see questions/prompts); example:

What	Details (and/or sketch)
Summary:	

3. Set up for notetaking. Consider a guided practice before observing outside.
4. Pairs share: What advice can you give about observing nature? (be quiet, still, patient, look around, be gentle etc.)
5. Whole group debrief and review expectations for outdoor behavior.
6. Move to the observation area!

(continued)

Table 12.8 Noticing Nature: Looking For Harmony (continued)

Questions & Prompts		
Emerging	Intermediate	Advanced
Draw a picture of what they are observing.	Identify the 'what' to observe.	Sketch and write down what they notice in note-taking format. Use three columns:
Label (initial sounds, inventive spelling, words) what they notice.	Sketch observations and add labels.	What / Sketch-label / Description
	Add key details and ideas.	Encourage students to be specific (sensory) with their language.
Support dictation.	*Geese:*	*Oak Tree:*
The ants are in a line following each other.	• *taking turns in front*	• *Five brown acorns, wearing little hats*
	• *flying south for the winter*	• *Each leaf and acorn connect*
I notice the geese flying together in a V.	• *staying together in a V*	• *Small, red insect holds to underside of leaf*
		• *Leaves – neon green to dusty yellow*
Check for Understanding	**Closing**	**Extension**
Pairs: share their observation notes and discuss.	Add summary to end of notes (or orally share):	Build in mindful walks with your class for "mini" observation and calming lessons.
How does this demonstrate harmony, collaboration and/or teamwork?	____ is showing harmony because ____.	Express observations through art, music, poetry, theater or movement.
	Remind students that by observing nature and taking time to pause and notice will help them show gratitude for the environment and the world around them.	

Table 12.9 Identifying Injustices & Empowering Action

Analyze Text & Oral Report (Speech)

Identifying Injustice & Empowering Action

Peace Actions & Pursuits	Setup	Hook & Identity
Be A Responsible Citizen Of The World • I reflect and wonder about (system) causes of the hurt and harm that I see in our world. I consider the effect of this on myself, others and the environment. (justice) • I embrace (show) patience with myself, others and in the vision (hope) I have for the future. *Reach Out In Service* • I ask questions and stand up for the needs and rights of myself, others and the planet.	1. Preview the lesson(s) and materials. *Wangari's Trees of Peace* by Jeanette Winter (2018) *Wangari's Seeds of Hope* a digital resource from Global Peace Heroes (2020): https://globalpeaceheroes.org 2. Reflect, plan and take action: How will you learners share their speeches (partner, small, whole group)? How can students be empowered to act on their speech topics? What support will they need?	*Being a responsible world citizen means that we notice needs, hurts and harms in people and our natural world. When we do, we take peace action to help.* • Have you ever encountered a problem that made you want to take action to change it? • What is special to you in your community? What if this were taken away? What would you do?

(continued)

Table 12.9 Identifying Injustices & Empowering Action (continued)

Vocab & Mini Lesson
Community: A community is a place where people live, work and play. It has homes, businesses and schools.

Injustice: Something that is unfair or wrong, such as someone's needs and rights not being valued, met or being taken away or denied.

Empowerment: Having a sense of hope and confidence in asking for help or meeting needs. Feeling freedom or the ability to help yourself and others.

1. Introduce vocabulary and add to your word wall, journals and/or digitals.
2. Share *Wangari's Trees of Peace* and/or *Wangari's Seeds of Hope* and prompt learners to listen for connections they have (self, community, text, world).
3. Analyze the text through discussion (pairs share). Prompt learners to provide evidence from the story.
   ○ What was the injustice?
   ○ How did it affect the community?
   ○ Why was Wangari empowered to help?
   ○ How did Wangari empower others?
4. Set up learners to identify an injustice they care about and to prepare a speech or oral report about it. Brainstorm:
   ○ What have you noticed in our school/neighborhood that you would like to change?
   ○ What have you noticed in our world that you would like to change?
   ○ What are the positive impacts of making these changes?
   ○ What would be hard about making these changes?
   ○ What action could you take to help make this change?
5. Students can use a claim, evidence and reasoning to outline their ideas (see Lesson: We Are Protectors, p. 267).

Example: *There is a lot of trash at the park in my neighborhood. There are not enough garbage cans and the ones that are there are always full. If there were more empty cans, we could clean up the park and then keep it clean. I can help by organizing a trash pickup day. I will also ask my dad to help me call the park (city) about the cans.*

(continued)

Table 12.9 Identifying Injustices & Empowering Action (continued)

Questions & Prompts		
Emerging	Intermediate	Advanced
Support shared writing in small groups. Draw a picture or a series to show the injustice they are empowered to help change. Label (inventive spelling). Support dictation.	Work in small groups or partnerships to create a speech or oral report. Use the question, claim, evidence and reasoning process to write out the speech (~ one paragraph).	Journal individually and then join with a small group or partnership to create a speech or oral report (~ one page). Prompt learners to provide specific actions that can be taken to address the injustice. • What can you do? • Who will you contact? (Have students research local, national or international leaders.)
Check for Understanding	**Closing**	**Extension**
Guide students to practice speaking with confidence, fluency and expression and then provide an opportunity for them to orally share.	Reflect together: • Why is it important to make changes in the world? • What will you do the next time an injustice arises? • How will you empower yourself and others to stand up for your beliefs? • What might happen if your actions didn't work? How could you handle that and still have hope?	Support students in creating a presentation that shows the injustice and walks through their ideas to help make change. Create opportunities for learners to take peace action about injustice.

Table 12.10 How Do I Belong?

Writing Process (Personal Narrative)
How Do I Belong?

Peace Actions & Pursuits	Setup	Hook & Identity
Seek Peace Within Yourself • I have awareness of what makes me, me. • I explore and share ideas about happiness, love and safety. *Seek Peace With Others* • I belong to a community. With others I learn, connect & show respect. *Be A Responsible Citizen Of The World* • I celebrate life (mine, others, environment).	1. Preview the lesson(s). 2. Reflect, plan and take action: What belonging story will you share to model the writing process along the way? Be sure to draft near the development of your students and leave opportunities for revising and editing! What will the published piece look like (exemplar)? Pencil in your dates for each part of the writing process. Note: whole, small group or conferring. How will you support students in tracking progress? How will materials be organized (e.g., writing process tracker, editing symbols, edit-revise checklist)? How will the final product look? (prepare exemplar)	*Having a sense of belonging is an important need of all humans. Belonging means we feel included, accepted or a part of something else. Belonging begins with knowing ourselves (awareness) and often changes as we grow, learn and have different experiences.* • Model. Look at your heart map (journal-joy write lesson) and share all the people, groups, places or times you've felt belonging. • Add to your heart map more examples of belonging; you might be inspired by what your peers share (e.g., playing, sports, team or group work, family events or customs, birthdays and sharing stories). • What can we do to help others feel they belong? (e.g., inviting them in, asking questions to learn interests, sharing about yourself)

(continued)

Table 12.10 How Do I Belong? (continued)

Mini Lessons	Prompts & Focus Areas		
	Emerging	Intermediate	Advanced
Draft: Choose a story from your heart map that shows a time you felt a sense of belonging. Draw/write all about it, zooming in on the most important part.	From shapes and lines of a single sketch and then expand to three sketches (beginning, middle, end) Add details and inventive spelling labels.	Stretch your writing across three pages/paragraphs: beginning – middle – end Add details and describe: Who was there? Where were you? What happened? How did you feel?	Show, don't just tell (descriptive details, five senses) Elaboration of the most important part (heart/climax) Dialogue and figurative language to show how belonging feels
Revise: Choose a focus area(s) based on benchmarks and student needs. Recommend going deeper with structural elements (organization, lead, transitions, ending). Peer-revise, too!	I belong when/with __. It feels _ to belong. Oral Storytelling Dictation and/or Tracing words, sentences (adult uses a highlighter) Show more details (see draft)	Lead: hook the reader or get their attention; connect to setting. Middle: transition words that show the order End: wrap it up, how did you feel to belong? Show more details (see draft)	Lead: hook the reader and connect to belonging. Middle: transition words that show tone/mood End: sense of closure, feelings and insights about what it means to belong

(continued)

Table 12.10 How Do I Belong? (continued)

Mini Lessons	Prompts & Focus Areas		
	Emerging	Intermediate	Advanced
Edit: Choose focus area(s) Peer-edit, too!	Label spelling, simple phrases and sentences Space between words Lower and uppercase letters usage Spelling: high frequency/sight words	Punctuation & capital letters Spelling, using tools (word wall, lists, dictionary) Possessive ('s or s')	Dialogue punctuation Sentence structure: complete sentences, eliminated run-ons Grammar and syntax
Check for Understanding	**Closing**		**Extension**
After each mini lesson (session), set up the opportunity for a consistent partnership to share progress on their piece and to set a mini-goal for the next session.	Final drafts! Practice reading aloud with confidence, expression and fluency. Determine how the writing will be celebrated and shared with the community.		Discuss: • Why is having a sense of belonging important to you? • What is the opposite of belonging? How does that feel? • What can we do to help others feel they belong?

References

Anderson, T. (2019). *The hoop dancer's teachings (Von Innerebner, J., Illus.).* Medicine Wheel.

Common Core State Standards Initiative. (2024). *Common core state standards.* Corestandards.org. https://corestandards.org/

Fletcher, R. (2017). *Joy write: Cultivating high-impact, low-stakes writing.* Heinemann Educational Books.

Frayer, D., Frederick, W. C., & Klausmeier, H. J. (1969). *A schema for testing the level of cognitive mastery.* Wisconsin Center for Education Research.

Global Peace Heroes. (2020). *We let peace tell the story.* Peace Heroes. https://globalpeaceheroes.org

Harjo, J. (1983). *Remember.* Poets.org; Poets.org – Academy of American Poets. https://poets.org/poem/remember-0

Heard, G. (2016). *Heart maps: Helping students create and craft authentic writing.* Heinemann Educational Books.

@HoopDanceProductions. (2009). *Teddy A.* YouTube. https://www.youtube.com/channel/UCSZJ6fX-3RdkLPVLS-VEvWg

Kaagegaabaw, J. V. (2022, July 17). *How do you say all of my relatives in Ojibwe?* YouTube. https://www.youtube.com/watch?v=ZBIc3Lv7j1Q

Lindstrom, C. (2020). *We are water protectors (Goade, M., Illus.).* Roaring Brooks Press.

Marshall, A. D., & Zimanyi, L. (2023). *Walking together.* Annick Press.

Medicine Wheel Publishing. (2023). *Teddy Anderson.* https://medicinewheelpublishing.com/teddy-anderson/

Native Voices. (n.d.). *Medicine ways: Traditional healers and healing.* Nlm.nih.gov. Retrieved January 6, 2024, from https://www.nlm.nih.gov/nativevoices/exhibition/healing-ways/medicine-ways/medicine-wheel.html

Nelson, S. D. (2015). *Black elk's vision: A Lakota story.* Abrams Books for Young Readers.

PBS. (2018, August 15). *Haudenosaunee's Legendary Founding.* Public Broadcasting Service (PBS). https://www.pbs.org/video/haudenosaunees-legendary-founding-ziahzz/

Six Nations Indian Museum. (1993). *Haudenosaunee thanksgiving address: Greetings to the natural world*. Americanindian.si.edu. https://americanindian. si.edu/environment/pdf/01_02_Thanksgiving_Address.pdf

Symphony of Science. (2009, October 19). *We are all connected*. YouTube @melodysheep. https://www.youtube.com/watch?v=XGK84Poeynk

United Nations Children's Fund (UNICEF). (2021, November 12). *We all have rights. UNICEF*. Unicef.org. https://www.youtube.com/watch?v= 6F7ie1Z07aM&t=1s

Verde, S. (2017). *I am peace: A book of mindfulness (Reynolds, P.H., Illus)*. Abrams Books for Young Readers.

Winter, J. (2018). *Wangari's trees of peace: A true story from Africa*. HMH Books for Young Readers.

Conclusion

Gratitude to You

Hope, empowerment, culturally relevant pedagogy and trauma informed peacelearning are keys for creating environments that allow all children to see and share their many geniuses, experiences and wonders. Peace educators build upon children's assets, model care, embrace critical thinking, peaceful problem-solving and highlight the interconnectedness of all. Creating an environment anchored in democratic practices, kindness and empathy are essential. We are grateful that you are joining us in co-creating just cultures of peace and nonviolence through education!

Dismantling and transforming systems and structures of oppression and violence is possible. As a peace guide, you are often called upon to support others on their paths. This happens in your home, classroom, school, district and community. As we've discussed, seeking peace is a personal and collective journey. It is important to continually celebrate and reflect on progress, challenges and goals, in regard to living in accordance with the Five Peace Actions.

You make a world of difference! We extend our heartfelt appreciation for all you do to help raise awareness and foster the attitudes, behaviors, skills and knowledge that are required to actualize a more just and peaceful society. Keep flowing in your journey. The waters of change are already underway and we each have a precious role in raising our collective consciousness.

Remember, we may not see the acorn grow into the mighty oak in this lifetime. Yet, we are planting and caring for the seeds that will become the anchored roots of an evolutionary way of living – in just, positive peace.

DOI: 10.4324/9781003449249-14

Appendix A

Peace Action Framework (Visual)

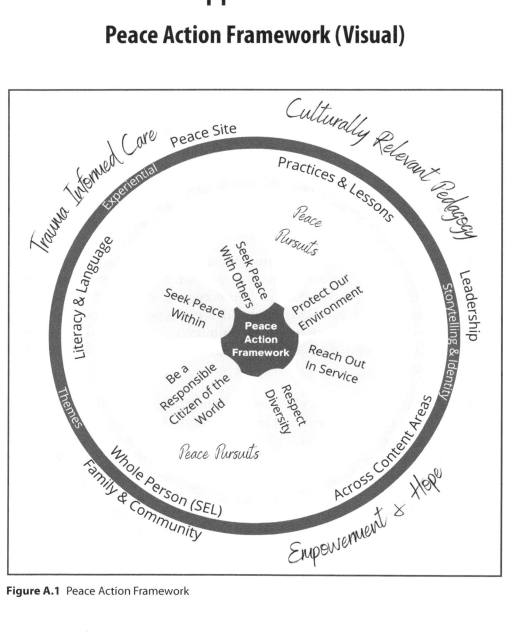

Figure A.1 Peace Action Framework

Appendix B

Peace Actions & Pursuits

Five Peace Actions

- SEEK peace within yourself and others

- REACH OUT in service

- PROTECT our environment

- RESPECT diversity

- BE a responsible citizen of the world

The Peace Pad

www.thepeacepad.org

World Citizen Peace

www.worldcitizenpeace.org

Figure B.1 Five Peace Actions

Peace Actions & Pursuits	
This table outlines all of the peace pursuits with the corresponding peace action. This cumulative view is supportive for collaborating with stakeholders, creating units, lessons and/or evaluating existing curriculum and resources for implementation of peace and justice education.	
Peace Action	**Peace Pursuits**
Seek Peace Within Yourself	I identify my emotions and explore their messages.
	I use strategies to calm and ground myself.
	I recognize how my values, needs and wants impact my behavior and decisions.
	I feel empowered that as I learn and grow, my opinions, ideas and understanding of myself and the world may change.
	I explore and share ideas about happiness, love and safety.
	I have a sense of hope for my future and for what the world will be like for those who come after me.
	I have awareness of what makes me, me.
Peace Action	**Peace Pursuits**
Seek Peace With Others	I belong to a community. With others I: • learn • connect • show respect
	I practice peaceful (nonviolent) communication and actions when: • I disagree with someone • I feel hurt or wronged • My needs or wants are not being met
	I practice cooperation and collaboration with others (problem-solving).
	I practice active listening, empathy and compassion.
Peace Action	**Peace Pursuits**
Respect Diversity	I view and am inspired by stories of peaceful people from around the world.
	I listen to and consider others' ideas or opinions. I honor the ideas, views or perspectives ('truth') of others, even if it is different from mine.
	I understand that every person experiences the world in their own unique way.
	I describe similarities and differences between myself and people with different experiences, histories or cultures from my own.

(continued)

Peace Action	Peace Pursuits
Protect Our Environment	I describe the habitat(s) near my community and explain why it is important.
	I respect all forms of life.
	I learn about the interconnectedness between myself, others and our environment.
	I consider the impact my choices have on our environment.
Peace Action	**Peace Pursuits**
Reach Out In Service	I respect all forms of life and show this through my actions.
	I ask questions and stand up for the needs and rights of myself, others and the planet (empowerment, justice).
	I try to help others in need (advocacy, justice).
Peace Action	**Peace Pursuits**
Be A Responsible Citizen Of The World	I identify people's basic needs and universal human rights.
	I reflect and wonder about (system) causes of the hurt and harm that I see in our world. I consider the effect of this on myself, others and the environment (justice).
	I peacefully share my ideas or opinions.
	I celebrate life (mine, others, environment).
	I consider my needs and the needs of others in my choices and actions.
	I embrace (show) patience with myself, others and in the vision (hope) I have for the future.

Appendix C
Sample Theme Calendar

Adapted from *Onward: Cultivating Emotional Resilience in Educators* (p. 15–16) (Aguilar, 2018).

Align social emotional (SEL) and peacelearning lessons to this monthly theme calendar. Kick-off each month with a special themed event to create a shared understanding of the theme. Honor learner strengths with a theme-connected student of the month celebration.

August/September: *Belonging & Community*
Working together to build a positive classroom and school community.

October: *Caring*
Caring for yourself and others.

November: *Belief*
Believing in yourself.

December: *Empowerment*
Trying new things.

January: *Perspective*
Accepting another's point of view.

February: *Curiosity & Wonder*
Demonstrating curiosity and wonder in learning and in life.

March: *Bravery*
Showing bravery, innovation and problem-solving.

April: *Persistence*
Persisting in the face of challenges.

May/June: *Pride*
Showing pride and confidence in your accomplishments and believing that you can succeed!

Reference

Aguilar, E. (2018). *Onward: Cultivating emotional resilience in educators*. Jossey Bass.

Appendix D
Sample Unit Themes

Inspired by *Onward: Cultivating Emotional Resilience in Educators* (p. 15–16) (Aguilar, 2018).

Align curriculum, social emotional (SEL) and peacelearning lessons to these unit themes. The first unit is designed for the first six to eight weeks of school. The remaining units can be moved around and may vary in their duration. Create a shared understanding of the theme through a special unit launching event. Celebrate the end of the unit with a showcase highlighting the theme.

Unit 1: Belonging & Harmony: Building a positive & inclusive community. Appreciating the connection within all of life (self, others, nature). Note: See Chapter 12 for this unit of lessons!

Unit 2: Caring & Compassion: Showing support, patience and love for yourself and others. Respecting all forms of life.

Unit 3: Hope & Empowerment: Believing in yourself and knowing your value in the world. Having a positive view of what the future can bring. Learning from others & creating the world you hope for all.

Unit 4: Gratitude & Kindness: Feeling thankful for the possibilities, opportunities and gifts in life's journey and from all on the planet. Showing gratitude toward others.

Unit 5: Empathy & Perspective: Listening to, communicating and considering another's point of view and feelings. Having awareness of your own thoughts, feelings and actions and how they may differ from others.

Unit 6: Curiosity & Wonder: Demonstrating curiosity and wonder in learning and in life. Trying new things and observing the results. Noticing the interconnectedness of all on Earth.

Unit 7: Bravery & Courage: Using our strengths (gifts) to face problems, try new things and help all on Earth. Showing innovation and speaking up for others and the environment.

Unit 8: Persistence & Resilience: Persisting and/or learning (growing) and healing in the face of challenges. Appreciating that everyone's experiences are unique and connected.

Unit 9: Pride & Humility: Celebrating and sharing the growth and gifts of yourself, others and nature! Being aware of the balance and connection of all of life.

Unit 10: Advocacy & Justice: Honoring the needs and rights of others and the environment. Using peaceful actions to help make the world more just.

Reference

Aguilar, E. (2018). *Onward: Cultivating emotional resilience in educators.* Jossey Bass.

Appendix E

Best Practice of Peace Guides, Educators & Leaders

These culturally relevant, trauma aware and sensitive best practices and strategies will support your ongoing peacelearning implementation. **As you review, reflect on your practice, strengths and areas for growth and support.**

For more insights on (*) indicated strategies, *The Supportive Classroom: Trauma Sensitive Strategies for Fostering Resilience and Creating a Safe, Compassionate Environment for All* by Anderson & Bowen (2020) is a great resource.

Self	Attentiveness to own stress levels, well-being & self care needs*	Being present; practicing non-judgement and giving grace	Assuming positive intent and/or not taking things personally*	Exploring and honoring intersectionality (identity)	Leaning in with curiosity; examining implicit & explicit biases
Democratic Principles	Choice, voice agency & autonomy is crucially important - in every area	Co-creating physical environment & learning agreements	Empathetic and reflective listening practices	Ample opportunities for exploration, caring & being in service of others, nature & the environment	Co-created non-verbal communication channels
Communication & Relationships	Clear, calm and kind body language, tone of voice and communication	Boundary setting and de-escalation techniques Use of proximity*	Positive and proactive relationships and ongoing communication with families & caregivers*	Relationship building and learning about others; Create trusting and safe relationship(s)*	Consistent & predictable routines and expectations*
Self & Social Awareness	Self-regulation practices, tools, spaces & emotional intelligence*	Flexible grouping, cooperative learning structures & role playing	Peace circles (peer meditation) & relationship problem-solving	Guiding exploration and honoring of intersections of identity & culture	Modeling and emphasis on hope, connection, empowerment & resilience
Instruction	Scaffolding from zone of proximal development; towards shared expectations	Differentiation based on needs, strengths and universal design of learning	Supporting visuals, prompts & language stems (available at time of use)	Utilizing a variety of input & output opportunities	Information, interaction & processing in multiple modalities

(continued)

Environment & Materials	Texts & materials represent the diversity of the world	Safe & soothing space setup that allows for flow, movement, varied seating options and safe breaks*	Clean, organized spaces with limited visual stimulation & as much nature access as possible	Available sensory materials and regular opportunity for expression through journaling, art, music and movement	Experiential & project-based learning
Reflection, Assessment, Feedback	5:1 ratio of positive to negative contacts, corrections or feedback* Private and empathetic behavior or error correction	Instruction informed by ongoing formative assessment, observation, pre/post summatives	Dynamic feedback loops that empower learners and encourages questions	Flexible goal setting & ongoing reflection* Feedback on effort; positive reinforcement that fosters a growth mindset*	Balancing opportunity, encouragement, mistakes or errors & support
Peace Actions	Modeling and naming progress towards peace actions; honoring that progress is not always linear	Exploring the interconnectedness between self, others & environment	Learning & critical thinking connected to identity, human rights, needs & real-world application	Raising consciousness through active dialogue & action	Reflecting & problem-solving on progress towards peace pursuits
	Ongoing exploration of peaceful solutions & possibilities to social and global problems	Being informed about the complexities of peace, conflict, war, violence and environmental justice	Infusing & embedding peace, justice and sustainability across all content areas	Advocating, building connections & joining networks dedicated to peace	Reexamining behaviors, thoughts, patterns and current events related to peace and justice

Reference

Anderson, L. & Bowen, J. (2020). *The supportive classroom: Trauma-sensitive strategies for fostering resilience and creating a safe, compassionate environment for all*. Berkeley, CA. Ulysses Press.

Appendix F
The Peace Pad

We invite you to visit our website www.thepeacepad.org

The Peace Pad is for anyone who is passionate about peace and justice education and wants to make a positive impact in their learning environments and communities. We believe peace education is for everyone – at all ages and stages of life!

- Digital slides and printables for select lessons.
- Guided video series of the Five Peace Actions (for adults).
- Resources, including other sites and organizations for peace education.
- Consulting: Collaboratively customized (virtual and/or in person) leadership, coaching and support to create cultures of peace and justice in schools, organizations and communities – with adults, youth and children.
  - Professional Learning (Development)
  - Project/Strategy Leadership & Coaching
  - Speaking
  - Peacelearning Programs
  - Learning Experience Designer
- Happenings: workshops, gatherings, special features
- Newsletter: writings, ideas, videos, lessons, opportunities, events and resources to support us all on our journey of seeking peace.
- Social Media: peacelearning content and engagement.

Index of 'Put It Into Practice'

About the Authors

Julie Lillie has over 15 years of experience in diverse school settings as an elementary teacher, literacy interventionist, coach, curriculum coordinator and leader with PreK-12 teachers across all content areas. She has a Master of Science (M.S.) as a Reading Specialist and for over a decade has facilitated professional learning with an emphasis in literacy, trauma informed and sensitive practices, equity, culturally relevant pedagogy and social emotional learning. Julie is dedicated to evolving our education systems. Co-founder of The Peace Pad, she is a peace- and justice-centered educational consultant, writer, speaker, content creator, coach, leader, learning designer and facilitator. Julie believes that peace education is for all ages and stages of life.

Dr. Carey Seeley Dzierzak is a dedicated educator who has been involved in education for 25 years working in diverse settings. She has been a first-grade teacher, literacy teacher, an instruction and literacy coach, elementary curriculum director, assistant principal and principal. Through these various roles, she has remained committed to culturally relevant peace education and rigorous instructional practices. As an educator, she is committed to creating inclusive peace-centered environments for students, staff and families. She earned her Education Doctorate (Ed.D.) from Hamline University focused on culturally affirming practices. Co-founder of The Peace Pad, she is a peace- and justice-centered volunteer and advocate. She is also a parent to some amazing children with her husband, who is also a writer.